# HIGHLY EFFECTIVE THERAPY

# CONTENTS

# FOREWORD

Since the age of three, I have been a ballet dancer. Ballet training was rigorous. Classes were daily and there were set exercises that became increasingly complex and demanding as I became more advanced. Feedback, albeit sometimes critical, was designed to make us technically superb, graceful, and agile. Reflecting back on my ballet training, I realize that in many ways it was highly competency-based; there were specific competencies that we were expected to acquire and the nature and extent of the acquisition varied based on our developmental phase of training. To be successful, we were not only expected to be competent, but also to demonstrate capability. That is, we were expected to adapt our skills, be creative using our knowledge, and continue to improve our performance. In other words, we were encouraged to become highly effective.

My passion for psychotherapy, just like my love for ballet, also developed very early on. I even developed my theoretical orientation, or at least part of it, by second grade. In first grade, I heard my mother give a lecture on Freud and I took notes. My notes said: Superego = mommy and daddy, ego = me, and id = my feelings. Then, in second grade, I attended a lecture my mother gave on Skinner. Afterwards, I said, "Mommy, I think Freud is more interesting than Skinner." Today, although I am an integrationist and have strong cognitive-behavioral training, having been mentored by some of the leading behaviorists and cognitively oriented psychologists (Marty Seligman—undergraduate advisor, Lynn Rehm—graduate school advisor), I more often integrate psychodynamic thinking into my clinical endeavors. My strong psychodynamic orientation is not only influenced by the lecture I attended in first grade, but also by my own psychoanalysis, which I have found to be meaningful and enlightening. Other orientations have influenced me heavily, including family systems thinking, my mother's dominant framework.

Although I have been dedicated to research since my undergraduate years, what engages me most professionally is being a psychotherapist and teaching and supervising future generations of psychotherapists. As a trainee, I appreciated most those supervisors who gave me confidence as a therapist by conveying that I possessed some basic personal attributes that would allow me to effectively interact with and even help my patients. These same individuals provided me a developmentally sensitive roadmap for case conceptualization, forging and maintaining a therapeutic alliance, and understanding and directing the therapeutic process. Of course, my best teachers have been my patients, particularly those individuals who forced me to think and act outside the realm of traditional intervention techniques to connect with them and to enable them to trust me and change. For example, when I worked at a long term hospital, I saw an adolescent three days a week for therapy and in addition to swearing at me, her only other comment was to say "sewer rat, sewer rat, here comes the sewer rat." I calmly visited with her for months on end and one day, I lost my patience and swore back at her. She yelled to staff to come quickly because her therapist had just cursed at her. I was ashamed, humiliated, and confused and immediately sought supervision. I was fearful of showing up for our next scheduled appointment, dreading her reaction, as well as the response of the staff and other patients. However, her response when she saw me was shocking; she calmly and appropriately greeted me, for the first time in almost a year and invited me to her room to teach her how to put on makeup. It was a turning point in our relationship. Months later she said that my "losing it" showed that I was a real person, with real feelings, who wasn't perfect. This was one of many times in which I realized that a therapeutic error could be turned into a therapeutic success if I let my patients guide me and help me navigate the murky therapeutic waters. Further, I recognized through the interaction how valuable it was for me that I had a conceptual understanding of her interpersonal interactions, which also guided us onto more solid therapeutic ground.

Since 1984, first at Yale and for the past 19 years at Emory, I have been fortunate to teach and supervise psychology interns, postdoctoral fellows, and graduate students, as well as psychiatry residents in individual, couples/family, and group therapy. My students' feedback has led me to appreciate how helpful it was for supervision to focus on assisting them in articulating their own theoretical model that is consistent with their personal predilections, facilitating their processing of transference and countertransference dynamics, and developing and implementing a wide range of intervention techniques. My students have helped me to realize that effective psychotherapists are not just individuals with lots of knowledge or skill, but people who integrate their knowledge and skills with attitudes that reflect a value on scientific mindedness, self-assessment, individual and cultural diversity, ethical practice, productive interpersonal interactions and interdisciplinary systems, and professionalism.

In addition to my day-to-day activities as a therapist, supervisor, and teacher, I have come to genuinely recognize the need for a shift toward a culture of competence in professional psychology through my national involvements through the Association of Psychology Postdoctoral and Internship Centers (APPIC), as Past Chair and Board Member Emeritus; the American Psychological Association (APA) as Past President of the Society of Clinical Psychology (Division 12) and the Division of Family Psychology (Division 43) and current President of the Division of Psychotherapy (Division 29); and through the American Board of Professional Psychology (ABPP), as President of the American Board of Clinical Psychology and President-Elect of the ABPP Board of Trustees. While I have been dubbed by the profession as "the Queen of Competencies", a term of endearment I guess, I do not take credit for the competencies movement. Many individuals and groups came before me and laid the stage for the 2002 Competencies Conference that I chaired. This multinational, multiconstituency group conference paved the way for current efforts at delineating the foundational and functional competencies, ascertaining the essential components of these competencies and benchmarks for their successful attainment at various stages of development, and determining appropriate strategies for competency assessment.

Sperry's engaging book, *Highly Effective Therapy*, represents a continuation of the competencies movement. This well-organized, concise, and thorough book sets a standard at the outset for how therapy should be conducted—like an expert. The author masterfully presents an intelligent, developmentally sensitive, and competency-based approach for teaching individuals how to formulate and utilize a conceptual framework to guide the therapeutic process, regardless of theoretical orientation. This global perspective, which cuts across schools of thought, provides novice and experienced therapists alike with essential insights and a gold mine of practical advice regarding dealing with challenging therapeutic encounters, determining diagnosis, developing case conceptualizations, planning and implementing intervention strategies, and evaluating treatment progress. The author offers illustrative, in-depth, and lucid case examples that highlight many essential components of the psychotherapy competency and that clarify many of the nuances of effective psychotherapeutic practice. *Highly Effective Therapy* draws together the most current thinking in competency-based psychotherapy practice and as such is an outstanding resource that will enable therapists to both more competently understand and implement psychotherapy. It is a must-read for any individual who aspires toward excellence in the practice of effective psychotherapy.

**Nadine J. Kaslow, PhD, ABPP**

# INTRODUCTION: DEVELOPING ESSENTIAL CLINICAL COMPETENCIES

What exactly is Highly Effective Therapy? Highly Effective Therapy is not a new approach to psychotherapy or a set of treatment interventions. Rather it is a *way of practicing psychotherapy based on how expert therapists practice*. It is also a way of developing the competencies that highly effective therapists utilize. Practicing like a highly effective therapist is possible because highly effective therapy is basically a competency-based therapy. One doesn't have to be a "born therapist" to learn the ways in which expert therapists think and act.

Thinking and acting more like expert therapists is what fosters the practice of Highly Effective Therapy.

Is there a need for the practice of Highly Effective Therapy today? It should come as no surprise that in the current era of accountability and evidence-based practice, the training and practice of psychotherapy is expected to become increasingly competency-based. Thus, it is becoming less acceptable for therapists to practice conventional therapy that is standards-based. It is also harder to justify standards-based training with its focus on the core curriculum when the need and demand for competency-based training with a focus on core competencies is so evident. This need and demand are reflected in the movement toward competency-based training by the American Psychological Association, the American Association of Directors of Psychiatry Residency Training, the American Counseling Association, and the American Association of Marital and Family Therapy. This book also reflects this demand for preparing therapists for competency-based practice.

This chapter provides a brief introduction to competency and how competency-based practice and training learning differ from conventional practice training. Highly Effective Therapy is based on 5 core competencies and 20 essential clinical competencies. Both core and clinical

1

competencies are briefly introduced along with an overview of the structured learning format utilized in this book to help readers develop these clinical competencies.

## DEFINITION AND COMPONENTS OF COMPETENCY

Competence has been defined as the consistent and judicious use of knowledge, technical skills, clinical reasoning, emotions, values, and reflection in clinical practice. Competency involves the capacity for critical thinking, analysis, and professional judgment in assessing a situation and making clinical decisions based on that assessment. Furthermore, it is the ability to evaluate and modify one's decisions, as appropriate, through reflective practice (Kaslow, 2004). Clinical competencies are composed of three interrelated components, *knowledge, skills, and attitudes*, which are essential for effective professional practice. Such competencies are reflected in the quality of clinical performance, can be evaluated against professional standards, and can be developed or enhanced through professional training and personal growth (Kaslow, 2004; Kaslow et al., 2004).

## COMPETENCIES VERSUS SKILLS

Too often the terms *competency* and *skill* are used synonymously. Although there is some similarity, they are notably different. As described earlier, a clinical competency is composed of knowledge, skills, and attitudes components that are necessary for professional practice (Kaslow, 2004), whereas a skill is simply a capability that has been acquired through training but does not have knowledge or attitudinal components.

To illustrate how a competency is more than a skill or skill set, let's examine the concept of empathy. Many individuals besides therapists can and do exhibit empathy. These include salespersons and psychopaths. Defined as a competency, empathy has three components: empathy knowledge (knowledge), empathy communication skills (skill), and *empathic stance* (attitude). The presence of all three components is involved in what is called "therapeutic empathy." So what is the empathic stance? This component refers to an attitude of benevolence and a desire to promote the client's well-being. Consequently, for empathy to become therapeutic empathy the therapist must respond and act out of a stance of benevolence, interest, and respect toward clients (Thwaites & Bennett-Levy, 2007). Effective and successful therapists exhibit therapeutic empathy and would be considered *empathically competent*.

Defined as a *skill*, empathy involves one component: empathy communication skills (skill). Sales personnel who have developed the skill of empathic communication are likely to be very successful because they can effectively "read" and respond to customers. However, their success would fade to the extent to which they possessed an empathic stance. Why? Because sales personnel who are really concerned about customers' well-being will not use empathic influence to sell items that customers do not really need, or that might be unhealthy or harmful. Accordingly, successful sales personnel are not empathically competent. Similarly, therapists who engage in sexual misconduct with clients demonstrate a lack of empathic stance by their harmful rather than benevolent behavior. Although they may have mastered the skill of empathy, they are incapable of therapeutic empathy and are *empathically incompetent*.

## COMPETENCY AND DEVELOPMENTAL STAGES

Being a competent therapist involves the capacity to appropriately and effectively utilize the knowledge, skills, and attitudes necessary to perform a wide range of therapeutic tasks and clinical tasks. Becoming a competent therapist involves the development of essential competencies. This developmental process has been described in terms of five stages across the various professions (Dreyfus & Dreyfus, 1986). A description of these stages has been modified to reflect training for the practice of psychotherapy.

1. *Beginner stage.* At this stage trainees possess a limited knowledge and understanding in analyzing problems and intervening. They are reliant on basic principles and techniques, are rule-bound, and are too inexperienced to flexibly use these principles and techniques.
2. *Advanced beginner stage.* In this stage trainees possess a limited capacity for pattern recognition and application of interventions but have difficulty generalizing this capacity to different clients and new situations. Rules and principles previously learned now become guidelines. They need considerable support and clinical supervision.
3. *Competent stage.* At this stage therapists can function independently albeit at a minimal level of competence. They are consciously

aware of long-range goals and plans for their clients and can adapt to the changes in the client with appropriate changes in the intervention plan. They recognize patterns more easily and begin to tailor intervention. They experience a feeling of mastery and are able to cope with and handle crises or other problems as they arise, and are able to integrate theory and research into every aspect of their practice applications.

4. *Proficient stage.* At this stage therapists possess a more integrative understanding of their clients, and their performance is guided by flexibility and a clear understanding of the nuances of therapeutic interventions and the impact of the intervention on the client and others. At this stage, therapists are able to train and supervise others in intervention skills.

5. *Expert stage.* At this stage therapists possess an intuitive grasp of clinical situation and can rapidly assess problems and design appropriate interventions. They quickly recognize when an intervention is not working and are able to modify the treatment accordingly.

## DIFFERENT WAY OF PRACTICING PSYCHOTHERAPY

The expectation is that formal didactic training and internship training should facilitate the trainee's movement from the beginner stage to the initial level of the competent stage. Typically, licensed therapists function at or above the initial level of the competent stage, and licensure boards assume that those whom they license meet minimal levels of competence. However, competency and the developmental view espoused in this book refer to an aspirational striving toward excellence. "Aspirational competencies are those for which one strives to achieve, and those who achieve them often are considered the experts" (Kaslow, 2004, p. 775).

Highly Effective Therapy is associated with aspirational competence rather than with minimal competence. As designated in this book, those practicing Highly Effective Therapy are more likely to function at the high level of the proficient stage or expert stage of professional development. By comparison, those practicing effective therapy are more likely to function in the high level of the competent stage or in the low level of the proficient stage.

Throughout this book readers will become increasingly aware of how highly effective therapists function differently than less effective therapists. For example, highly effective therapists are guided by cognitive maps for assessing, conceptualizing, planning, and implementing treatment interventions. They quickly and intuitively know if they are connecting with the client, if their case conceptualization is accurate, and if treatment is on target. They are also able to improvise and modify their ideas and actions when clinical circumstances change. Furthermore, compared to less proficient therapists, they are likely to excel in dealing with complex situations and difficult clients (Lambert & Okishi, 1997).

In short, highly effective therapists *think, act,* and *reflect* differently than less effective therapists. They *think* differently because their grasp of declarative knowledge is more differentiated. They *act* differently because their procedural knowledge and skills are better developed. And, they *reflect* differently on clinical situations and dilemmas including ethical ones, because of their capacity and experience as effective, reflective practitioners (Schön, 1983).

## COMPETENCY-BASED LEARNING AND PSYCHOTHERAPY

A major shift is occurring today in graduate training programs. It involves a shift from standards-based learning, with a focus on the core curriculum, toward competency-based learning, with a focus on core competencies (Kaslow et al., 2004). Four core competencies for psychotherapy practice have been identified in the professional psychology literature. They are (a) foundational competencies, including theoretical models and relationship building; (b) intervention planning competencies; (c) intervention implementation competencies; and (d) intervention evaluation competencies (Kaslow, 2004; Spruill et al., 2004)

In this book, 5 core competencies and 20 essential clinical competencies are discussed and illustrated. Before turning to these specific competencies, I will describe an approach to learning that favors the development of clinical competencies.

The process of developing clinical competencies can best be understood in terms of three kinds of learning: declarative, procedural, and reflective (Bennett-Levy, 2006; Binder, 1993, 2004). *Declarative learning* involves conceptual, technical, and interpersonal knowledge. This kind of learning is largely facilitated by lectures, presentations, discussions, and reading. *Procedural learning* is the application of knowledge to the clinical practice and is largely facilitated by clinical experiences and supervision. It occurs when declarative knowledge becomes actualized in practice and refined. Procedural learning is essentially skill-based, clinical learning. *Reflective learning* differs markedly from declarative and procedural learning. It involves reflecting on declarative and procedural knowledge and coming to a decision about a course of action. Various processes are involved in this type of learning. They include analyzing experiences, comparing them with others, identifying a plan of action as necessary, and possibly changing previous information and insights in the light of the analysis. The reflective system is mostly facilitated by client and supervisor feedback of counselor performance in addition to counselor self-evaluation during clinical training (Bennett-Levy, 2006). The interaction of these three types of learning is required to develop and master a competency (Bennett-Levy & Thwaites, 2006).

Another difference between skills and competencies is evident in terms of these three kinds of learning. Typically, skill learning is primarily procedural learning, although some declarative learning may be involved. In contrast, competency learning involves all three types of learning: It involves knowledge (i.e., declarative learning), skills (i.e., procedural learning), and attitudes, values, and standards (i.e., reflective learning). It has been noted that reflective learning is essential to becoming a highly proficient therapist or an expert therapist (Bennett-Levy & Thwaites, 2006).

The current approach to training therapists involves didactic instruction in the classroom followed by clinical experience and supervision. The assumption is and has been that clinical experience and supervision provide the bridge between theory and practice and that the therapy session is the best place to learn how to do therapy by practicing basic therapy methods.

For the great majority of trainees it is not. Supervision also has limited value in learning and practicing basic therapy methods. Rather, supervision "is a teaching format best suited for refining therapeutical skills and elaborating procedural knowledge across more and more clinical situations after the initial foundation of declarative knowledge and therapy skill components have been laid" (Binder, 2004, p. 266).

## A STRUCTURED APPROACH TO LEARNING CLINICAL COMPETENCIES

What is needed is a structured means of learning essential clinical competencies during the didactic phase of training and during the clinical phase of training in the practicum and internship. Structured learning, also called "deliberate practice," is essential to the development of expertise (Erickson, 1996). There is evidence suggesting that "more structured teaching, including structured supervision, produces more effective learning than less structured approaches" (Binder, 2004, p. 264). Unfortunately, there is a dearth of such structured learning approaches and formats. This book offers such a learning format. It provides a series of structured learning experiences that can help one develop essential clinical competencies of psychotherapy. The format consists of brief descriptions of each competency, followed by clinical guidelines for developing the competency and extensive case material with session-long transcriptions that illustrate how a highly effective therapist thinks, acts, and reflects.

## ESSENTIAL CLINICAL COMPETENCIES

Table 1 lists the 20 essential clinical competencies described and illustrated in this book.

These clinical competencies are categorized in terms of their corresponding five core competencies. These core competencies are foundations, relationship building and maintenance, intervention planning, intervention implementation, and intervention evaluation.

**Table 1**  Core and Essential Clinical Competencies

**I. Conceptual Foundation**

  1. Apply a conceptual map to understand and direct the therapeutic process.

**II. Relationship Building and Maintenance**

  2. Establish an effective therapeutic alliance.
  3. Assess readiness and foster treatment-promoting factors.
  4. Recognize and resolve resistance and ambivalence.
  5. Recognize therapeutic alliance ruptures.
  6. Recognize and resolve transference–countertransference enactments.

**III. Intervention Planning**

  7. Perform an integrative diagnostic assessment.
  8. Specify a DSM diagnosis.
  9. Develop an integrative case conceptualization.
  10. Specify a cultural formulation.
  11. Plan treatment interventions and predict obstacles to their implementation.
  12. Draft a clinical case report.

**IV. Intervention Implementation**

  13. Establish a treatment focus.
  14. Maintain the treatment focus.
  15. Modify maladaptive cognitions, behaviors, affects, and interpersonal relations.
  16. Plan and implement culturally sensitive interventions.
  17. Recognize and resolve treatment-interfering factors.

**V. Intervention Evaluation**

  18. Monitor progress and modify treatment accordingly.
  19. Evaluate progress and prepare clients for termination.
  20. Utilize supervision effectively to enhance and evaluate competencies.

# 1

# Apply a Conceptual Map to Understand and Direct the Therapeutic Process

Of all the essential competencies, having a "conceptual map" or theoretical framework is arguably the most basic. Such a conceptual map is a "working model" that guides the therapist in determining which clinical data to observe and elicit and how to understand that data. It guides the therapist in recognizing client patterns and framing diagnostic, clinical, cultural, and treatment formulations, on the basis of which the therapist specifies a treatment focus and intervention strategies and then implements and evaluates them (Binder, 2004).

Even though therapists may consider themselves "eclectic" in orientation, research indicates that these therapists espouse at least one basic theoretical orientation, which informs their understanding of personality, psychopathology, and the therapeutic process (Binder, 2004). Therapists need a conscious "conceptual map" of the immediate therapeutic situation that sharpens and guides their thoughts and actions about a specific case in terms of five key therapeutic tasks:

- Therapeutic Relationship
- Assessment
- Intervention Planning and Case Conceptualization
- Intervention Focus, Strategy, and Implementation
- Intervention Evaluation and Termination

9

This chapter describes five basic theoretical approaches and their underlying "conceptual maps." These five basic approaches are cognitive–behavioral, dynamic, experiential, relational-systemic, and integrative. For each approach five key therapeutic tasks are briefly noted. Table 1.1 summarizes the very brief discussion of each of these approaches specifically in terms of the tasks of therapeutic focus, therapeutic goals, therapeutic strategy, and interventions.

## COGNITIVE–BEHAVIORAL APPROACH

Cognitive–behavioral therapy (CBT) is the most commonly used psychotherapeutic approach in the United States today. It represents the merging of various cognitive therapy and behavior therapy approaches (Wright et al., 2006). In addition, CBT has been adapted to nearly all diagnostic conditions and is also the most commonly utilized therapeutic approach with culturally diverse clients.

## 1. Basic Orientation

### Personality
Personality is shaped by innate dispositions—particularly cognitive schemas and temperament—interacting with environment. These schemas develop early in life from personal experiences and identification with significant others, and are reinforced by further learning experiences which then influence the formation of specific beliefs, values, and attitudes. In short, the constraints of one's neurobiology and personal learning determine how one develops and responds.

### Psychopathology
There are multiple causes of psychological distress, including neurobiological vulnerability, learning history, and schemas. Psychological distress is experienced when situations are perceived as threatening; cognitive, emotional, motivational, and behavioral schemas are activated and may be expressed as symptoms and functional impairment. Specifically, such distress leads to interpretations that are selective, egocentric, and rigid and results in impaired cognitive processes such as distorted thinking, poor concentration, and poor recall. Maladaptive or negative behaviors (deficits or excesses) further reinforce maladaptive cognitions.

10

Table 1.1   Treatment Factors in the Common Psychotherapeutic Approaches

| Therapeutic Approach | Basic Goal | Treatment Focus | Basic Therapeutic Strategy | Interventions |
|---|---|---|---|---|
| Cognitive–behavioral (*Cognitive–behavior therapy*) | Change maladaptive beliefs and behaviors | Analyze situations and modify specific maladaptive beliefs and behaviors | Cognitive restructuring and behavior modification | Socratic questioning Disputation Skill training Behavioral rehearsal |
| Dynamic (*Time-limited dynamic therapy*) | Experience insight and corrective interpersonal experiences | Analyze and interpret troublesome interpersonal relationships and plan corrective experiences | Facilitating new relational experiences and understandings that replace maladaptive relational pattern | Interpretation Transference analysis Incisive questioning Coaching practice |
| Experiential (*Emotionally focused psychotherapy*) | Modify emotional responsivity, schemas, and self-narrative to live a more vital and adaptive life | Analyze and process client's core pain | Accessing and utilizing adaptive emotional functioning | Empathic attunement Empathic exploration Focusing Two-chair technique Empty-chair technique Empathic affirmation |
| Relational-Systemic (*Solution-focused therapy*) | Facilitate the smallest changes needed for better functioning | Find exceptions and implement solutions | Goal clarification and solution amplification | Exceptions Miracle question Scaling |
| Integrative (*Adlerian psychotherapy*) | Increase social interest and modify faulty convictions | Analyze and process situations involving specific maladaptive beliefs and behaviors | Cognitive restructuring, fostering insight, and constructive action | Lifestyle assessment Interpretation Encouragement Acting "as if" Paradox |

**Psychotherapy**

CBT is a problem-focused, here-and-now approach that endeavors to modify maladaptive cognitions and behaviors using a variety of cognitive and behavioral methods to change thinking, mood, and behavior. Because behavior is learned, negative behavior can be unlearned and new behaviors can be learned. The mark of successful treatment is healthier ways of thinking and behaving.

## 2. Therapeutic Relationship

The therapeutic relationship is considered collaborative in that the client provides thoughts, images, emotions, and behaviors that occur in various situations and shares the responsibility of setting the agenda for the session, providing feedback to the therapist, and doing between-session homework. The relationship facilitates change rather than being the primary mechanism of change.

## 3. Assessment

In addition to establishing a diagnosis, the second goal of assessment is to develop case conceptualization. Accordingly, *cross-sectional* and *longitudinal* information is collected. Also identified are clients' perception of their control over thoughts and images, and their expectations for treatment.

## 4. Intervention Planning and Case Conceptualization

Case conceptualization is a theoretical understanding or map that serves as a guide for treatment. It is based on a *cross-sectional view*, that is, the presenting problem, precipitants, perpetuants, and consequences, and a *longitudinal view*, that is, an explanation of the underlying mechanisms and origins of the maladaptive beliefs, schemas, and behaviors. In addition, the case conceptualization specifies treatment goals and sequencing of interventions and predicts obstacles to treatment based on the conceptualization. Intervention planning is based on this conceptualization, and direct intervention strategies and tactics are chosen based on the client's key problems and strengths (Wright et al., 2006).

## 5. Intervention Focus, Strategy, and Implementation

The focus of treatment is the pattern of maladaptive thinking and behavior. The basic goal is to modify maladaptive thoughts and behaviors. Cognitive restructuring is a primary strategy to help clients recognize maladaptive beliefs and behaviors, teach them skills for changing these beliefs and behaviors, and perform in-session and between-session (homework) exercises to generalize this new learning. Various intervention tactics as Socratic questioning, role-playing, reattribution, and rehearsal are employed with this strategy. Psychoeducation and replacement of thoughts and behaviors, that is, in cognitive–behavioral analysis system of psychotherapy (CBASP), are other intervention strategies. Ongoing practice is usually necessary to change ingrained, maladaptive thoughts and behaviors.

## 6. Intervention Evaluation and Termination

Because CBT is a problem-focused approach, assessing progress toward goal attainment is relatively straightforward. In addition to the therapist monitoring progress, the client is encouraged to engage in self-monitoring. CBT endeavors to prevent relapse by developing a prevention plan and what clients can do if symptoms reemerge. Termination decisions, follow-up sessions, and the possibility of reentering treatment are discussed with the client.

## DYNAMIC APPROACH

Of the several psychodynamic approaches, time-limited dynamic therapy is highlighted here as it represents a commonly utilized and well-researched interpersonal-dynamic therapy approach. Basic to time-limited dynamic therapy is the observation that over time, clients unwittingly develop a self-perpetuating maladaptive pattern of relating to others, and this pattern underlies their presenting problem. The therapist's task is to use the therapeutic relationship to facilitate a new experience of relating that allows the client to break the old pattern, thereby resolving the presenting problem (Levenson, 1995).

## 1. Basic Orientation

**Personality**
Human relatedness, that is, belonging, is a person's basic need and motivation. Personality is viewed as interactional structures, that is, self-object representations, resulting from the internalization of particular

interpersonal experiences. Early factors such as temperament influences interactional styles, just as later internalizations can modify these internal structures.

Whereas these internalizations approximate what occurs when interpersonal stress is minimal, when such stress is significant, perceptual and cognitive functions are impaired and distortions of interpersonal occurrences are internalized and can significantly affect personality development.

### Psychopathology

Disturbances in adult interpersonal relatedness typically stem from faulty relationship patterns with early caregivers. These early experiences result in dysfunctional mental representations, also called mental models or schemas, which are maintained in the present. These mental models engender maladaptive patterns of interpersonal interactions or relationship styles, which are reflected in symptoms and occupational and interpersonal distress and dissatisfaction.

### Psychotherapy

The client's maladaptive interpersonal patterns are reenacted in therapy, and the therapist will be influenced by the client's enactment and will reciprocally respond. Thus, treatment is focused on modifying both the mental model and the maladaptive interpersonal pattern. This central focus on interactions distinguishes this approach from other psychoanalytic approaches that emphasize personality reconstruction.

## 2. Therapeutic Relationship

As with other psychodynamic approaches, the therapeutic alliance is considered the principal mechanism for change. The therapist's role is that of participant observer, who relates to the client in a nurturing and supportive as well as directive and active manner. Therapists anticipate and work to resolve resistance such as transference–countertransference enactments and ruptures in the therapeutic alliance.

## 3. Assessment

Emphasized is an interpersonal diagnosis rather than a diagnosis based on the *Diagnostic and Statistic Manual of Mental Disorders* (*DSM*). Central to this is a careful inquiry of the interpersonal context of the client's symptoms and problems as well as past and current interpersonal relationships. From this information, the therapist then constructs a mental model of the client's interpersonal functioning. Also assessed is the client's readiness to form a working alliance and his or her expectations of therapy. The outcome of this inquiry is a case conceptualization that elucidates the "cyclical maladaptive pattern" that characterizes the client's repetitive, maladaptive interactions, particularly the inflexible, self-defeating expectations, behaviors, and negative self-appraisals (introjections) that lead to dysfunctional interactions with other people.

## 4. Intervention Planning and Case Conceptualization

Specifically, it means explicating the client's mental model and corresponding maladaptive interpersonal pattern. Treatment is planned, tailored, and tracked because a consistent correspondence between therapist's interventions and the identified therapeutic focus treatment results in optimal treatment outcomes.

## 5. Intervention Focus, Strategy, and Implementation

The primary goals of treatment are to foster insight, enhanced interpersonal problem-solving skills, and corrective emotional and interpersonal experiences. The basic treatment focus is the client's current most important troublesome relationship pattern. The principal treatment strategy is to utilize the therapeutic relationship to facilitate new relational experiences and understandings that replace the maladaptive pattern. Besides the traditional dynamic interventions of clarification, confrontation, and interpretation, this approach utilizes incisive questioning, transference analysis, coaching, skill training, and practice.

## 6. Intervention Evaluation and Termination

Although treatment outcomes are not formally evaluated, in this approach ongoing progress is monitored in terms of achievement of treatment goals. Client readiness for termination is assessed in terms of the client's improved interpersonal functioning, increased understanding of interpersonal dynamics, and the capacity to maintain treatment gains. Since this is a brief therapy, clients are helped to view therapy as a resource to which they can return over time.

# EXPERIENTIAL APPROACH

Among the various experiential therapies, emotionally focused therapy (EFT) is probably the most researched and utilized of these approaches today. EFT treatment protocols have been developed for individuals, couples, and families and have relatively few contraindications.

## 1. Basic Orientation

### Personality

Experiencing is posited as the basis of one's thoughts, feelings, and actions. Although persons are whole, they are made up of various parts or self-organizations. Nevertheless, persons function best when they possess an integrated understanding of, and relationship, to all of their parts. Achieving this integrated awareness maximizes one's potential for personal choice and adaptiveness.

### Psychopathology

The experience of emotion is constrained by the degree to which it is attended and by the processes, that is, language, narrative, and explanations, used to symbolize it in awareness. All persons have an innate emotional responding system consisting of responses, such as sensations, autobiographical memory, and facial expressions, which function automatically to organize a person's higher order experiences, including self experiences. Called "emotion schemes" or schemas, these responses are not available to self-awareness, and the activation of these maladaptive schemas results in dysfunction. Psychologically healthy persons experience congruence between their awareness and experience in the moment, whereas less healthy persons experience incongruence due to activation of primary maladaptive emotion schemas (Pos & Greenberg, 2008).

### Psychotherapy

Emotion is central to the therapeutic process, and therapy is viewed as a collaborative process in which clients are assisted to better identify, experience, explore, make sense of, transform, and flexibly manage their emotion schemes. The expected outcome is that clients become more skillful in accessing important information and meanings and more skillful in utilizing that information to live vitally and adaptively. Therapy is best facilitated by a therapist who is psychologically present and establishes an interpersonal environment that is empathic, unconditionally accepting, and authentic.

## 2. Therapeutic Relationship

In this approach, effective treatment is based on two factors: first, establishing a genuinely empathic relationship; and second, the therapist being highly present, respectful, and responsive to the client's experience.

## 3. Assessment

Mindful of the humanistic-experiential tradition's wariness of diagnosis creating a power differential between therapist and client, adherents of EFT utilize a diagnostic process to identify client suitability for EFT. Strong biological and systemic factors, as well as psychosis and severe personality disorders, are contraindicated. Assessment is process diagnostic rather than person diagnostic, meaning that the client's experiential processing style, degree of emotional arousal, and other markers of emotionality are emphasized in the assessment. Process diagnosis is privileged over person diagnosis, that is, DSM diagnostic categories and criteria.

## 4. Intervention Planning and Case Conceptualization

Case conceptualization is viewed as a dynamic process that identifies clients' presenting problems, how they are currently experienced, and how they interfere with their own experience. A therapeutic focus is co-constructed with the client because EFT holds that an optimal treatment focus involves core issues that are collaboratively identified.

## 5. Intervention Focus, Strategy, and Implementation

The focus of treatment is the client's core pain. The basic treatment goal is to modify emotional responsivity and emotional schemas and create a new self-narrative in order to live a more vital and adaptive life. The primary therapeutic strategy is to access and utilize adaptive emotional functioning. There are two fundamental interventions: the therapeutic relationship, which promotes safety and fosters client emotional processing, and the therapist's verbal empathic exploration of the client's verbal and nonverbal narrative. Intervention choice is based on identified problems and markers of emotional processing. Marker-driven interventions that are utilized include empathic attunement, empathic exploration, focusing, two-chair technique, empty-chair technique, and empathic affirmation. Three phases of treatment are delineated: bonding and awareness; evocation and exploration; and transformation, which involves generating new emotions and meanings and a new self-narrative.

## 6. Intervention Evaluation and Termination

The identified emotional markers serve as means of assessing and monitoring progress. As the transformation phase of treatment unfolds, progress is mutually evaluated and a decision about termination is collaboratively discussed and made.

## RELATIONAL–SYSTEMIC APPROACH

Among the various relational and systemic approaches, Solution-Focused Therapy (SFT) (de Shazer, 1985) is one of the most commonly used approaches throughout the world. Unlike most of the other approaches identified in this chapter, SFT is based on a postmodern perspective of the therapeutic process.

## 1. Basic Orientation

**Personality**
This approach does not posit a theory of personality development or how individuals come to be the way they are. However, it does posit that individuals are unique and so are their problems and symptoms. In line with its social constructivist philosophy, clients are understood to be experts on their own lives, and they have the strengths and resources necessary to resolve any difficulties.

**Psychopathology**
This approach does not recognize pathology and refuses to pathologize individuals or assign diagnoses. Rather, problems are understood to arise when clients continue to apply solutions that don't work rather than

solutions that do work. "Exceptions" is a key construct in SFT. There are times when the problem does not occur even though the client may expect it to occur.

**Psychotherapy**
This is a brief form of therapy that lasts only as long as necessary to get the client on track toward achieving his or her goals. Goals do not need to be actually achieved for treatment to be finished; rather treatment is finished when the client is satisfied with changing direction and understands what is needed to change even without therapy. This approach holds that change constantly happens, that small changes lead to big changes, and that solutions may not seem related to problems.

## 2. Therapeutic Relationship

The therapist functions as a participant observer. Clients are understood to be experts on their lives while therapists support and encourage clients' movement toward finding and implementing solutions. Unlike other approaches, which view resistance negatively, this approach views clients' unique way of cooperating with the therapist, that is, providing information that will help them work toward their goals.

## 3. Assessment

Therapist and client work together to identify, amplify, and increase exceptions in the direction of problem resolution. Unlike other assessment approaches, SFT's emphasis is in on the client's uniqueness and the therapist's understanding of the client's life experiences from the client's perspective. Assessment focuses on inherent strengths and unique resources.

## 4. Intervention Planning and Case Conceptualization

Unlike other therapeutic approaches, SFT is not concerned with understanding clients' problems, providing explanations, or solving problems. Instead, case conceptualization in SFT is organized around solutions and achievement of goals. Emphasized is how to help clients identify changes that are meaningful to them and indicators that a problem is resolved or no longer causing distress.

### 5. Intervention Focus, Strategy, and Implementation

The basic goal of treatment is the smallest changes needed for clients to function better. The treatment focus is solutions, and the primary intervention strategies are goal clarification and solution amplification. Interventions include exceptions, the miracle question, presuppositional questions, and scaling.

### 6. Intervention Evaluation and Termination

The criterion for problem resolution is that therapist and client agree that the presenting problem is no longer problematic or is sufficiently improved. Monitoring change is easily accomplished with scaling. The therapist and client plan for termination by reevaluating the problem and goal and determining the extent to which the exceptions represent an attainment of the client's treatment goals and if further sessions are indicated.

## INTEGRATIVE APPROACH

Integrative refers to combining or incorporating to produce a whole. Adlerian psychotherapy (Adler, 1963) is most representative of the integrative approaches because of its compatibility with a wide range of cognitive–behavioral, dynamic, systemic, and experiential models and approaches. In large part, this is because its basic constructs permeate and, in most cases, predate many of these other approaches.

### 1. Basic Orientation

**Personality**

The individuals' basic motivation is to belong, and they develop within a family environment (constellation). In this context individuals create their own subjective interpretation of life events based on their unique private logic, which becomes their lifestyle or cognitive map, which subsequently guides their perceptions and actions. This map contains subjective convictions about self-view, world-view, and conclusions and life strategies that reflect their life narrative. Healthy functioning is an outcome of social interest, that is, concern for others.

**Psychopathology**

Psychopathology reflects the manner in which an individual "arranges" symptoms that serve as excuses for failing to meet life tasks and responsibilities and for safeguarding self-esteem. Psychopathology reflects clients' self-interest and discouragement and is manifested in their faulty lifestyle convictions (core convictions that run counter to social interest), also called maladaptive schemas, and summarized as their "basic mistakes."

**Psychotherapy**

The process of therapy has four aims: establishing and maintaining a good (i.e., effective) therapeutic relationship, lifestyle investigation, insight and constructive action, and reorientation. These processes are continuous throughout the course of treatment. The primary goal of treatment is to increase social interest.

## 2. Therapeutic Relationship

The relationship is characterized by mutual respect and equality. Client and therapist are considered collaborative partners wherein clients are expected to assume an active role in the change process.

## 3. Assessment

Assessment focuses on both the current situation and predisposing factors, that is, lifestyle analysis. This analysis includes elicitation of family constellation and early developmental experiences, including early recollections, to derive the individual's lifestyle convictions.

## 4. Intervention Planning and Case Conceptualization

Lifestyle information is summarized into a conceptualization that is collaboratively discussed and modified with the client. The conceptualization helps clients understand who they are and how they became who they are and to increase their awareness of their faulty logic and patterns.

## 5. Intervention Focus, Strategy, and Implementation

The focus of treatment is faulty lifestyle convictions and basic mistakes. The basic goal is to increase social interest and modify faulty lifestyle convictions, while the basic therapeutic strategy is cognitive restructuring and fostering insight and constructive action. Interventions include lifestyle assessment, interpretation, encouragement, acting "as if," paradox, and reframing.

## 6. Intervention Evaluation and Termination

No particular method of monitoring and evaluating progress or of planning and implementing termination is advocated.

# 2

# *Establish an Effective Therapeutic Alliance*

Effective therapy typically begins with the establishment of an effective therapeutic alliance, a therapeutic relationship with specific characteristics. The therapeutic alliance can have a profound effect on the treatment process and outcomes. Research consistently demonstrates that the therapeutic alliance is the best predictor of therapeutic outcome (Horvath & Symonds, 1991; Orlinsky, Grawe, & Parks, 1994; Orlinsky, Ronnestad, & Willutzi, 2004). A meta-analysis showed that treatment outcomes were clearly a function of the therapeutic alliance rather than of the length or type of treatment (Horvath & Symonds, 1991). It also showed that collaboration and negotiation of mutually agreeable goals and plans were essential to treatment success. Yet, trainees and beginning therapists are often unaware of the importance of the therapeutic alliance. It may be they came from graduate programs that focused on counseling micro-skills, or they may have come from programs that emphasized empirically supported treatments (ESTs) and did not emphasize the value and importance of effective therapeutic alliances. Even though ESTs do impact treatment outcomes, without an effective therapeutic alliance the best treatment interventions are unlikely to succeed. Thus, this essential clinical competency is one of the first and most important competencies for therapists to develop.

This chapter discusses several aspects of therapeutic alliance, including its development, an integrative view of the alliance, and therapist attributes and skills in developing therapeutic alliances. Next, it describes the challenge of developing a therapeutic alliance with difficult clients. Finally, it illustrates the development of a therapeutic alliance with two case examples.

## THERAPEUTIC ALLIANCE AS A PROCESS

The therapeutic alliance is not the beginning of a treatment event; rather it is a process, an ongoing process that begins with the first contact between client and therapist and continues through the last contact. Although initial interactions are especially important, as first impressions usually are, the development of the therapeutic alliance is intertwined with all aspects of the treatment process and evolves and changes over time. An effective therapeutic alliance may develop as quickly as the first session but must be in place by the fifth session if treatment is to be successful (Orlinsky et al., 2004). Needless to say, every client–therapist contact, either positive or negative, influences the development and maintenance of the therapist alliance.

## AN INTEGRATIVE VIEW OF THE THERAPEUTIC ALLIANCE

Historically, there have been several theories and viewpoints about the nature and role of the therapeutic alliance in psychotherapy. Although differing views of the alliance have been championed, an integrative view has recently emerged (Bordin, 1979). These differing views can be understood on a continuum. One end of the continuum represents the view that the therapeutic relationship or alliance is the primary element of change in therapy. In this view, the alliance is itself an intervention and the primary corrective and curative factor in change. The other end of the continuum represents the view that intervention strategies in general, and ESTs in particular, are the primary agents of change. In this view, the therapeutic relationship can play a role in eliciting the client's collaboration, but it is the therapist's interventions that effect change. The midpoint on the continuum represents a more integrative view. Called the "common factors" approach, it contends that, irrespective of the theoretical orientation, both relationship and intervention factors effect change (Lambert, 1992).

An integrative view of the therapeutic alliance operationalizes this in terms of three factors of a therapeutic alliance: bond, goals, and tasks

24

(Borden, 1979). Another way of saying this is that an effective therapeutic alliance involves a "meeting of hearts" (bond) and a "meeting of minds" (goals and tasks) between clinician and client.

Important to the formation of a strong therapeutic bond is that clients feel understood, safe, and hopeful. It also means that they are more likely to take the risk of disclosing painful affects and intimate details of their lives, as well as risk thinking, feeling, and acting in more adaptive and healthier ways. Besides the therapeutic bond, clinicians need to attend to mutually agreed upon therapeutic goals and tasks or methods. This entails recognition of the client's explanatory model and expectations for treatment goals and methods and the way treatment will be provided. Such expectations are influenced by cultural factors and norms. Among some cultures, it is customary for family members to accompany the designated client to appointments. Because there may be the unspoken expectation that family members be included in the treatment process, effective clinicians will inquire about such expectations. Similarly, there may be "silent expectations" about the type of intervention utilized. Sometimes, the silent expectation is that healing requires some measure of touch or contact. Some clients prefer action-oriented approaches over strictly talk-oriented approaches. In short, an effective therapeutic alliance involves a "meeting of hearts" and a "meeting of minds" between clinician and client. The basic constructs involved in developing an effective therapeutic alliance are further elaborated here.

**Table 2.1** Elements of an Effective Therapeutic Alliance

| | |
|---|---|
| **Bond** | Bond is the affective quality of the relationship between therapist and client. It reflects how the client feels understood, respected, valued, and cared for. The more the first nine attributes and skills described in the following section are present in the relationship, the better the bond. |
| **Goals** | Goals are the targets toward which an intervention is directed. For instance, achieving insight and a corrective emotional experience are two basic goals of time-limited dynamic psychotherapy. |
| **Tasks** | Tasks refers to the in-therapy and between-session behaviors and activities that the client must engage in to benefit from the treatment. For example, an important task in cognitive–behavioral therapy might be to engage in a behavioral rehearsal role plan in session or to complete a mutually agreed upon homework activity between sessions. |

| | |
|---|---|
| **Explanation** | Explanation or explanatory model is the client's theory or best guess for what is causing his or her presenting problems, symptoms, or impaired functioning. It is akin to the therapist's case conceptualization. |
| **Expectations** | Expectations are what the client wants and anticipates of treatment, both its process and outcomes. It involves role and responsibilities the client expects the therapist will assume, as well as the role and responsibilities the client is willing to assume in the treatment process. Expectations flow from the client's explanatory model. For example, if a client believes his or her panic attacks result from a chemical imbalance in his or her brain, the client may expect that treatment will consist of medication to correct the imbalance. |
| **Negotiation** | Negotiation is a reciprocal communication process between client and therapist for arriving at mutually agreeable treatment goals and tasks. To the extent that treatment goals and tasks offered by the therapist are consistent with the client's explanation and expectations, the client is likely to agree and collaborate with treatment. However, if the therapist's treatment goals and tasks do not match the client's explanation and expectations, the client's agreement and collaboration in the treatment process is unlikely, and noncompliance is the result. For this reason, negotiation plays a central role in achieving a mutually agreed treatment plan, the result of which is a "meeting of the minds." |

## THERAPIST ATTRIBUTES AND SKILLS IN DEVELOPING THERAPEUTIC ALLIANCES

Clinical lore holds that therapists who embody the core conditions of effective treatment, empathy, respect, and acceptance (Rogers, 1961), and who demonstrate active listening and responding, facilitate the development of an effective alliance. In such a relationship, clients will feel accepted, supported, and valued, and they will believe that their therapist cares about them and is worthy of their trust. As a result, they become hopeful and confident that treatment will be successful.

Research has validated much of the clinical lore of the therapist's contribution to the alliance. But it does not support Carl Rogers's claim that three core conditions are the necessary *and* sufficient conditions for therapeutic change (Rogers, 1961). However, a review of the literature shows that certain therapist attributes and skill sets are positively related to an effective therapeutic alliance. Therapists in an effective alliance present themselves in a *warm* and *friendly* manner and appear to be *confident* and *experienced*. They are *interested* in and *respectful* toward the client, and they relate with *honesty, trustworthiness,* and *openness*. During treatment they remain *alert* and *flexible* and provide a safe environment in which clients can discuss their issues. They are *supportive*, use active and *reflective listening, affirm* the client's experience, and demonstrate an *empathic understanding* of each client's situation. Furthermore, they *attend to the clients' experiences* and *facilitate the expression of affect*, to enable a *deep exploration* of concerns. Finally, they *provide accurate interpretations* of the client's behavior and are *active* in treatment and *draw attention to past therapeutic successes* (Ackerman & Hillensroth, 2003; Orlinsky et al., 1994, 2004).

## ILLUSTRATIONS OF DEVELOPING AN EFFECTIVE THERAPEUTIC ALLIANCE

### Case 1: Meeting of the Hearts

Inspired by Hill (2004), the following is a transcription of a first therapeutic encounter in which the therapist endeavors to develop a positive therapeutic alliance, starting with the "bond" dimension. Through active listening and responding, the therapist creates a safe, trusting, and caring, environment for the client to explore her concerns and connect or bond with the therapist.

Lori is a 36-year-old, never married Caucasian female who is a junior faculty member in an advanced practice nursing program at a local university. She is proud of her job and the extraordinary efforts involved in the 7 years it took to complete her Ph.D. Like other junior faculty, Lori is expected to conduct research, publish articles on her research, and give presentations at national meetings of professional nursing organizations. She was surprised when her proposal was accepted for a presentation at the annual conference of one of those organizations. Even though her presentation reports on her dissertation research, she has become increasingly anxious and "stuck" in her efforts to prepare the presentation, which is scheduled in approximately 1 month. She is referred for therapy by a colleague to a large private practice that has a

27

good reputation in the community for working effectively and discretely with executives and professionals.

Th.: It's good to meet you, Lori. (shaking hands with client) I'm Dr. Setter. We have the next 50 minutes to begin to get to know each other and talk about your concerns.

The therapist starts by making visual, verbal, and physical contact with the client and provides information about the structure of their time together and what the client can expect.

Cl.: Great! I'm glad I was able to get this appointment so soon.
Th.: So, what brings you here?
Cl.: Well, I've been feeling quite anxious about a professional presentation I have to make soon. Time is passing quickly, and all I have to show for 5 weeks of preparation is a one-page outline and some ideas about two or three handouts. (pause) I'm even imagining it will be the day before the presentation and I won't have the PowerPoint slides done and won't be ready. That thought is panicky. (pause) I just can't get myself to get this project ready.
Th.: You're very upset with yourself.

A reflection of feeling response that both acknowledge and that helps the client experience her feelings.

Cl.: Yes. I am worried that I'm going to fail or make a fool of myself in my first national presentation to my professional peers. If I can't do something as simple as this without falling apart, I'll never get promotion and tenure.
Th.: You're feeling nervous because your current efforts might interfere and limit your career plans.

Another reflection of feeling response to encourage the client to stay with her feelings and to further explore her concerns.

Cl.: That's right. I really think I could succeed in an academic career, but that means I'll have to be proficient at publishing papers and making professional presentations. It scares me to think that I could blow my career at this national presentation.
Th.: I hear you. (pause) Can you describe your most recent presentation to professionals? If you would, please take me through what was taking place inside you.

28

The therapist endeavors to elicit specific information about exactly what happened and wants the client to talk more concretely about the problem, so he asks open-ended questions.

Cl.:     Well, it was at a meeting of advanced practice nurses in the city about 6 weeks ago. I was asked to make a 20-minute presentation on evaluating adolescents who present with fever of unknown origin. I know that subject inside out because I deal with it all the time in one of our community clinics. Someone even gave me some commercial PowerPoint slides from a drug company on fever in young adolescents. So, the day before the presentation, all I really needed to do was modify some of those scanned slides. But, after several hours I finished it. I did it.

Th.:     So, you did finish the preparation for the presentation. Great!

An encouragement response that acknowledges the client's accomplishment fosters client confidence, and encourages her to continue pursuing her goals.

Cl.:     Yes, after what seemed like an eternity, I finished the preparation and the next day I gave the presentation without a hitch. (smiles) It was well received.

Th.:     Wonderful!

Cl.:     (pause with head down) But I went through hell, besieged by doubts and fears over my capacity to present on a topic that I really have considerable expertise. (deep sighs) I stayed up most of the night doing what should have taken no more than a half hour of preparation time. But for the life of me, there were stretches of time when I couldn't seem to put the presentation together. I couldn't concentrate, I couldn't think straight, and … I started to feel numb.

Th.:     I can sense the panic in your voice.

Cl.:     I'm scared that I won't be able to pull together and give this presentation in time. This last time I worked around the clock to get the presentation ready. But the national presentation seems too big this time. I've been working on it for over 5 weeks and I seem to be falling behind.

Th.:     Exactly how much have you completed on the preparation?

An open-ended question is asked to gain more precise information about the challenge the client is facing.

**29**

*Cl.:*      Well, I'd say I'm about a third of the way finished. But, the way I feel right now I just don't want to work on it anymore.

*Th.:*      Might there be other things going on in your life that are making it difficult for you to focus on the presentation right now?

The therapist recognizes that the client seems stuck and wonders if a complicating factor is operative. Thus, an open-ended question is asked.

*Cl.:*      (pause) Well, I suppose there is. My significant other for the past 3 years had proposed to me a while back. Gary wants to get married and have a family soon because he's 40 and he says it's now or he'll be too old to take on family responsibilities. I told him that I'm just getting my career off the ground and having a family right now would effectively put my career on hold. I've seen that happen so many times for female faculty. I mean, I want kids but not right now.

*Th.:*      So you're feeling conflicted between the marriage proposal and developing your career.

It is noteworthy that the client feels sufficiently comfortable and trusting to share information about a personal dilemma in her life. In order to facilitate the client talking about her feelings regarding this conflict, the therapist uses a reflection that focuses on both parts of the dilemma.

*Cl.:*      That's it. It's like everything has to go his way and on his time line. Just because he's already established in his career, he expects me to meet his needs at the expense of mine.

*Th.:*      So how does this make you feel?

A question that encourages the client to take the risk of identifying and expressing her feelings.

*Cl.:*      As I think about it, I feel angry. Why should I have to give up my career for his? My mother did it, and some of my friends and colleagues have done it, and they are all unhappy or even bitter. (pause) I want to have a career, but I don't know. It's not fair. But I don't want to lose my relationship with Gary.

*Th.:*      It sounds like you are really torn up inside.

The therapist realizes that the last intervention was inaccurate and shifts focus back to the client's feelings by using a reflection.

*Cl.:*    (tearful) Maybe I'm having so much trouble preparing these presentations because I'm so confused about my conflict with Gary and my fear that I'll end up as unhappy as my mother.

*Th.:*    (Silence)

The therapist is silent to give the client time to experience her feelings of sadness.

*Cl.:*    (cries and wipes her eyes with a tissue)

*Th.:*    (softly) This is so difficult and painful for you to talk about.

The therapist provides emotional support to the client with this reflection of feeling.

*Cl.:*    (still tearful) Yeah, it sure is.

**Case Commentary**

A therapeutic bond of caring and trust has begun to develop. It is at this point that the focus of the interview conversation can begin to shift to the other aspects of the therapeutic alliance, namely, goals and tasks, that is, the meeting of minds.

## Case 2: Meeting of the Minds

Jessica is a 24-year-old, single Caucasian female who was referred for therapy for "anxiety attacks" that are interfering with her study preparation for the nursing licensure exam. She has had asthma since she was a young adolescent, and it has been well controlled with medication and an inhaler. She had asked Dr. Wheeler, her family physician, for a prescription of Ativan to curb her anxiety attacks, but he was reluctant because of reported difficulties of combined use of Ativan and her asthma medications. After discussing this with her, he suggested she talk with a psychologist affiliated with his practice. If that didn't "work," he was willing to consider other possible medications. Jessica agreed that she would meet with Lillian Benzer, Ph.D., but wasn't hopeful it would really help. It was comforting to know that her physician, under whose care she had been for over 10 years, wanted the best for her and would help her if the therapy didn't work. If need be she was willing to "tough out" any medication side effects in the remaining weeks before her exam. About halfway through her first session with Dr. Benzer, Jessica began to feel understood and cared for. As Dr. Benzer recognized that a bond was forming with Jessica, she began to shift the conversation more to goals and tasks.

| | |
|---|---|
| *Th.:* | How much would you say your asthma affects your life? |
| *Cl.:* | Until lately, not very much. I'm so thankful that Dr. Wheeler has been pretty good at controlling it with changing my medications as the allergy season comes and goes. But lately, I've become almost a basket case with all this anxiety and worry. |
| *Th.:* | So, using a 10-point scale, where 1 is very little and 10 is very high, how much control would you estimate you have had over your asthma before this anxiety started? And, how much control would you say you have now? |
| *Cl.:* | I'd say about an 8 or 9 before, and about 3 or so now. |
| *Th.:* | Thanks, that helpful. So, what do you think has caused your asthma? |

Here Dr. Benzer begins to elicit Jessica's explanatory model.

| | |
|---|---|
| *Cl.:* | Well, it seems to run in the family. Heredity. My mother and sister have it. I've had it since I was 13, and I was told that allergies to tree pollen and mold just make it worse. |
| *Th.:* | Do you see a connection between the stress you experience as anxiety and your allergy symptoms? |
| *Cl.:* | Definitely. |
| *Th.:* | How do you understand that connection? |
| *Cl.:* | Well, I guess that stress aggravates it. The more stress and worry I have, the worse my asthma gets and the harder it is to control it. |
| *Th.:* | So, psychological stress activates your asthma just as environmental stress like pollen and mold do. Psychological factors can affect your asthma in addition to environmental and hereditary factors. Is that what you're saying? |

Dr. Benzer endeavors to expand Jessica's perception of causality to include both biological *and* psychological factors. A positive response to his question suggests that she is more receptive to a multiple cause explanation (i.e., biological and psychological formulation) as compared to a single causative one (i.e., biological formulation).

| | |
|---|---|
| *Cl.:* | Yes. (pause) I suppose I am. |

*Th.:*    So, generally speaking, biological treatments like your asthma medication and inhalers are the usual treatment for biologically caused aspects of a medical condition like asthma. And, while medications can be a treatment for more psychologically caused aspects of it, psychological treatments like stress management and counseling are the usual treatments for it, particularly when medications are contraindicated, such as the potential for causing serious side effects. Does that make sense?

Here Dr. Benzer helps Jessica to see that her treatment expectations for medication were connected with her biologically oriented explanatory model. He also helps her link a more psychologically oriented explanation with more psychologically oriented treatment expectations (goals and tasks).

*Cl.:*    (pause) It does. But I told Dr. Wheeler I was willing to put up with any side effect problems.

*Th.:*    Dr. Wheeler mentioned to me that the Ativan you wanted prescribed has been shown to cause short-term memory loss and concentration difficulty in a number of people who take it. Such side effects are most likely to occur in the first two weeks of use. Are you saying that you're willing to take the chance of having memory loss and even failing your exam by taking a medication that has such side effects?

*Cl.:*    Well, if you put it that way … no. I guess that isn't what I want. Dr. Wheeler didn't tell me that memory loss was such a big problem.

*Th.:*    That's not the kind of news you were expecting. (Yes.) You seem to be viewing yourself more as having a medical problem and wanting a biological treatment than as someone with a psychological problem and needing a psychological treatment. Would that be accurate?

*Cl.:*    Yes, it is.

*Th.:*    Well, then I think I can be of some help to you. Since medication seems out of the question at the present time, I suggest we do an experiment where we'll use some powerful stress reduction strategies to reduce your anxiousness. We can start right now and then follow up as needed. Are you willing to give it a try?

**Case Commentary**

Jessica's objective was to get relief from the anxiety symptoms that were interfering with her exam preparation. Her explanatory model was that there was a biological cause for her anxiety, and so her treatment expectation was that she needed a biological treatment, such as Ativan or a similar medication. As Dr. Benzer increased Jessica's awareness of an additional causative factor, psychological stress, Jessica became receptive to a more psychologically based intervention. In short, Dr. Benzer helped Jessica expand her explanatory model, which changed her expectations of treatment. As a result, her receptivity to psychological treatment was significantly increased. It turned out that her work with Dr. Benzer was short and successful, two sessions in 1 week, and she was able to continue preparing for and passing the exam with minimal anxiety. Among other things, this case example illustrates how Dr. Benzer began to work with Jessica to achieve a reasonable degree of a "meeting of the hearts" before proceeding to work at developing a "meeting of the minds."

# 3

# *Assess Readiness and Foster Treatment-Promoting Factors*

While developing an effective therapeutic relationship, the therapist needs to consider the various treatment factors that can promote or impede the treatment process as well as progress in therapy. This means that the therapist must attend to such critical factors as the client's readiness for change, capacity for collaboration, expectations, and other treatment-promoting factors.

This chapter focuses on a variety of treatment-promoting factors, beginning with readiness for change. It briefly describes the *stages of readiness for change* model and some markers for assessing readiness. Next, it describes *common factors*, that is, nonspecific curative factors that are common to all forms of psychotherapy. Then, *treatment-promoting factors* and strategies are described. Finally, case material illustrates a key treatment-promoting strategy: optimizing readiness for treatment.

## ASSESSMENT OF TREATMENT READINESS

### Stages of Readiness for Change

Prochaska, DiClemanti, and Norcross (1992) found that individuals who change their behaviors, on their own or with a therapist's help, typically proceed through five stages of change. The stages are precontemplation,

contemplation, preparation, action, and maintenance. This stage model is quite useful in understanding and predicting client change across a wide array of client concerns in psychotherapy.

A preliminary assessment of readiness for change can be extremely valuable and useful in treatment planning. Because most clients cycle in and out of these stages several times before achieving their goals, it is helpful to gauge the current stage during the initial session and to monitor movement through these stages. Ideally, the client enters therapy at the preparation or action stage, which means that treatment outcomes will be predictably positive. When the client enters at the precontemplative or contemplative stage, the therapist's primary task is to tailor treatment in order to move the client toward the action stage.

Readiness is typically assessed through observation or interview. Markers, by stage, to elicit or observe when assessing readiness include the following:

| | |
|---|---|
| **Precontemplation** | The client does not consider his or her behavior to be a problem and/or does not currently consider making any change. |
| **Contemplation** | The client is considering that his or her behavior may be a problem and contemplates, that is, seriously considers, making a change *within the next 6 months*. |
| **Preparation** | The client has made a commitment to change a behavior considered problematic and intends to make the change soon. The client can have a specific plan or a target date set for change *within a month*. |
| **Action** | The client is already making changes and is considered to be *in this stage for up to 6 months* from the start of the initial change. |
| **Maintenance** | The client works to stabilize the new change to prevent a return of the problem behavior. (Prochaska et al., 1992) |

## Interventions to Optimize Readiness for Change

The treatment implications of the concept of readiness for change are immense. Several strategies for fostering readiness have been proposed, implemented, and researched. Currently, motivational interviewing (MI) has become a useful strategy. The following outline, adapted from Miller,

Duncan, and Hubble (1997), indicates some of the targets for MI and suggests other possible interventions.

| Stage | Interventions |
|---|---|
| Precontemplation | 1. Explore the client's explanatory model. |
| | 2. Suggest the client think about the situation from another perspective. |
| | 3. Provide education and information. |
| Contemplation | 1. Encourage the client to think about making changes. |
| | 2. Suggest an observational task (i.e., what happens to make the situation better or worse). |
| | 3. Join with the client's ambivalence to action with a "go slow" directive. |
| Preparation | 1. Offer several viable treatment options. |
| | 2. Invite client to choose from among these options. |
| Action | 1. Elicit details of the client's successful efforts. |
| | 2. Reinforce those efforts and encourage other efforts. |
| Maintenance | 1. Support the client's successful efforts. |
| | 2. Predict relapse and setbacks. |
| | 3. Help client make contingency plans. |

## TREATMENT-PROMOTING FACTORS AND STRATEGIES

Lack of treatment progress typically reflects *treatment-interfering behaviors,* which are behaviors that the client brings to bear and that impede the progress of therapy (Linehan, 1993). In Chapter 17 a broader designation, *treatment-interfering factors,* is described, which includes not only client-interfering behaviors but also other impediments to treatment progress such as therapist factors, client–therapist relationship factors, and treatment factors. The other side of treatment-interfering factors is *treatment-promoting factors,* and this section focuses on such factors.

Treatment-promoting factors include a range of client factors, therapist factors, client–therapist relationship factors, and intervention factors that promote progress in therapy (Sperry, Carlson, & Kjos, 2003). In this and previous chapters, a number of treatment-promotion strategies have already been described; others will be introduced in subsequent chapters. Table 3.1 provides a listing of some of these strategies. A

**Table 3.1**   Treatment-Promoting Factors and Strategies

| Factors | Treatment-Promotion Strategies |
| --- | --- |
| Client–therapist relationship | Optimize treatment readiness. |
| | Demonstrate clinician credibility. |
| | Provide active listening and empathic responding. |
| | Elicit client's explanatory model and treatment expectations. |
| | Negotiate mutually agreeable goals, focus, and intervention methods. |
| Intervention | Tailor interventions to client need, capacity, and expectations. |
| Faith and hope | Reverse demoralization. |
| | Trigger the placebo effect. |

particularly critical treatment-promotion strategy that therapists would do well to develop is clinician credibility. Clinician credibility is the client's perception that the therapist is effective and trustworthy based on how the therapist instills hope, confidence, and trust in the client (Sue & Zane, 1987).

# ILLUSTRATIONS OF OPTIMIZING TREATMENT READINESS

The following case examples illustrate how MI techniques can be used to increase a client's involvement in the therapeutic process as well as increase therapeutic alliance. These case examples, inspired by Lambie (2004), demonstrate how therapists can work with clients in the stages of precontemplation, contemplation, and preparation.

## Case 1

Jerrod is a 19-year-old male sophomore. Facing expulsion from the university, the Dean of Students has suspended Jerrod but because this is his first violation of the code of student conduct, Jerrod has been given the chance of being reinstated if he undergoes a course of counseling. Jerrod was arrested by university police after vandalizing property while drinking beer in the dorm, both actions being grounds for expulsion. The staff psychologist who evaluated Jerrod quickly recognized that this client was at the precontemplation stage of change.

38

*Th.:* Jerrod, what's your understanding of why Dean Simpson referred you to the counseling center?

*Cl.:* He said if I went for counseling I could avoid being expelled.

*Th.:* Do you believe there is any reason for the dean to be concerned about your recent behavior?

*Cl.:* No, there is no reason.

*Th.:* So, everything is fine with you. But, is it true that you were arrested for underage drinking and vandalizing dormitory property?

*Cl.:* Yes, some stuff did get broken. But it's no big deal. I already paid restitution. (pause) I've been under a lot of pressure lately.

*Th.:* Jerrod, could you tell me about the pressure you have been under lately?

The therapist emphasizes the client's personal choice.

*Cl.:* It's no big deal. (pause). Sara, my girlfriend has been on my case.

*Th.:* What has she been on your case about?

*Cl.:* Different stuff.

*Th.:* Would you mind giving an example of what Sara's been on your case about?

*Cl.:* Well, Sara is always telling me that I go out too much.

*Th.:* Going out too much?

*Cl.:* Yeah, going out too much with my friends.

*Th.:* Do you think this is a problem?

*Cl.:* No, but she does.

*Th.:* So while your girlfriend and the dean think that your behavior has become a problem, you don't think it is a problem. Any idea about why they think this is a problem for you?

The therapist assists Jerrod in perceiving a discrepancy, a key MI strategy.

*Cl.:* Because they're uninformed.

*Th.:* So you think they are worrying about nothing.

*Cl.:* Definitely.

*Th.:* Do you have any other ideas about why Sara is so concerned about you?

*Cl.:* Probably because I've been drinking a lot more and we haven't been getting along lately.

*Th.:* So it sounds like your girlfriend and the dean are concerned about you and recent changes in your behavior.

*Cl.:* Yes.

**Case Commentary**

Clients at the precontemplation stage are often not aware that a problem exists. At this stage the client may need information and feedback to raise his or her awareness. In this example, Jerrod seemed unaware that he was having any type of problem. A basic premise of MI is that aggressive confrontation is counterproductive and engenders resistance. Therefore, the therapist used active listening techniques and gently drew out discrepancies in what Jerrod was saying—there is no problem, but your girlfriend and the dean are concerned about you. The therapist also emphasized to Jerrod a sense of choice and control in the session by asking his permission to answer a question (Would you mind ...?). At the end of the meeting, it seemed that Jerrod's awareness had risen about his going out being a possible problem. Raising awareness is a step forward in contrast to efforts to confront Jerrod about his drinking and vandalism being a problem and slipping into an emotional power struggle.

Future sessions with Jerrod would focus on strengthening the therapist–client relationship, while continuing to increase Jerrod's awareness of his possible problem through gentle confrontation where incongruences would be identified and explored. Once Jerrod's awareness has increased, the therapist would work with and support Jerrod in the resolution of his ambivalence toward change. Throughout the process, collaboration between therapist and client would foster improvement in Jerrod's current situation.

## Case 2

Suzanne is a 20-year-old college junior who is majoring in marketing. She lives in an off-campus apartment and is self-referred for counseling. She reports that her parents have threatened to cut off her tuition and living expenses if her grades don't improve and she "doesn't settle down." During the first session, the staff therapist who evaluated Suzanne soon recognized that she was at the contemplation stage of change. Before the session the therapist received a call from the client's mother, who indicated that Suzanne said that she was getting counseling as a sign that she was "settling down." The mother wanted to provide information and ask questions of the therapist, but mindful of client privilege, the therapist listened but said she could not comment but thanked the mother for her concern. Near the beginning of the second session, Suzanne asked if her mother had called the therapist.

*Th.:*    Yes. Your mother did call. Would you like to talk about that call?

Anticipating resistance, the therapist begins by emphasizing the client's personal choice rather than providing an agenda to which the client might resist.

*Cl.:*    Sure.

*Th.:*    Suzanne, what's your guess as to why your mother would want to talk to with me?

*Cl.:*    Probably to see if I really followed through with the counseling?

*Th.:*    Followed through?

*Cl.:*    Yeah, I told her you were my therapist and that counseling might help me settle down and focus on my grades.

*Th.:*    So, she's concerned about your grades and your well-being.

*Cl.:*    Yes, both my parents are concerned about me getting my grades up and that I'm not taking things seriously enough. That's why they gave me this ultimatum. My dad says he's not going to continue to throw money down a rat hole if things don't improve.

*Th.:*    Have your grades dropped?

*Cl.:*    Yeah, my grades dropped last semester.

*Th.:*    Do you think your grades dropping and not settling down is a problem?

The therapist recognizes a self-motivational statement and reinforces the client's "change talk," another key MI strategy.

*Cl.:*    Well, I am not all that sure. My parents keep telling me it is a problem.

*Th.:*    What types of things do they tell you?

*Cl.:*    That I could do so much better if I applied myself and tried to stay focused.

*Th.:*    So, it sounds like your parents think it is a problem but you are unsure.

The therapist offers a reflection of content and assists the client in perceiving a discrepancy.

*Cl.:*    Yeah. (pause) I know I could do much better if I tried but I just don't know.

*Th.:*    Well, Suzanne, what do you think are some good reasons to change your behavior?

**41**

Several MI strategies are demonstrated here: intention to change, self-motivational statement, and decision balance.

*Cl.:*     My parents would be off my back and I would get better grades. (pause) And, I could come back next fall and be with my friends.
*Th.:*     Those sound like really good reasons. What do you think are some good reasons for you not to change and to keep things the way they are?

Again, decision balance.

*Cl.:*     Well, it sure would be easier.
*Th.:*     Could you say a little bit more about how it would be easier?
*Cl.:*     Well, I like to be with my dorm friends and sorority sisters. It's great to spend time with them at the student union and other places. But if I spend hours in the library, I probably won't see them much.
*Th.:*     So Suzanne, it sounds like if you were to change, you would have less time to spend with your friends, but your parents would be off your back and your grades would likely improve, which means you'd be academically eligible to return for the fall semester. Is that correct?
*Cl.:*     Yeah, probably.
*Th.:*     Is it possible that if you choose to change, you could still spend time with friends, but maybe in a different way for some of the time? (pause) For example, some students who are friends arrange to study together. But there are a lot of other ways that students have figured out how to meet different needs at the same time. (pause) If you did find a way to do this, you could probably still spend time with friends, improve your grades, and get your parents off your back.

Again, the therapist recognizes the client's self-motivational statement and change talk.

*Cl.:*     I guess.
*Th.:*     Do you have any ideas what might work for you if you decided to make a change?

The therapist attempts to promote self-motivational statements and change talk.

*Cl.:*     Probably. I need to find a way to study without becoming a hermit and never seeing my friends. (pause). Studying with friends is an interesting idea. Jenny Burns is a real fun person, and she's smart and gets high grades. Maybe I could study with her.

*Th.:*     So, it sounds like you see change as a real possibility for you if you choose to make that choice.

The therapist offers a reflection which emphasizes the client's personal choice.

*Cl.:*     Yeah, I could do it if I really want to.

**Case Commentary**

Clients at the contemplation stage are aware that others perceive a problem but are ambivalent about changing. At this stage, the therapist's goal in utilizing MI is to collaborate with the client to tip her ambivalence toward change. In this example, Suzanne seemed aware that others see her having a problem, but she was unsure. Therefore, the therapist used active listening techniques and asked Suzanne to look at both sides of changing, bringing to her awareness that if she chooses to make the change she may gain some benefits but also may lose something she likes. The therapist attempted to emphasize Suzanne's choice and provided her with information about changing using self-motivational statements and change talk while presenting incentive to change and accentuating the positive aspects of changing. At the end of the brief session, it appeared that Suzanne's scale to change was vacillating more toward change than at the start of the meeting. The one thing the therapist needs to remember when counseling clients at this level is that if the therapist moves to the action stage before the client is ready, resistance will likely be engendered.

# Case 3

Derrin is an 18-year-old freshman who is a commuter student who lives with his parents. The Dean of Students referred him to counseling because although Derrin had been placed on academic probation after the first semester for failing grades, he is now facing academic dismissal from the university since his second semester mid-term grades have not improved. The irony is that Derrin was a scholarship student, having received a full-tuition Knights of Columbus scholarship for outstanding community involvement. The therapist met with Derrin for three sessions about his academic difficulties, which he attributed to commuting long distance (about 2 hours per day), not having developed a realistic plan for studying, and not feeling connected to fellow students on campus, most of whom lived in dorms. During the third session, the staff therapist soon recognized that Derrin was now at the preparation stage of change. The fourth session progresses as follows:

*Th.:*    Hey Derrin, how are you doing today?
*Cl.:*    I'm doing okay.
*Th.:*    I am happy to see you. How do you feel about the prospect of improving your grades and returning as a sophomore next fall?

The therapist emphasizes the client's personal choice.

*Cl.:*    I think it is something I really want to do. I want to get a college degree so I can get a great job.
*Th.:*    Have you thought about any specific things that you could do to raise your grades in the remaining 6 weeks?

Here the therapist recognizes the client's intention to change and encourages his self-motivational statement and change talk.

*Cl.:*    Yes, I've talked to someone about getting tutoring at Student Services. My mom had an idea and talked to my aunt about staying at her place 3 nights a week, on the days I have most of my courses: Monday, Wednesday, and Thursday. My aunt and uncle live about 5 minutes from campus. That means I could stay and study at the university library and maybe even study with some kids in my classes. So, the 2 hours a day I now waste on commuting I can use for studying and stuff.
*Th.:*    Those sound like realistic and specific plans. Do you think you have addressed all the study targets we talked about last week:
*Cl.:*    I think so.
*Th.:*    As I remember it, there were three. A regular, dedicated place to study. Spending 2 hours a day in the university library seems to fit that, at least on the days you can stay in town at your aunt's house. Tutoring in physics and precalculus with a tutor sounds right. There was a third target. Do you recall?
*Cl.:*    Yeah. It was study skills.
*Th.:*    Would you be willing to make a change in your plan to add the study skills part?

Therapist again emphasizes the client's personal choice and encourages collaboration with the therapy process.

*Cl.:*    Sure, I would.

*Th.:*    Would you be willing to sign up for the half-day "Sharpen Your Study Skills" workshop that the counseling center offers a couple of Saturdays a month? There's actually one this Saturday.

*Cl.:*    (nods) That shouldn't be a problem. I'll sign up.

*Th.:*    Derrin, are you willing to do an experiment between now and when we meet next week?

Again, the therapist emphasizes the client's personal choice.

*Cl.:*    What kind of experiment?

*Th.:*    The experiment is for you to do the plan we just discussed between now and next Tuesday when we meet next. So you would study in the library 2 hours a day on Thursday, Monday, and Tuesday. You'd get tutoring at least twice, and you'd go to the study skills workshop this Saturday and start applying what you learned. Then when we meet next Tuesday you let me know how you did and how it was for you.

*Cl.:*    Sure. That shouldn't be a problem at all.

*Th.:*    So you understand the experiment and don't have any questions?

*Cl.:*    No, I don't. (pause) Wait, I do. Where do I sign up for the workshop?

They discussed how and where to sign up for the workshop. The therapist offered to walk Derrin over to the registration desk. When they found that the workshop for Saturday was already full, the staff therapist was able to sign a waiver permitting Derrin to register to attend it.

*Th.:*    Everything set now?

*Cl.:*    Oh yes. I'll see you next Tuesday at 11:30.

**Case Commentary**

Clients at the preparation stage are considered motivated for change. Frequently they use statements like "It is time to make a change" or "How can I make a change?" The therapist's job is to work with the client to develop a change plan that is acceptable, accessible, appropriate, and effective (Miller & Rollnick, 2002). In the example, the therapist collaborated with Derrin to develop a plan that the client accepted and that was realistic and possible. Beginning the plan with an "experiment" allows the client to try the strategy for a short time and return to the therapist for support and possible modification in the plan. The experiment takes the blame off the client if he is unsuccessful at the first attempt to change and allows him to receive the additional support and make accommodations to the strategy. The therapist needs to match the client as well as possible at this stage to reduce the likelihood that the client will move back to the contemplation stage.

# 4

# Recognize and Resolve Resistance and Ambivalence

## AN OVERVIEW STATEMENT FOR CHAPTERS 4, 5, AND 6

There is no question that therapeutic impasses and roadblocks can play havoc with the therapeutic process and negatively impact treatment progress. Table 4.1 lists the five most common types of impasses and their sources. It is noteworthy that while clients are the most common source of these therapeutic roadblocks, there are other sources, including therapists and the therapeutic relationship. Each of these impasse types is addressed in this book. This and the next two chapters focus on various types of impasses and various therapeutic strategies for resolving these impasses. This chapter focuses on resistance and ambivalence. Chapter 6

**Table 4.1**  Therapeutic Impasses and Sources

| Type of Impasses | Source |
| --- | --- |
| Resistance | Client |
| Ambivalence | Client |
| Alliance strains & ruptures | Client–therapist relationship |
| Transference | Client, sometimes client–therapist relationship |
| Countertransference | Therapist, sometimes client–therapist relationship |

emphasizes alliance strains and ruptures, and Chapter 5 focuses on transference–countertransference enactments.

These impasses present a formidable challenge for many therapists and an overwhelming challenge for most trainees and beginning therapists. Relatively few training programs formally address these impasses, which means that therapists have been left to their own devices to find ways of coping with and resolving them. Experienced supervisors and savvy colleagues have been the primary resource therapists have turned to for help with these challenges. Because resolving resistance, ambivalence, alliance ruptures, and transference–countertransference enactments are considered essential competencies in psychotherapy, it is unconscionable that training programs—and most basic texts—fail to formally incorporate these competencies in didactic coursework and clinical training experiences. Accordingly, this book endeavors to provide a solid overview and introduction to these competencies.

## RESISTANCE AND AMBIVALENCE

Resistance to change is a problem that complicates psychotherapy, particularly for trainees. Understanding why clients don't change is a complex issue because it has multiple determinants, many of which are often outside of conscious awareness. Because it is associated with a sense of unpredictability and uncontrollability, change is often resisted, whereas nonchange is perceived as relatively safe (Arkowitz, Westra, Miller, & Rollnick, 2007). This chapter briefly describes an integrative view of it. Next, it describes two interventions and illustrates their application to different cases.

## AN INTEGRATIVE PERSPECTIVE OF RESISTANCE

Because therapy models have different understandings of resistance, an integrative context for understanding and working with resistance has been proposed and appears to have considerable clinical utility. This integrative view has been proposed by Engle and Arkowitz (2006) and is briefly described here. The basic premise is that resistance manifested as outright refusal by a client is not common. Instead, most instances of what is called resistance or noncompliance can better be understood as ambivalence. Such ambivalence is usually manifested as defensive avoidance or a repetitive pattern of interpersonal behaviors that cause distress or result in limited gratification. Engle and Arkowitz (2006) call this type of ambivalence *resistant ambivalence*. It reflects discrepancies among self-schemas relevant to change, that is, schemas associated with movement toward change and those associated with movement away from change. Most often clients are not fully aware of their self-schemas and the discrepancies among them that cause resistant ambivalence (Arkowitz et al., 2007).

Because resistant ambivalence is also an interpersonal phenomenon, it is best understood in the interpersonal context in which it occurs. When it occurs in a therapeutic setting, it is essential that the therapist be mindful of this fact and view it as a temporary state rather than a personality trait. A therapist recognizes that resistant ambivalence is operative when the following elements are observed:

1. The client believes or agrees that the anticipated change is in his or her own best interest.
2. The client has sufficient information and the capacity to make the change happen.
3. The client demonstrates initial movement toward change with words and other behaviors.
4. The client, at the same time, demonstrates movement away from change with words and other behaviors.
5. The client experiences a negative emotional reaction to the failure to change. (Engle & Arkowitz, 2006)

To effectively resolve ambivalence, two therapeutic interventions can be used, which ultimately facilitate the change process. The interventions are the two-chair approach and motivational interviewing. A third intervention strategy that can also be utilized with ambivalence resistance is Solution-Focused Therapy.

## INTERVENTION STRATEGIES FOR RESOLVING AMBIVALENT RESISTANCE

### Two-Chair Approach

The two-chair approach has its roots in Gestalt therapy and has been adapted by Greenberg and Watson (2006) and by Engle and Arkowitz

(2006) for resolving resistant ambivalence. This approach presumes that each individual has at least two selves or voices that coexist and often conflict. Utilizing this approach, the therapist endeavors to create a dialogue between the two discrepant selves of the client regarding change. In the so-called conflict split, one self advocates for change, while the other self struggles against making a change. In the therapy session, the client is invited to participate in a dialogue in which each self occupies a separate chair (Engle & Arkowitz, 2006). The therapist's role is to facilitate dialogue between the differing selves. The self that struggles against change typically operates outside of the client's awareness; thus the client requires the therapist's assistance to foster greater awareness such that a productive dialogue can develop and possibly lead to change.

## Motivational Interviewing (MI)

Whereas acceptance of the status quo is a reasonable outcome in the two-chair approach, MI is more focused on moving the client toward change. MI utilizes a number of interventions to resolve ambivalent resistance, among them decisional balance, value–behavior discrepancies, and development and reinforcement of "change talk." With the *decisional balance method*, the client is encouraged to lists the pros and cons of change. With the *value–behavior discrepancies method*, the therapist subtly uses reflections of the client's own values and behaviors to help move him or her toward change. For example, the therapist might say: "You really want to be a good father, but your drinking interferes with that desire." Such reflections point out the inconsistency of what the client desires to happen and what actually happens, and are a powerful cognitive dissonance that the client feels compelled to resolve, at least to some degree. The therapist can also develop and reinforce "change talk," which further tips the decisional balance toward change. Change talk is particularly important since it indicates that the client is in the process of schema change. Accordingly, the therapist would listen for and then reinforce the client's change talk. Four types of change talk clients make that therapists should recognize and effectively respond to are disadvantages of the status quo, advantages of change, optimism for change, and intentions to change (Miller & Rollnick, 2002). Furthermore, it is important to note that the therapist's role in MI is that of consultant rather than as change agent. The client is the final decision maker in the change enterprise.

## ILLUSTRATIONS OF RESOLVING AMBIVALENCE

The following two cases illustrate two different approaches for dealing with ambivalence. As noted above, motivational interviewing and the two-chair technique are powerful interventions for resolving resistance and ambivalence. The first case was inspired by Westra (2004) and the second by Watson and Greenberg (2000).

## Case 1: Motivational Interviewing

Sondra is a mother of three younger children who was referred for psychotherapy for depression, social anxiety, and vague suicidal ideation, which she had not yet acted on. Her primary concern was depressive symptoms, particularly low energy. Medication management had begun 3 months previously but with limited response. The hope was that psychotherapy would be beneficial. She appeared to be a good candidate for cognitive–behavioral therapy, and it was begun. By the third session it became clear that Sondra was ambivalent about engagement in the treatment process, particularly with regard to homework assignments. She was noncompliant with intersession tasks even though she agreed to do them. Recognizing her ambivalence, that the client wants help to make her depression go away but is afraid and unwilling to be involved in the treatment process, the therapist suggested MI because she was of "two minds" about her depression. It was explained that treatment would focus only on the "battle" in her mind, rather than on monitoring and restructuring her beliefs or her homework tasks. She agreed to meet for four sessions toward this end. In their subsequent MI session a decisional balance exercise was undertaken on the pros and cons of remaining depressed in contrast to eliminating the depression. The therapist's role in this exercise was to assist Sondra in specifying each pro and con so she could fully appreciate, validate, and understand the value behind it.

*Th.:*    So, can you tell me some of the reasons there could be for remaining depressed.

*Cl.:*    Not changing means that no one will pressure me. That's important because I don't like others always telling me that I need to do things differently. That I should get out of bed and be more active. That I should stop crying, and stuff like that. I just want to be left alone. I don't have the energy to do anything else. It's

| | |
|---|---|
| | all I can do to just manage my kids' activities. I can't do anything else. I don't want to do anything else! |
| *Th.:* | So if I'm hearing you correctly, it would be great if others would just leave you be. You don't need the stress and aggravation of others trying to make you do things that you're not feeling up to doing. Life is hard enough, without all that added pressure. |

The therapist expresses empathy, a key MI strategy.

| | |
|---|---|
| *Cl.:* | Exactly! They should just leave me alone. |
| *Th.:* | So one "pro" is that staying the way you are, and not making any changes, reduces your stress level. It's also a lot easier than the alternative. (pause) How important is it to you to have reduced stress and less hassle in your life, on a scale of 1 to 10 where 10 is extremely important and 1 is not important at all? |
| *Cl.:* | Eight. |
| *Th.:* | Why 8 and not 10? |
| *Cl.:* | Well, there is a part of me that thinks that I do have to do those things eventually. I know I have to push myself, just not yet. |
| *Th.:* | What are the other good things about staying depressed? |
| *Cl.:* | Well, I get to sleep all day and that takes my negative thoughts away. |
| *Th.:* | What might some other reasons be? |
| *Cl.:* | (pause) No risk of disappointment if I try and fail. |
| *Th.:* | So how would you rate your pros on a 0 to 10 scale with 0 meaning no reason to change and 10 meaning every reason to change. |
| *Cl.:* | Well, it's a zero. I see no reasons to change at all. There's a down side to making any right now. |
| *Th.:* | Well, then you're free to stay depressed, you don't have to struggle with trying to get better. |

Here, the therapist sides with the client's resistance, another key MI strategy.

| | |
|---|---|
| *Cl.:* | Thanks ... it's good to hear that. |
| *Th.:* | Still, there can be some down sides for individuals to be depressed. Imagine this, if there were absolutely no down sides, you probably wouldn't be coming to our sessions. But you do come and are involved in our sessions. (pause) You know I am |

curious as to why you would continue to make the effort to attend sessions. Is it a hassle to come in to these sessions?

The therapist utilizes developing discrepancy, another key MI strategy.

Cl.: Yeah, there is sometimes.

Th.: So what are some reasons for working to overcome that "hassle"?

Cl.: So I can be a really good mother and provide for my kids. Another is that my kids won't have to suffer.

Th.: Suffer?

Cl.: (silence followed by tears welling up) My depression hurts my kids.

Th.: Uhm hmm. How exactly does it hurt your kids? What's an example of that?

Cl.: Well, last week Jamie [her older daughter] said she needed $18.00 for a class trip to a museum the next day. I told her I didn't have the money. She started to cry and said if I really cared about her I would give her what she needed. I started screaming at her and she ran outside and didn't come home till after it was dark. I was worried to death that she had run away.

Th.: She was hurt and when she ran out of the house it really scared you. How are you feeling as you talk about the impact of your depression on your kids?

Cl.: Pretty bad.

Th.: How important is it to you to be a good mother?

Cl.: Really, a lot.

Th.: On a 1 to 10 scale how much does it bother you to see yourself hurting your kids?

Cl.: (Crying) A 9 or 10. (pause) I'm mad at you for making me think about how my depression is affecting the kids.

Th.: This is really painful for you. I can see that it is. (pause) You don't have to keep talking. In fact, you don't even have to stay here right now. (pause) What would be the advantages to continuing to explore the impact of your depression, and what would be the disadvantages?

Cl.: I do want to talk about it. (pause) I feel guilty for not being able to play with my kids. I haven't been able to go with them on school outings for a while. I don't take them to the park anymore. (pause) And, I've been so miserable about it that I even thought that the kids might be better off if I was gone. But then

|  |  |
|---|---|
| | I got really scared thinking about those kids being alone without anybody and thinking that I must have been a real loser for offing myself. I don't want them to think that about me, because all my life I've wanted to be a great mom. That's what I want them and everyone to remember me as. |
| *Th.:* | I hear that loud and clear. |
| *Cl.:* | My kids are so great. They really care about me. When they found me crying last week they were so sad and kept asking me: "Mommy, what's wrong?" I felt even worse. I hated myself for putting my kids through all this. |
| *Th.:* | They're really worried about you, and you're mad at yourself for putting them through this. |
| *Cl.:* | I'm becoming more worried that if my depression and anxiety aren't going to get better that the kids are really going to be harmed. And little Eddie [her youngest son] has got some of the same fears as mine. It's like my illness is contagious. (pause) He doesn't deserve this and neither do the other kids. |
| *Th.:* | They don't deserve it. |

The therapist again expresses empathy.

|  |  |
|---|---|
| *Cl.:* | And they can't get the clothes they need to look decent at school or even have a small allowance. My disability check is nothing. If only I was able to go back to work and earn the pay I had three years ago. Things could be much better. |
| *Th.:* | Things could be better. (pause) As we talked before, staying the same allows you freedom from hassle, but it seems like it creates real problems for you and your family. |
| *Cl.:* | (in a saddened voice) Yeah. I see that. |
| *Th.:* | How does your wanting to be a great mom "fit" with your not being there for your kids because of the depressive and withdrawing behaviors you've been describing? |

The therapist utilizes developing discrepancy.

|  |  |
|---|---|
| *Cl.:* | (pause) It doesn't fit so well. |
| *Th.:* | So, on a scale from 1 to 10, how well is withdrawing helping you control negative thoughts? |

The therapist utilizes rolling with resistance.

In the next session Sondra announced that she had tried something different and played with her children more in the past week, as well as having forced herself to go to the store to do her own grocery shopping.

*Th.:* What was the effect on your mood?

*Cl.:* Well, I did it but I hated every minute of it. I'm not sure that I'll do it anymore. It's too hard.

*Th.:* This is very interesting. Now, you have some idea of the impact when you withdraw from situations and responsibilities. And, you also have some idea of the impact when you try to do something a bit different. I hear you saying that pushing yourself is not very enjoyable and probably will lead to no good. That makes sense to me given the big advantages of staying the same. What are your thoughts about where you go from here?

*Cl.:* I've been toying with that idea of continuing to push myself. ... It may not have paid off this week but I think if I just keep on, it just might pay off.

*Th.:* That's an interesting thought. Where did it come from?

*Cl.:* I'm not really sure but a week ago I taped my pro–con list on the refrigerator door. So I look at it every time I'm in the kitchen. (pause) Then I've been thinking about my kids and how they are being affected by my problems. (pause) I'm realizing that my depression is having a bad effect on them ... I don't like that. They deserve better.

**Case Commentary**

By the end of the fourth session, Sondra continued to report that she was being more active, especially with her children, and even noted that she was experiencing some enjoyment and hopefulness. A plan for continuing treatment with Cognitive–Behavioral Therapy was discussed and 10 sessions were agreed upon. Sondra evidenced significant improvement over the course of this treatment and was consistently compliant with homework, exposure, and relapse prevention exercises.

## Case 2: Two-Chair Technique

This case study illustrates a strategy for dealing with a client's ambivalence to active commitment in the treatment process. The therapist utilizes an experiential intervention, called the two-chair dialogue, to process and break through that ambivalence. Martina is a 40-year-old married female who sought treatment for depression, after being laid off from a faculty position at a community college due to budget cutbacks, and because of increasing marital discord. She had been in psychoanalytically oriented therapy previously and "didn't want to talk interminably" but only wanted symptom relief. She refused to discuss early life history, insisting that she already had worked on family dynamics in the previous therapy. While she came across as mature, analytical, and demanding, she could also present as childish, emotional, and frightened. She regarded her emotions as painful and disruptive and preferred to process her thoughts and beliefs. She did admit that she had difficulty asserting herself in close interpersonal relationships and with authority figures, and that she found herself becoming severely depressed quite frequently for no apparent reason after losing her job. During the fifth session, she indicated that she wasn't sure whether she would continue in therapy. The therapist acknowledged these feelings and concerns.

Cl.:    I don't I like it. I just want to get up and go somewhere else right now. I feel really split.

Th.:    It's really hard for you to be here.

Cl.:    I'm getting more agitated.

Th.:    Can you separate out the two parts, the part that wants to be here and the part that wants to leave?

Cl.:    I think so.

Th.:    Can the agitated side tell the side that wants to be here what it is that is agitating her?

After Martina states that she is torn between engaging in and leaving therapy, the therapist suggests a two-chair dialogue to understand the two sides of the conflict more fully.

Cl.:    (chair 1): Staying in therapy is going to change things and you're not going to be the same anymore. I can manage the way things are now, but I'm not sure I can manage the way things will be later.

Th.:    So you're afraid of the change. Can you tell her some of the things that frighten you?

Cl.:    (chair 1): I've worked hard to deal with this stuff, and now I'm afraid I'll disappear.

56

*Th.:* Please come over to this chair now. What's it like when you hear her say that she's afraid that she'll disappear?

*Cl.:* (chair 2): Well, she probably will, and I am afraid of that, too. And, I'm sorry, too.

*Th.:* So you feel sorry, too. (To chair 1) How do you feel when she expresses fear and sadness that you'll disappear?

*Cl.:* (chair 1): I feel angry. ... No, it's more like feeling annoyed. She's going to do it anyway.

*Th.:* (To chair 1) So you feel angry.

*Cl.:* (chair 1) Yeah.

*Th.:* Now, what do you need from her?

*Cl.:* (chair 1): Reassurance that she'll stop taking swipes at me. I'm feeling trapped in this chair and I don't want to be hurt.

*Th.:* You're feeling trapped over there. Do you mean that I'm trapping you?

*Cl.:* (chair 1): No, not you, it's her trapping me. (pause) No, I'm really trapping myself ... I just don't feel like I have any control over what she will do.

*Th.:* (To chair 2) What happens when you hear this part say, "I'm trapped and unable to control you"?

*Cl.:* (chair 2): (tearful) I know that's what I 'm doing. ... But I'm not going to destroy it all. There'll be something left. I wish she wasn't so afraid.

*Th.:* (To Chair 1) What is it like when you hear her say there will be something left?

*Cl.:* (chair 1): I feel a bit better ... I don't feel quite so trapped.

*Th.:* (To Chair 1) What do you need from her?

*Cl.:* (chair 1): I need to know that it will all be worthwhile and that she'll keep some of my things, like my ideas and stuff.

*Th.:* Like your intelligence ... your vision.

*Cl.:* (chair 1): (pause) Yes.

*Th.:* (To chair 2) What is it like to hear her say that she will save these parts of you and take care of them?

*Cl.:* (chair 2): I'm not sure. ... That they're important to me, too.

*Th.:* You value those aspects, too. (To chair 1) How does it feel when you hear her say that?

*Cl.:* (chair 1): I feel calmer ... and ... the separation is starting to disappear a little bit.

## Case Commentary

The session was a turning point in resolving the client's ambivalence to fully engaging in the treatment process. Martina recognized that she was in control of the process and able to negotiate conditions of safety that enabled her to proceed further. A key issue for her was in expressing her own needs in relation to others, as well as learning to accept her emotional self, which was previously subjugated to her rational self. While she had discounted the role of her emotions at the onset of therapy, at termination she was able to integrate these two warring selves into a more fully functioning personality. After this session, Martina was able to engage in therapy more easily and examine her depression more closely. Subsequently, she could identify the antecedents of her depression and choose alternative strategies to preempt her depressive symptoms.

# 5

# *Recognize and Resolve Transference and Countertransference*

The quality of the therapeutic alliance is the foundation upon which all other therapeutic endeavors are based. While there are conditions that facilitate the development and maintenance of an effective therapeutic alliance (see Chapter 3), there are also conditions that militate against its development and maintenance. This chapter focuses on one set of these conditions, transference and countertransference, that can and do interfere with the therapeutic relationship as well as therapeutic outcomes. This chapter begins by describing transference, countertransference, and their enactments. Then it describes how transference and countertransference can be recognized and resolved. Finally, it illustrates how these enactments can be recognized and resolved in session transcriptions from two cases.

## TRANSFERENCE AND ENACTMENTS

Past experiences with relationships affect subsequent relationships and so a woman can meet a man today who reminds her unconsciously of someone, such as her father or a male teacher, from her past. Often, individuals have little or no conscious awareness that they are "transferring" feeling and thoughts from past relationships onto current ones or that they are reliving or enacting unfinished business from the past. Furthermore, in addition to transferring feelings and thoughts, expectations to act in certain ways are also transferred and enacted. Thus, a graduate student may meet a professor for the first time and react to that professor with the same or similar set of thoughts, feelings, and expectations that she had for her high school biology teacher. She may be surprised and even experience slight confusion when her new professor is friendlier but more academically demanding than she expected. This confusion is because a transference is an interpersonal distortion that often does not fit present role expectations (Good & Beitman, 2006).

## TRANSFERENCE AND COUNTERTRANSFERENCE

Just as there are active elements like trust and collaboration in *current* relationships, there are also active elements of *past* relationships that both clients and therapists bring to the client–therapist relationship. It is these active elements of past relationships that can negatively impact the treatment process. Transference is such an element. Transference is a phenomenon in which clients inaccurately transfer thoughts, feelings, and expectations about past interpersonal experiences onto their current relationship with the therapist. These *distortions* tend to be considerably potent and can negatively impact the process of therapy (Good & Beitman, 2006).

Transference can be either positive or negative. It is a form of reenactment of the client's old and familiar pattern of relating, a pattern that often involves *unfinished business*. In this reenactment, clients demonstrate how they felt in the past when they were treated in a particular manner. Transference typically occurs when a therapist, often inadvertently, says or does something that triggers the client's unfinished business.

Countertransference is a similar phenomenon, in which therapists inaccurately transfer thoughts, feelings, and expectations from past experiences onto clients. Similarly, these distortions can impact the treatment process. Countertransference can be either positive or negative. There is increasing consensus of clinicians from all therapeutic orientations that countertransference can be a useful source of information about the client (Gabbard, 1999).

## TRANSFERENCE–COUNTERTRANSFERENCE ENACTMENTS

Whereas in the past transference and countertransference were considered "separate" phenomena, today an increasing number of researchers and clinicians consider transference and countertransference as best understood from a relational perspective or model. The emphasis in this model is not on the client as in the past, but on the interaction between client and therapist. In this view client and therapist are participants who *co-create enactments* that represent configurations of transference and countertransference. Both client and therapist have roles in the transference reenactment. The client's role is to respond, while the therapist role is to trigger and shape that response. In other words, transference has two aspects. The first is the client and the client's past, and the second is the interpersonal dynamic between therapist and client. Thus, transference involves "the here-and-now experience of the client with the therapist who has a role in eliciting and shaping the transference" (Ornstein & Ganzer, 2005, p. 567). For example, a client who was raised by a mother who alternated between being emotionally distant and angry and abusive may be reluctant to disclose and discuss feelings in therapy. When encouraged by the therapist to discuss feelings, the client may react by becoming aloof and withdrawn or by becoming irritated and angry.

## RECOGNIZING TRANSFERENCE AND COUNTERTRANSFERENCE

Manifestations of transference and countertransference are not uncommon in therapeutic settings. It is more likely to be expressed in longer term therapies that emphasize feelings and the here-and-now (Gabbard, 1999). As previously noted, transference and countertransference can be either positive or negative. It behooves the therapist to recognize the signs or indicators of both. Table 5.1 lists several such indicators in terms of feelings, behaviors, and fantasies and thoughts.

**Table 5.1**  Common Indicators of Transference and Countertransference

| Transference | Countertransference |
|---|---|
| **Feelings** | **Feelings** |
| Awe | Awe |
| Anger | Anger |
| Hostility | Irritation |
| Hurt | Criticalness |
| Envy or jealousy | Boredom |
| Distrust | Disappointment |
| Concern | Envy or jealousy |
| Appreciation | Excessive pride in client progress |
| Sexual attraction | Fear about seeing client |
| | Resentment about seeing client |
| | Excitement about seeing client |
| **Behaviors** | **Behaviors** |
| Excessively criticizing therapist | Planning to socialize with client |
| Calling therapist at home | Criticizing the client |
| Writing love letter to therapist | Excessively reassuring the client |
| Coming late for sessions | Extending session time |
| Sending gifts to therapist | Ending session early |
| Seeking personal information about the therapist | Making fun of the client |
| | Reducing fee or not charging the client |
| Trying to meet with therapist outside of sessions | Attempting to impress the client |
| | Asking the client for favors |
| | Coming late for a session |
| | Failing to deal with client boundary violation, e.g., making excessive phone calls |
| **Fantasies and Thoughts** | **Fantasies and Thoughts** |
| Dreaming about therapist | Dreaming about client |
| Having sex with therapist | Going out or dating client |
| Marrying the therapist | Having sex with client |
| Being in love with therapist | Being best friends with client |
| Becoming a colleague of therapist | Traveling with client |
| Having a family with therapist | Marrying the client |
| Harming the therapist | Harming the client |

Adapted from *Counseling and Psychotherapy Essentials: Integrating Theories, Skills, and Practices,* by G. Good and B. Beitman, 2006, p. 202.

## DEALING WITH TRANSFERENCE–COUNTERTRANSFERENCE ENACTMENTS

Unfortunately, recognizing and resolving transference and countertransference issues do not appear to be a priority in the didactic portion of therapy training programs today. Unless a trainee initiates the discussion, transference and countertransferences may not come up in supervision either. Based on the conviction that effectively dealing with transference and countertransference enactments is essential for trainees to practice therapy competently, this section and subsequent case material discuss and illustrate these clinical issues. Because therapists can too easily get blindsided by transference–countertransference enactments, it is critical to deal with these concerns proactively and directly.

Various methods of managing transference have been proposed. For instance, Gelso, Hill, Mohr, Rochlen, and Zack (1999) describe five such methods: focusing on the immediate relationship; interpreting the meaning of the transference; using questions to promote insight in the transference enactment; educating the client about transference; and therapist self-disclosure.

Similarly, various strategies for managing countertransference have been proposed to help therapists avoid acting out their countertransference. Gelso and Hayes (2007) provide a research-based set of strategies for preventing such acting out as well as for managing the therapist's internal countertransferential reactions. The strategies are self-insight; self-integration (i.e., possession of a healthy character structure); empathy; anxiety management; and conceptualizing ability (i.e., use of theory to grasp the patient's dynamics in the therapeutic relationship). Of these, self-insight and self-integration are critical for the therapist in gaining greater self-understanding of the treatment situation in which the countertransference arose, including client–therapist boundary issues. Furthermore, self-insight and self-integration are necessary for the therapist's work on his or her own psychological health and for managing and effectively using the therapist's own internal reactions.

The therapist's level of self-integration plays a pivotal role in whether countertransference is acted out or utilized therapeutically. It is axiomatic that resolution or completion of unfinished business is a prerequisite for a therapist to provide optimal therapeutic assistance to clients. Focused reflection and clinical supervision are two common ways of understanding and managing, although personal therapy may be necessary when counter-transference is a chronic problem (Gelso & Hayes, 2007).

These and other methods of dealing with transference and counter-transferences can be very helpful, *after the fact*. But what about dealing directly with transference enactment as they arise within a particular session? A more *proactive*, here-and-now approach and protocol will be briefly described. The purpose of this approach is not only to address and presumably resolve the immediate transference enactment but also to effect a corrective emotional experience, that is, to experience the client–therapist interaction in a way that reverses or changes the maladaptive pattern underlying the transference enactment (Levenson, 1995).

## PROTOCOL FOR RESOLVING TRANSFERENCE ENACTMENTS

This is a four-step process for recognizing and effectively dealing with transference enactments. Basically, the therapist

1. Makes explicit the emotionally charged context of the origins of the transference in the client's past.
2. Helps the client recall how a significant other reacted to the client in the *past* emotionally charged context.
3. Helps the client describe how the therapist reacted in the *present* to him or her.
4. Helps the client *compare and contrast* the therapist's behavior with that of the significant other and emphasizes the new (and corrective) emotional experience.

A similar method is offered by McCullough (2005). This protocol is illustrated in the case examples that follow.

## ILLUSTRATIONS OF RESOLVING TRANSFERENCE–COUNTERTRANSFERENCE ENACTMENTS

Over the years, I have found it fascinating to ask experienced clinicians about the types of countertransference reactions they have found most common and troublesome in their therapeutic work. Almost without exception, clinicians indicate the same two countertransferences. The first is the experience of being exasperated with a client's reactions. For example, clients will expect therapists to punish them for enacting unfinished business. The second is that of being sexually attracted to or "falling in love" with a particular client. Following are examples of transference enactment of both types in which the therapists quickly recognize and effectively resolve them. In the first case there seems to be less countertransference enactment than in the second, but in both cases the situation is resolved and both clients experience a corrective emotional experience. The first case is inspired by McCullough (2005) and the second by Beitman (1999).

## Case 1: A Punitive Transference Enactment

Dory is a 37-year-old, never married Italian American female who was referred by her primary care physician, Mark Belker, M.D., for evaluation and treatment of anxiety and worry. This was her first experience with psychotherapy and she was uncertain it would help, but because of her confidence in Dr. Belker, who had been her doctor for most of her life, she followed up on the referral. Dr. Virginia Jonas had practiced psychotherapy for several years and had received many referrals from Dr. Belker. In her initial evaluation she learned that Dory was the only child of her parents, both of whom had passed away over a year ago in a car accident. She reported that she was a "worrywart" her whole life, but that worry had increased dramatically following the death of her parents. Dory described her father as a demanding and critical father who regularly chastised his wife, described as a self-effacing alcoholic. Although she denies being physically or sexually abused by her parents, it appeared that Dory sustained considerable verbal and emotional abuse from her father and emotional neglect from her mother. Since she was a child, Dory worried that she could not do anything right in the eyes of her father and was never sure that she could count on her mother to protect her. Nevertheless, she finished college and worked as a nurse in an extended care facility. While Dory denied the use of alcohol and other substances, she admitted to being a chain smoker "to calm my nerves." It is noteworthy that in her treatment plan Dr. Jonas not only indicated that resolving relationship issues with parents was a mutually determined treatment goal, but that based on Dory's relationship history that negative transference enactments were likely to arise in the course of treatment. In the beginning of their fifth session, Dory begins by saying the following:

*Cl.:*   Why is it that I screw up so much?

*Th.:*   What are you referring to?

*Cl.:*   You know, last week I got here so late that we couldn't meet.

*Th.:*   I'm really sorry that we couldn't meet at all last week.

*Cl.:*   You're mad about it, aren't you?

*Th.:*   About what?

*Cl.:*   That I messed up. You know, I overslept and got here really late for our appointment.

*Th.:*   You made a mistake. (pause) Guess what, other people make mistakes. I make mistakes.

*Cl.:*   But I'm expecting you to punish me or something. I did come really late and it probably really threw off your schedule for the rest of that day (client becomes tearful).

The conversation up to this point suggests that transference is operative. To verify this and begin therapeutically processing it, Dr. Jonas prompts Dory's recall of hurtful memories associated with experiences of her father's anger and criticalness.

*Th.:*   I have a question for you. How did your father react when you slept through a planned activity with him?

*Cl.:*   (pauses, sobs and breathes deeply) Oh, my God, he went nuts! He'd hit me and curse me. Then I'd start crying and running to my room. I wouldn't come out for hours because I was terrified of what he'd do to me. (pause) He really hurt me.

*Th.:*   You feel that hurt now. (pause) I'm going to ask another question, if I might. But it is important for you to look at me when you answer it.

*Cl.:*   (blows her nose) Alright.

*Th.:*   What did I say to you about last week?

Dr. Jonas helps Dory to differentiate between her reactions to Dory's failure to arrive on time and the way her father reacted to her for failures and mistakes.

*Cl.:*   You said you were sorry that we couldn't meet last week.

*Th.:*   Okay. Now please look straight at me and describe my reaction to your missed appointment. Describe, in as much detail as you can, my reactions to you last week and this week, especially about my words, tone of my voice, and facial expression.

*Cl.:*   (stops sobbing and looks confused) I'm not really sure how I'd describe it.

*Th.:*   It's very important for you, so please try.

*Cl.:*   Okay. (pause) Well last week you said you were sorry we couldn't meet, and it sounded like you really meant it. Today, you said that all people make mistakes, even yourself. You looked calm and didn't yell at me or make me feel stupid. (pause) I'm not sure I know what to make of your reaction. This is all so new to me. I'm not used to having someone treat me like this way.

*Th.:*   Did I do anything like your dad used to do?

*Cl.:*   Absolutely not! You're not like him at all. (pause) And, I'm not afraid of you.

Now the therapist endeavors to facilitate the client's new experience, a corrective emotional experience.

*Th.:*   Why wouldn't you be afraid of me, particularly after you made a mistake?

*Cl.:*   I guess I've never thought about it before now. I guess I'm not afraid of you because I don't believe you'd intentionally hurt me. (pause) It feels weird. I'm not used to trusting other people, but I think I trust you. It's a new experience for me.

*Th.:*   I'm so glad you've experienced these feelings of trusting me! (pause) So what do you suppose this means for our relationship now?

*Cl.:*   It means that I can let my guard down and be myself with you. It's funny, in a way. I don't think I've ever had a relationship with a man when I wasn't afraid.

*Th.:*   You're in a different place in your life right now. What you've just learned about yourself and shared with me is so important. (pause) As we continue to work together, we'll be able to build on this insight and corrective experience.

*Cl.:*   When I first came in today I felt terrible. But right now, I'm feeling calm and confident and happy. I can't remember when I last felt this way.

*Th.:*   Have you ever felt happy when you were with someone else before?

*Cl.:*   No. Don't think I have.

*Th.:*   Well, savor the feeling, Dory, I'm happy for you too.

**Case Commentary**

In this session Dory enacted her unfinished business in the therapeutic setting but had a much different cognitive and emotional experience than she had with her father. Such a corrective emotional experience can significantly supercharge the course of treatment. The fact that the therapist anticipated that transference enactments were likely, given Dory's early life and ongoing verbally and emotionally abusive experiences, meant that Dr. Jonas was not surprised or unprepared for the transference. In so doing, Dr. Jonas not only avoided the likelihood of premature termination by Dory, but she facilitated important growth.

## Case 2: A Sexualized Transference Enactment

Laura W. is a 29-year-old divorced Caucasian female who works as a sales associate for a national real estate company. She sought therapy to work through her hurtful relationship with her narcissistic father and confusion about her relationships with men. She married at age 22 and sought a divorce after 2 years on the grounds of irreconcilable differences. Since then she has been involved in a number of affairs with married men. The therapist she contacted was Gerard Givens, Psy.D., a 40-year-old married male clinical psychologist.

Because her insurance company provided reimbursement for up to 18 sessions per year, Laura and the therapist contracted for 18 sessions. In the course of therapy sessions with the 40-year-old married male therapist before the transcription of the 13th session that follows, the therapeutic focus had been on her relationship with her father and with her unsatisfying relationships with other men. She began to understand her father better and was able to gently confront some of his insensitivities to her and accept that he would probably not change much if at all.

Beginning in the fourth session there were some clues that transference was operative. She was, at times, flirtatious and dressed somewhat suggestively. The therapist experienced occasional involuntary sexual fantasies about her. Subsequently, he discussed this matter with a senior colleague to help him separate his own feelings from those the client might have induced in him. The senior colleague encouraged Dr. Givens to monitor his reactions and continually ask: "How can my feelings and reactions be put in the service of this client—and not to meet my own needs." The therapist agreed and continued to monitor his reactions in terms of that therapeutic question. His colleague also suggested that Dr. Givens should directly address the client's flirtatiousness and the core beliefs behind it.

As treatment progressed, Laura experienced some improvement in her relationship with her father. About that time she asked Dr. Givens to accompany her to a reception to launch an upscale condominium complex that her company was promoting. He politely refused the invitation. Recognizing that only six sessions remained and in view of the progress she had made in relation to her father, Dr. Givens felt that the time was right to more directly address the client's thoughts and feelings about him. The 13th session begins with the client saying:

*Cl.:* It was really weird. Driving over here today I completely forgot your name.

*Th.:* Forgot my name?

*Cl.:* Yeah. Earlier today I was trying to figure out how to do something for myself that you usually do for me. And then coming over here I just blocked on your name. Isn't that weird?

*Th.:* Unusual reactions like that mean that we probably should talk about your reaction to me. I say that because your responses to me seem to reflect your responses to other important individuals in your life. What do you think?

*Cl.:* (pause) I'm not sure. I mean I guess it makes sense. (pause) What should I say?

*Th.:* Well, you have started to do some important work on your relationship with your father. It may be that some of your difficulties with relationships are being repeated here with me.

*Cl.:* I suspect you are right. But, how do I talk about it?

*Th.:* Well, you said you were trying to figure out how to do for yourself what I had been doing for you. It sounds like you are giving me credit for the changes you have made. Is that right?

*Cl.:* No, it really is not. You have listened and helped me make sense of my life. And it has really helped. But, I've been the one who has made changes with my father and others.

*Th.:* Exactly. So now we have to look at that part of your self that thinks and says what you know is not true. (pause) Why did part of your self give me more credit for your changes than you know that I deserve?

*Cl.:* Probably because my opinions of myself depend so much on what others think of me. I seemed to get into relationships by

|        |                                                                                                                                                                                                                               |
|--------|-------------------------------------------------------------------------------------------------------------------------------------------------------------------------------------------------------------------------------|
|        | being what the person wanted me to be. But, after the relationship was over, I would feel so bad about myself.                                                                                                                 |
| *Th.:* | So what led you to give me the credit for the changes you made?                                                                                                                                                                |
| *Cl.:* | That's how I hold onto others. I do and become what they expect me to be. I give them power over me so they know that I need them and so they won't leave me. I hate that so much.                                              |
| *Th.:* | I hear that. So, what were my expectations that you were trying to meet?                                                                                                                                                       |
| *Cl.:* | I don't know really what they were, but I think you wanted me to be strong, to take care of myself, and to be attractive and interesting to talk to. I think you wanted me to become what I needed for myself.                 |
| *Th.:* | I agree with some of what you've said. But, is there anything else that I expected from you that you did?                                                                                                                      |
| *Cl.:* | (pause) I can't think of anything.                                                                                                                                                                                            |
| *Th.:* | Were you aware of being somewhat seductive with me about 4 months ago?                                                                                                                                                         |
| *Cl.:* | Yeah. I was trying to seduce you. Isn't that what all men want, for women to be sexual?                                                                                                                                        |
| *Th.:* | How much do you believe that all men want women to be sexual?                                                                                                                                                                  |
| *Cl.:* | A lot. I mean, wouldn't having sex with my shrink prove how powerful I was?                                                                                                                                                    |
| *Th.:* | Would it?                                                                                                                                                                                                                      |
| *Cl.:* | Well, maybe not. (pause) But I would be terrified if you said you wanted to.                                                                                                                                                   |
| *Th.:* | It's good that you could admit that you were being seductive with me. I was not sure that you were aware of it or would be willing to admit it.                                                                                 |
| *Cl.:* | I recall that you did seem to notice. That you seemed interested.                                                                                                                                                              |
| *Th.:* | Do you mean that I seemed interested in you sexually?                                                                                                                                                                          |
| *Cl.:* | Not that you said anything, but you seemed to be responding.                                                                                                                                                                   |
| *Th.:* | What specifically did you notice?                                                                                                                                                                                             |
| *Cl.:* | The way you talked to me, looked at me. Kinda the way men react to me when I'm flirting with them. (pause) This has something to do with my father. I know it, but I can't explain it. I don't know what it was, but it's confusing and upsetting. |
| *Th.:* | It is very confusing and upsetting for you not to know.                                                                                                                                                                        |
| *Cl.:* | I put so much energy into talking and smiling and flirting with men just to get their approval and acceptance. Why can't I just                                                                                                |

accept myself? (cries) I've never said that about my father before. (pause) Talking about my reaction to you is hard. I've told you so much about myself, but I know so little about you. I'm vulnerable and you might hurt me. You haven't yet.

*Th.:*   It is hard to talk about these things. No, I haven't hurt you because I'm here for your best interests. As you learn to trust me more and become more vulnerable, the more you can learn to trust yourself.

*Cl.:*   (pause) I think that trust is building … but it's not good to trust something so totally. Bad things can happen.

*Th.:*   You're saying that giving complete trust to another gives that individual total power over you, and you've been hurt by that, is that right? (Yes.) When has that happened?

*Cl.:*   (Dory gives examples of relationships with several men for which sex seemed to be a common feature)

*Th.:*   It sounds like you have to have the kind of sexual energy and power that men are attracted to. That seems to be both a blessing and a curse.

*Cl.:*   A curse? What do you mean?

*Th.:*   It means it can be harmful if not used properly. So, you have a responsibility with this sexual power to attract men, certain men and not others.

*Cl.:*   I guess I do. It is certain men, married men.

*Th.:*   I'm one of those men. (client nods) What were you trying to accomplish by flirting with me?

*Cl.:*   I guess I was testing you. You know, to see if you really cared about your wife and kids. (pause) Like my father. He was having an affair while married to my mom. I was only 8 at the time when he left us for that woman. (pause) So if I was able to seduce you, it would prove that all men only want sex. That they can't be trusted.

*Th.:*   What about your father and you flirting with me, what does it mean to you?

*Cl.:*   It means I'm glad that you didn't respond to my sexual overtures. Thank you. But, if you had I would have continued to have come on to married men just to prove that I was right and men never could be trusted.

*Th.:*   Yes. Now that's the negative side. Is there anything positive that you have learned?

71

Cl.:    (pause) I learned that I am in control of the cues I give and the responses I get from men. I can influence how they respond, and I am responsible for my actions. (pause) In some way that makes me less dependent on them.

Th.:    Hopefully, you also can conclude that I am one of the exceptions to your rule that men only want sex, aren't loyal to their families, and cannot be trusted.

Cl.:    Maybe, because I'm not sure there are others.

Th.:    Well, you previously believed that there were none. Now there is at least one exception. Me. Maybe there are more.

Cl.:    Right now, I cannot imagine getting married again. My belief about men is still pretty strong.

Th.:    Hopefully, I've added some doubt to the certainty of that belief.

Cl.:    Yes, you have.

The session winds down and a subsequent appointment is made. Some further discussion of the transference occurred in the next session, and the process of consolidating gains, reviewing progress, and planning for relapse prevention ensued in preparation for termination. Resolving this transference was essential in achieving a positive treatment outcome.

**Case Commentary**
A key factor that contributed to the success of this treatment was the input Dr. Given received from a senior colleague on dealing with his sexual feelings for the client. Regularly reflecting on the question "How can my feelings and reactions be put in the service of this client—and not to meet my own needs" was critical in his review and planning. It helped him in understanding and maintaining appropriate boundaries with the client.

# 6

# *Recognize and Repair Alliance Ruptures*

Chapter 4 focused on two formidable impasses to therapeutic progress: resistance and ambivalence. Chapter 5 focused on two other potential impasses: transference and countertransference. This chapter emphasizes another formidable impasse: alliance ruptures. Alliance strains and ruptures can and do occur in all forms of therapy. This chapter addresses the essential competency of resolving alliance strains and ruptures. First, alliance ruptures will be described. Then different strategies for resolving this major threat to client engagement and cause of premature termination are presented. Finally, these points are illustrated with case material.

## WHAT IS AN ALLIANCE RUPTURE?

As described in Chapter 2, the therapeutic alliance has been conceptualized in terms of three interdependent variables: an agreement on the therapeutic *tasks*, an agreement on *goals*, and the quality of the interpersonal *bond* between therapist and client (Bordin, 1979). An effective therapeutic alliance is a therapeutic relationship that is mutual and collaborative. Alliance ruptures are basically tensions or breakdowns in the *collaborative* relationship between client and therapist. Safran, Muran, Samstag, and Stevens (2002) conceptualize ruptures as either disagreements about the tasks and goals of treatment or as breaches in the therapeutic bond.

## THE ROLE OF TRANSFERENCE AND COUNTERTRANSFERENCE

Transferences and countertransferences, particularly negative ones, can significantly strain and even rupture the therapeutic *bond*. Ruptures often begin as transference–countertransference enactments between client and therapist (Safran, Muran, Samstag & Stevens, 2002). For instance, a client will enact a difficult or traumatic early experience and then try to hook the therapist into playing a role that conforms to the client's early experience. To the extent that the therapist unwittingly gets hooked and enacts this role, an alliance rupture results (Safran & Muran, 2000). However, that rupture can often be repaired if the therapist recognizes his or her contribution to it and then helps resolve the enactment, resulting in a corrective emotional experience.

Another way of putting it is that ruptures are breaches in relatedness and negative fluctuations in the quality of the relationship between therapist and client (Safran & Muran, 2000). Ruptures vary in intensity, duration, and frequency, depending on the nature of the particular therapist–client relationship. Intensity can range from relatively minor, that is, a "strain," to major breakdowns in understanding and communication, that is, a "rupture." When the rupture is extreme, the client may directly manifest negative sentiments to the therapist or even terminate therapy prematurely. Where the rupture is mild, only minor fluctuations in the quality of alliance are manifest, but they may be difficult to detect (Safran & Muran, 2000).

## ALLIANCE RUPTURE DIFFERENTIATED FROM RESISTANCE AND RELATED TERMS

Trainees often question the validity of the concept of alliance ruptures. They want to know if an alliance rupture is basically resistance or a form of resistance. This is a valid question that deserves an answer. Basically, an alliance rupture is defined as a tension or breakdown in the *collaborative relationship* between client and therapist (Samstag, Moran, & Safran, 2003).

> The interpersonal nature of alliance ruptures distinguishes the term from other definitions of impasses that emphasize either patient characteristics (e.g., resistance, negative transferences) or therapist characteristics

74

(e.g., empathic failure, countertransference reaction). In other words, a rupture is not a phenomenon that is located exclusively within the patient or caused exclusively by the therapist. Rather, a rupture is an *interactive process* that includes these kinds of defensive experiences as they play out within the context of each particular therapeutic relationship. (Samstag, Moran, & Safran, 2003, p. 188)

## TYPES OF ALLIANCE RUPTURES

Two categories of alliance rupture have been specified. The first category is called *withdrawal rupture*. In this type clients avoid or limit their participation and collaboration with treatment (Safran & Muran, 2000). Signs of withdrawal expressed by clients include denying obvious emotions, giving minimal responses, or providing overly detailed descriptions of situations. Other observable signs are rationalizing, intellectualizing, shifting topics often, and talking more about others than themselves.

The second category is called *confrontation rupture*. In this type, clients express frustration or question or lash out at the therapist (Safran & Muran, 2000). Signs of frustration expressed by clients include complaints about the therapist's questions, responses, or abilities. Other observable signs include clients questioning their need for therapy, their lack of progress, or the therapeutic tasks or interventions being utilized.

## STRATEGIES FOR RESOLVING ALLIANCE RUPTURES

There are several strategies for repairing alliance ruptures. These include therapeutic processing, supervision, role-playing, the two-chair technique (Watson & Greenberg, 2000), and metacommunication. One way of developing skill in metacommunication is reflective writing. Ruptures can be addressed either directly or indirectly. Some of these strategies are illustrated in the following case examples.

## ILLUSTRATIONS OF REPAIRING ALLIANCE RUPTURES

The first case illustrates that alliance ruptures are not always easily recognized. The trainee knew that something was wrong because the client was noncompliant with homework, but did not attribute it to a breach in the therapeutic alliance. It was during a videotape review of the session that the rupture was identified by the supervisor. The second case illustrates how clients can misconstrue a therapist's positive response which can cause both distress for the client and an alliance rupture. The third case highlights how a trainee's reflection in a journal helped her to recognize and set a plan for resolving a rupture. The first case is inspired by Bennett-Levy and Thwaites (2006) and the second by Arnkoff (2000).

## Case 1: Supervision and Repairing Alliance Ruptures

Jeremy, an intern, started his supervision session by noting concern for Jennifer, a depressed client he had been working with for the past 3 months. He indicated that Jennifer was not making the kind of progress to be expected. While she regularly attended sessions, she seemed a bit distant lately and there was notable noncompliance with homework. Watching the videotape of a recent session, the supervisor soon recognized a rupture in the therapeutic alliance. About 25 minutes into the session Jennifer began to cry, and rather than responding to her distress Jeremy quickly shifted into a problem-solving mode. As the supervisor paused the videotape, Jeremy noted that this had occurred in previous sessions.

The supervisor suggested they stop for a while and engage in a reverse role-play. In the role-play the supervisor assumed the role of therapist and Jeremy took on the role of his tearful client. As the supervisor assumed Jeremy's problem-solving mode, Jeremy experienced the hasty shift into problem-solving mode as hurtful and invalidating. As he reflected on the experience, he described himself as becoming angry, frightened, and withdrawing emotionally. As the supervisor and Jeremy reflected on the role reversal experience, they were able to derive a formulation of alliance rupture that had occurred. They identified the relational sequence in which (a) Jennifer's tearfulness "pulled" the problem solving from Jeremy and her resulting feelings of being ignored and invalidated; (b) Jennifer's emotional withdrawal; and (c) the effect on the therapeutic relationship in terms of limited cooperation and noncompliance with homework. Based on this formulation, they worked together to identify a strategy that Jeremy could utilize to repair the rupture.

The supervisor and Jeremy engaged in a number of role-play situations in which Jeremy sat in the therapist's chair and the supervisor role-played Jennifer. Jeremy's task was to practice responding with empathy to Jennifer and validate her distress before moving into a collaborative problem-solving mode. This was followed by the supervisor providing Jeremy with feedback on her experience in Jennifer's chair. They discussed what adjustments Jeremy could make to further enhance Jeremy's responsiveness. This continued until both agreed Jeremy was not only responding more effectively but also feeling more confident and comfortable.

In Jeremy's next session with Jennifer, the opportunity arose to employ this strategy with immediate positive results. One marker that this minor alliance rupture was repaired was that Jennifer's compliance with homework assignments improved.

## Case 2: Repairing an Alliance Rupture in the Session

Jill was a 31-year-old single account executive who, after having been offered a promotion, had becoming increasingly fearful that she would fail in this new position.

The position of regional manager would require her to supervise 10 account executives, most of whom were male and older than she. She doubted her ability to handle these new responsibilities. She reported insomnia, with anxious dreams and early morning wakening, and was having difficulty concentrating at her old job, in which she was usually quite effective and successful.

The first six sessions focused primarily on career issues, although occasionally interpersonal concerns were also discussed, such as her ongoing dependence on her parents. She had made considerable progress, and in the seventh session she reviewed the workplace changes she had made and her new confidence. Near the end of that session, the following exchange occurred.

Th.: The progress you're reporting is superb. Congratulations! I guess the question now is where do you want to go from here?

Cl.: (panic and terror are evident in her face and voice) Are you saying my therapy is over?

Actually, the therapist had been considering a shift in focus of therapy to interpersonal concerns and not termination. There was no question that the very possibility of termination terrified Jill. As the next session began, Jill was very anxious and inadvertently dropped her purse on the floor when she attempted to place it on the side table next to her chair.

*Cl.:*    I'm sorry for being so klutzy today. It's just not my day, I guess. (pause) I've been so preoccupied with things this week that I've been messing up. Everything that could have gone wrong this week went wrong.

*Th.:*    What went wrong?

*Cl.:*    Well, a bunch of little things, like letting a roast burn because I was too preoccupied, and getting a late fee for not returning a video on time. (pause) I've been so nervous.

*Th.:*    Did your nervousness about the week's events have anything to do with our possible termination?

*Cl.:*    I think so. (pause) As I was thinking about terminating, I imagined what might happen. Things seemed to be going well for a while and then I ran into a big problem and needed help. I imagined calling you and you said: "Sorry, our work together is over. You had your chance and now we're done."

*Th.:*    What did you feel when you imagined I said that?

*Cl.:*    Terrified! I felt I would die.

*Th.:*    Thinking about it now, do you think what you imagined is accurate? That if we terminated now and you called me later, I would say our work was done?

*Cl.:*    I don't know. I guess that's the way it works.

*Th.:*    What you imagined suggests that you might need a solid relationship for survival.

*Cl.:*    I'm not sure I'm following what you're saying.

*Th.:*    It seems similar to your experience of your parents packing your bags in preparation for sending you off to college; I was packing your bags and sending you away from therapy.

Jill appeared to be anticipating the loss or at least a major break in the therapeutic alliance, which would leave her, at least in her imagination, to rely only on her limited psychological and interpersonal resources. Her fantasy of being "rejected" by her therapist reflected the interpersonal consequences of her early relationships, specifically, what she learned early on about the support, and perceived withdrawal of support, of important people in her life. By repairing the rupture, or at least strain, in the therapeutic alliance, progress on important interpersonal issues in her life would be possible. However, because her anxiety was so high the therapist did not think Jill would be able to immediately process this loss, he first focused on reducing her anxiety to a manageable level. Only then did he explore it with her.

*Th.:*     It is not unusual for former clients to return for further therapy. And, I always make it a priority to schedule them as soon as possible.

*Cl.:*     (sighs and shows immediate relief) I'm so glad to hear that!

*Th.:*     I'm glad, too. (pause) Do you have any ideas about what led you to be so anxious and convinced that I would turn you away?

*Cl.:*     Well, it may be related to my early life experiences.

*Th.:*     Can you say a little more about that?

*Cl.:*     I think I've always had trouble seeing myself standing on my own two feet without the support of people who are important to me, like my parents, and, I guess, you.

## Case Commentary

While her need to depend on others in the workplace had been discussed previously, now she began to realize that she was depending on her therapist's support in other areas of her life. As the "termination" incident continued to be processed, she began to frame the next therapeutic goal: becoming interdependent, that is, being both independent and closely involved with others at the same time. Although independence had both positive and negative connotations for Jill, it frightened her because she felt so inadequate. At the same time, she realized the importance of developing a more interdependent relationship with parents and other important people in her life. It was mutually agreed that Jill and her therapist would continue working together with a shift in therapeutic focus. The experience of processing the alliance rupture resulted in Jill's recognition and willingness to shift the treatment focus to interpersonal issues.

## Case 3: Reflective Writing and Processing an Alliance Rupture

Liz is an intern in a state psychiatric inpatient unit. She is in the fourth week of the 15 weeks she will spend on that unit. So far she has liked the challenge of working with acutely ill patients. Dr. Monk, the director of clinical training, requires all interns to keep a daily journal to reflect and write about notable experiences with patients they have worked with that day. Today, after getting back to her apartment and finishing dinner, she sat down at her desk and wrote the following entry in her journal:

I don't know why I'm having so much trouble with some of these patients. I can't believe what I did this afternoon. How could I just sit there and say nothing and do nothing when Mrs. Jackson started crying. I just seemed to zone out when she was telling about her daughter running away. Here she is crying her head off and I didn't say a word. No empathic response. Nothing. Then she got up and walked back to her room. Then I sort of snapped out of it, but I felt too ashamed to go after her and process things. I guess this is what Dr. Monk meant when he was talking about alliance strains and ruptures in the intern seminar a couple weeks ago. I'm not sure this is a rupture but it is at least a strain. I'm not really sure what I should do about it. And, I don't know why I acted that way. Worse yet, I don't feel comfortable bringing it up in group supervision or in the intern seminar. I suppose I should bring it up in individual supervision, but then Dr. Arenna will probably ask me, "Where is that coming from?" and I don't really know.

I haven't been very comfortable talking to Dr. Arenna about my discomfort in dealing with the long pauses and periods of silence with another patient last week. But, it was helpful to process it with him. Still, I don't think I should bring up another one of my failures with him, at least so soon. I guess I don't want him to think I'm really not cut out to be a therapist. No, it's probably more my embarrassment. I probably have some countertransference going on here and it's embarrassing to have to talk about it. What if he recommends I need to do some personal therapy on this stuff? Who would I go to, and how would I pay for it? I don't think any of the other interns are in personal therapy. I really wouldn't want anyone to know. But, I've got to do something. I suppose I could just go up to Mrs. Jackson tomorrow morning and apologize or something. But then what would I say? Maybe I need to get some time with my supervisor first. We don't have our scheduled supervision for 2 days yet, but maybe I could get a quick consult with him tomorrow on what to do before talking to my patient later on. Then, in regular supervision I can get to the bottom of why I froze up. Mrs. Jackson is about my mother's age so maybe it is a transference–countertransference thing. If it is, I've got to get a handle on it. And, I've got to repair my alliance with Mrs. Jackson. So, I know what I need to do, and I'm going to do it.

The next day Liz did meet with Dr. Arenna for a short time and got some helpful advice for immediately dealing with the alliance breach. She subsequently met with Mrs. Jackson, apologized for not being more responsive, and processed their last session. Things went well. The next day she had her weekly supervision meeting with Dr. Arenna and began discussing transference–countertransference and how it can impact the therapeutic alliance.

**Case Commentary**

Rather than having a videotape of a recent session to review, Liz took the time to make an entry in her professional journal. It was while making this entry that she recognized an alliance rupture and that it may have been caused by her own countertransference. It has been conjectured that therapists who regularly engage in written reflection on their clinical work begin to "think" and practice like expert or master therapists (Bennett-Levy & Thwaites, 2006). In this case, Liz's journal entry reflects considerable uncertainty but her reflection, the same strategy commonly used by expert therapists, appears to have helped her considerably with this case.

# 7

# *Perform an Integrative Diagnostic Assessment*

A diagnostic assessment is a focused assessment of the client and the current and developmental context influencing the client. It is an essential competency in mental health practice. This chapter begins with a description of the diagnostic assessment. Then it discusses two different conceptual maps or ways in which the therapist "thinks" about the diagnostic assessment process. The second of the two ways, the integrative diagnostic assessment, is the one advocated in this chapter and is a key clinical competency in developing an effective case conceptualization. Next, the chapter outlines a "map" for performing an integrative diagnostic assessment. This procedure is illustrated with a transcription of an actual diagnostic interview.

## DIAGNOSTIC ASSESSMENT AND INTEGRATIVE DIAGNOSTIC ASSESSMENT

### Purpose

The purpose of this assessment is to discover the answer to the question of what accounts for the client's concerns, distress, and/or diminished functioning for which the client seeks therapeutic assistance. A relatively complete diagnostic assessment interview can often be accomplished within the first 30 to 40 minutes of the initial session between client and therapist. However, the time frame necessary to complete such an evaluation may take considerably longer depending on the client's previous history and treatment, language and other cultural factors.

The focus of the diagnostic assessment is to gather information about the client that is clinically relevant to the treatment process and outcomes. This includes data on the client's current problems, current functioning, and mental status; social, developmental, and medical history and health behaviors; and, particularly, the expectations and resources the client brings to therapy. In the past few years, it is has become the norm for therapists to collect relevant biological data in addition to psychosocial and cultural data pertaining to the client. For instance, it is important to elicit medical history and health behavior or health-related data because a client who complains of anxiety symptoms may regularly ingest caffeine and other stimulants that could trigger, exacerbate, or even cause the anxiety symptoms experienced by the client. Similarly, the diagnostic assessment emphasizes client resources, such as the client's coping skills and support system, previous success in making changes, readiness and motivation for change, and treatment expectations.

## Approaches to the Diagnostic Assessment

There are basically two approaches to performing this assessment. Both reflect differing cognitive maps that therapists have of the assessment process.

### Diagnostic Assessment

The most common for diagnostic assessment, and the approach used by most trainees and new therapists, is to interview all clients using the same intake form or interview protocol in which masses of data are collected by filling in blanks, checking items, and so forth. After the interview has been completed, the therapist sets aside time to sift through the accumulated data and search for themes and patterns that offer a reasonable explanation for the client's presentation. Although this approach can be quite comprehensive in scope, it is time consuming and may not provide a holistic and fine-grained portrait of the client and the client's concerns and context.

**Integrative Diagnostic Assessment**
The second approach is considerably different and basically the opposite of the first and reflects a different cognitive way of thinking about the assessment process. Instead of collecting volumes of data, a highly effective therapist begins with hypotheses and searches for a pattern or "map" that best explains the client and the client's current presentation, that is, concerns, symptoms, or functioning, and the precipitants, predispositions, and perpetuants or maintaining factors that explain that presentation.

## INTEGRATIVE DIAGNOSTIC ASSESSMENT MAP

This map is indispensable in developing a case conceptualization. Chapter 9 describes this process in detail. The following is a brief description of these five Ps: presentation, precipitants, predispositions, perpetuants, and pattern.

| | |
|---|---|
| **Presentation** | The client's characteristic response to precipitants; type and severity of symptoms, history, course of illness, diagnosis, and relational behaviors |
| **Precipitants** | The triggers or stressors that activate the pattern resulting in the presentation |
| **Predispositions** | All the intrapersonal, interpersonal, and systemic factors, including attachment style and trauma, which can render a client vulnerable to maladaptive functioning |
| **Perpetuants** | Also referred to as "maintaining factors," these are processes by which a client's pattern is reinforced and confirmed by both the client and the client's environment |
| **Pattern** | The client's characteristic way of perceiving, thinking, and responding, which is reflected in the client's presentation or presenting symptoms or concern as well as related precipitants, predispositions, and perpetuants |

Unlike the diagnostic assessment approach, information is selectively and strategically obtained (an iterative process) for the purpose of supporting or modifying the therapist's working hypothesis. This map is indispensable in quickly and accurately performing an integrative diagnostic assessment resulting in a holistic and fine-grained portrait of the client and the client's concerns and context. Just as important, it facilitates the process of developing an integrative case conceptualization, in real time. This means that the case conceptualization is developing with information bits as they are elicited. Furthermore, this approach is consistent with the way highly effective therapists "think" about eliciting information from their clients (Jennings & Skovholt, 1999; Skovholt & Jennings, 2004). With practice, supervision, and experience, trainees can learn and master this approach.

## DIAGNOSTIC ASSESSMENT INTERVIEW MAP

Table 7.1 provides an interview map for conducting a diagnostic assessment. It includes six components, plus "interview wind down and closing questions" component. An earlier version of this interview plan was presented in *Becoming an Effective Therapist* (Sperry et al., 2003). The use of this Diagnostic Assessment Interview Map is illustrated in the interview transcription that follows.

## ILLUSTRATION OF INTEGRATIVE
## DIAGNOSTIC INTERVIEW

### Case of Geri R.

This case example includes a transcription of a diagnostic interview with Geri R., a 35-year-old female administrative assistant of African American descent. Geri is single and lives alone. She was referred by her company's human resources director for evaluation and treatment following a 3-week onset of depressed mood. Other symptoms included loss of energy, markedly diminished interest, insomnia, difficulty concentrating, and increasing social isolation. She had not shown up for work for 4 days; her absence prompted the psychiatric referral. Cutbacks at her office led to her being transferred out of a relatively close-knit work team where she had been for 16 years—and had been an administrative assistant for 6 years—to a senior administrative assistant position for the new vice president of sales in the executive annex.

**Table 7.1** Diagnostic Assessment Interview Map

| Focus | Basic Screening Questions | Detailed Inquiry |
|---|---|---|
| 1. *Presenting problem and context* | 1. "What concerns brought you here?" | 1. Clarify concern or symptoms [*presentation*] and stressors or triggers [*precipitants*]. |
| [*Foster engagement and set stage for doing diagnostic assessment*] | 2. "Why now?" | 2. Elicit coping skills, social support, and related client resources. |
| | 3. "Have you (or relatives) ever experienced this or other psychological problems?" | 3. Elicit previous psychiatric and drug history and treatment outcomes and family history. |
| | 4. "How has this been affecting your daily functioning?" | 4. Elicit life functioning information, e.g., work, family, social, intimacy, health, self-management. |
| 2. *Mental status* | | |
| Presentation | [*observation*] | [Note age, dress and grooming, mannerisms, quality/rate of speech, psychomotor activity] |
| Orientation and attitude | 5. "How do you feel about being here today?" | 5. Assess orientation to time, place, person, and situation. |
| Mood and emotional status | 6. "How has this affected your spirits/mood?" | 6. Probe for mood and affect. |
| Perceptual status | 7. "Have you had any unusual experiences?" | 7. Probe for dissociative and/or psychotic processes. |
| Cognitive status | 8. "How has your memory been serving you?" | 8. Probe for the form and content and thought. |

*continued*

87

**Table 7.1 (continued)** Diagnostic Assessment Interview Map

| Focus | Basic Screening Questions | Detailed Inquiry |
| --- | --- | --- |
| Safety issues | 9. "Have you ever thought that life wasn't worth living?" | 9. Probe suicidal ideation, intention, and plan; violent impulses; and homicidal ideation. |
| Judgment and insight | 10. Proverb; letter on sidewalk *or* smoke in theater question | 10. Assess level of both factors. |
| 3. *Developmental history and dynamics* | 11. "How would you describe yourself as a person?" | 11. Clarify current self-view, level of self-esteem, personality style. |
| | 12. "You've told me how things are going for you lately. Now, I'd like to shift to how things were as you were growing up." | 12. Elicit developmental history: relations to parents [transference enactment w/therapist] and siblings, abuse or neglect, developmental milestones, school experience, best friends, first sexual experience, maladaptive *pattern, predispositions* and *perpetuants*. |
| 4. *Social history and cultural dynamics* | 13. "What is your current living [work] situation?" | 13. Jobs or military; any legal problems; current social support system: family, friends, peers at work or school; financial. |
| | 14. "What is your ethnic background?" | 14. Ethnic identity, race, age, gender and sexual orientation, religion, migration and country of origin, socioeconomic status, level of *acculturation*, language, dietary influences, and education. |

88

| | | |
|---|---|---|
| 5. *Health history and health behaviors* | 15. "Tell me about your health." | 15. Identify prescriptions, over-the-counter drug use, substance use/abuse, health status, medical conditions, and health habits. |
| 6. *Client resources and treatment Promoting Factors* | 16. "How have you tried to make things better (i.e., symptoms)?" "Results?" | 16. Probe client's own efforts to change; past efforts and successes in making changes; social support; therapy & *clinician credibility; placebo effect* potential. |
| [7.] *Explanatory model, treatment expectations, and readiness* | 17. "How would you explain why you're having these symptoms (problems)?" | 17. Clarify client's *explanatory model;* sets stage for negotiating a mutually agreeable case conceptualization. |
| | 18. "How is it best treated? What do you see as your part (role) in this process? Therapist's role?" | 18. Identify expectations for treatment and that client is motivated to change. |
| | 19. "When do you expect things will get better for you?" | 19. Specify *readiness for change.* |
| 8. *Interview wind down and closing* | 20. "Anything I haven't asked you about that would be important for me to know? | 20. Ask an open-ended question that permits client to add potentially useful information. |
| | 21. "I've asked you a lot of questions. Do you have any to ask of me?" | 21. Provide client a sense that the therapeutic relationship is reciprocal and collaborative. |

*Note:* Brackets around Focus number indicate that the basic screening questions are more treatment oriented than diagnostic oriented.

The interview basically follows the integrative diagnostic interview format (Table 7.1) wherein screening questions are followed by detailed inquiry questions.

*Th.:* I understand that Ms. Hicks, the director of human resources at your company, referred you to me. What's your understanding of why we're meeting today?

*Cl.:* She wanted me to see you because I haven't been feeling too well lately.

*Th.:* In what way haven't you been feeling well?

*Cl.:* Over the past 2 weeks, I've been feeling pretty sad. And, I guess it's been affecting my work a lot. I've got no initiative, no desire to get involved with anything.

*Th.:* So in the past 2 weeks you've been pretty sad, and it's been affecting you considerably. Has this been for brief periods over the past 2 weeks or has it been most of each day, every day during the past 2 weeks?

*Cl.:* Most of the day every day.

*Th.:* Have you ever felt like this before?

*Cl.:* Never. I've always been a pretty even-keeled person all my life.

*Th.:* How would you rate your moods now on a 1 to 10 scale, 1 being the worst and lowest, 10 being the best you could imagine yourself feeling?

*Cl.:* I'd say about a 3.

*Th.:* What's the lowest it's been recently?

*Cl.:* About 1 to 2.

*Th.:* When was that?

*Cl.:* After hearing that I was being transferred to a new boss in another department. It was the worst I've ever felt.

*Th.:* How would you rate your mood on the average over the past 12 months before this all happened?

*Cl.:* Between 7 and 8.

*Th.:* Has your sleep been affected?

*Cl.:* Oh yes. It seems I'm falling asleep really early and waking up about 4 a.m. and not being able to fall back asleep.

*Th.:* Is that a change from your regular sleep patterns?

*Cl.:* I usually had been able to go down at 11:00 p.m. right after the late night news and weather and fall asleep in a few minutes. I'd sleep through until 7 a.m. and wake up refreshed. I didn't even need an alarm clock.

*Th.:*   What about your energy level?

*Cl.:*   It's been pretty low. I feel drained and don't seem to have the energy to do anything except lay around.

*Th.:*   O.K. What about your interest and pleasure in life, such as with hobbies and recreation?

*Cl.:*   Well, I don't feel like doing much lately. I don't really have any hobbies except watching T.V. and reading novels, but I can't seem to get much interested in them anymore.

*Th.:*   How about concentrating, being able to keep your mind on things. Has it been affected?

*Cl.:*   Yes. It's been almost impossible. My mind drifts from one thing to the next.

*Th.:*   Has your weight changed?

*Cl.:*   I've lost about 10 pounds in the past 2 weeks or so.

*Th.:*   When some people feel really down, they may begin thinking that they're worthless and no good. Have you felt that way?

*Cl.:*   Well, I've occasionally had thoughts like that since I was a child. But not anymore so now, if that's what you mean.

*Th.:*   Yes, that's what I meant. What about guilt feelings?

*Cl.:*   Not really.

*Th.:*   How about thoughts of death, such as feeling life isn't worth living much anymore?

*Cl.:*   (pause) Well, some of those thoughts ... but suicide is against my religion, so I try to get them out of my mind.

*Th.:*   Have you been successful at keeping those thoughts out of your mind?

*Cl.:*   I've only had them four or five times, but I would never act on them.

*Th.:*   Has anyone in your family had similar symptoms to yours?

*Cl.:*   I don't think so. Not my parents or my brother.

*Th.:*   What about aunts, uncles, or grandparents?

*Cl.:*   (pause) Maybe my auntie, my mother's younger sister. She died in a car accident when I was young. Someone said it might have been suicide because she was depressed. But I don't know for sure.

*Th.:*   How's your overall health?

*Cl.:*   Pretty good. Thank God.

*Th.:*   Have you any medical conditions?

*Cl.:*   None that I know of. Except for being a little overweight, I've been pretty healthy.

*Th.:*   Do you take any medications, either prescribed or over-the-counter?

*Cl.:*   No. Except for a daily multiple vitamin.

*Th.:*   What about use of substances like alcohol, nicotine, or recreational drugs?

*Cl.:*   I'm Baptist so I don't drink alcohol. I've never used street drugs in my life. I used to drink a cup of coffee in the morning, but now I drink several just to get some energy.

*Th.:*   Would you say you're a nervous person?

*Cl.:*   Sort of. I used to worry a lot about what people might think of me.

*Th.:*   Has this changed recently?

*Cl.:*   Yeah. I don't seem to care what anyone thinks anymore.

*Th.:*   Have you ever had periods of tremendous energy, when you haven't needed much sleep, felt you were on top of the world, and could do anything you put your mind too?

*Cl.:*   No, not really.

*Th.:*   Have you had unusual experiences?

*Cl.:*   Like what?

*Th.:*   Feeling like you were outside your body or hearing or seeing things that others didn't see or hear.

*Cl.:*   No.

*Th.:*   Has your mind ever played tricks on you or your memory fail you: such as lost memory for events?

*Cl.:*   No it hasn't.

*Th.:*   How would you describe yourself as a person?

*Cl.:*   Well, I'm kind of quiet and reserved, but I'm a good worker or at least I used to be.

*Th.:*   You say quiet and reserved. Can you give an example?

*Cl.:*   Well, like at work a month ago, they asked if anyone would volunteer to go to another office and work for the vice president of sales. That's the last thing I'd do—volunteer. Even if there was a promotion in it.

*Th.:*   What did you anticipate might happen if you did?

*Cl.:*   That I'd get some new boss who would be really demanding and critical.

*Th.:*   Critical?

*Cl.:*   Yeah. Complaining that I made typos or that I didn't get a report or letter just right. And being around someone I don't know.

*Th.:*   What would that be like?

*Cl.:*   Uncomfortable … even scary. I'd rather be around people I've known a long time and can trust.

*Th.:*   It sounds like being around supportive and noncritical people is important to you.

*Cl.:*   Yeah. It is.

*Th.:*   Even if it means giving up a promotion and a raise?

*Cl.:*   Feeling safe is worth more to me than more money or promotion to senior administrative assistant.

*Th.:*   How about friendships at your company?

*Cl.:*   I have friends. Well, actually one for sure. Sally started about the same time I did. She's different than others. Kind, never a harsh word.

*Th.:*   You can count on her?

*Cl.:*   I sure can.

*Th.:*   How about the other secretaries and support staff?

*Cl.:*   They're pretty catty and gossipy. And they can tease, and I don't like that. I mean, I'm pretty thin-skinned.

*Th.:*   Have you done things socially with them?

*Cl.:*   Yes, I did. Well at least a time or two. Most of them just want to talk about men. And I don't like that kind of sharing. They want to get real close and find out everything about you. Secrets and all. I mean I really wanted to be at their parties, but it was so scary being around all those people. They're always ready to judge you before they know you. … I wouldn't know what to say to them. Whenever I opened my mouth I know I'd make a fool of myself. They were ready to laugh if I said anything.

*Th.:*   Did they actually laugh at you?

*Cl.:*   Well, no … but they could have.

*Th.:*   What would happen if they'd find out a little bit about you?

*Cl.:*   I feel that if they really got to know me they wouldn't like me … I don't have much to offer (long pause-head down).

*Th.:*   Are you in an intimate relationship now?

*Cl.:*   (pause and look of surprise) Are you kidding? I couldn't go through that after I saw what my parents did to each other. … I mean living so close to someone. Having someone judging everything you said or did.

*Th.:*   You mentioned your parents. How did they treat each other when you were growing up?

93

*Cl.:*    A lot of shouting, criticizing, and blaming. It was awful. It scared me so much. I just wanted to get away from all that. I needed to get away from it because after they fought, they would come after me and get on my case. There was nothing I did right. My grades weren't good enough. My room wasn't clean enough. I was too fat and not athletic enough. If only I had combed my hair better, the boys would like me ... All that stuff ... I couldn't stand it (voice raised).

*Th.:*    What was it like being around your brother and other kids in the neighborhood and around school?

*Cl.:*    The same. Teasing and making fun of me. I was the fat girl who couldn't do anything right. ... I'd get so nervous trying to answer the teacher in class that I'd freeze up even when I knew the answer. It was awful.

*Th.:*    Geri, can you tell me your earliest recollection?

*Cl.:*    (pause) Well I remember when my brother came home from the hospital after he was born.

*Th.:*    Can you tell me how old you were and the circumstances of his coming home?

*Cl.:*    I was about 4 or so. I remember my mother being gone for a while and not knowing where she went. I stayed at my auntie's house which I liked. But I was worried and nobody would tell me anything. Dad picked me up and took me home. Then I saw mom holding the baby and smiling and saying this was my new brother. Dad said this was the happiest day of his life. I guess I was whiny and upset and asking all kinds of questions. Dad told me to be quiet and go outside because Mom and the baby needed to be alone. I ran outside crying and hiding in my tree fort where it was safe.

*Th.:*    What do you remember thinking?

*Cl.:*    That I was confused. Didn't they want me anymore now that there was this new baby?

*Th.:*    And what did you feel?

*Cl.:*    (pause) That I was frightened, and probably angry, too.

*Th.:*    What does your brother do now?

*Cl.:*    He's a computer programmer. He's married and has two kids. I hardly even see him. We're not close.

*Th.:*    How about when you were growing up?

*Cl.:*    I had to take care of him. Babysit him … He used to tease me and call me names. The little brat. And so did his friends. We weren't close. My parents spoiled him rotten. He got whatever he wanted.

*Th.:*    Is there anything else you can think of that helps describe what it was like growing up in your family?

*Cl.:*    Well, we were supposed to be "seen and not heard," and never were we to "hang our dirty wash out in public." Like they say today, we were supposed to stuff our feelings. Also, we were expected to work hard and achieve. My brother was a lot better at that than I was … and, my parents got into some knock-down-drag-out fights. They didn't happen too often. And no outsiders would have guessed it, but they scared me. I really thought they'd get divorced and I'd end up in some foster home or something. I guess living by myself now is a lot more tolerable than what it was like living with my family when I was growing up.

*Th.:*    I've asked you a lot of questions so far and would like to know if there is anything I haven't asked you about, that you believe would be helpful for me to know?

*Cl.:*    (pause) No, I think you've pretty much covered it.

**Case Commentary**

With the diagnostic evaluation segment of the interview completed, the therapist now shifts the conversation to treatment considerations. He first explores her explanatory model and treatment expectations. Then the discussion turns to treatment goals and methods, and roles of both client and therapist. Because this will be Geri's first experience with therapy, the therapist provides a frame for treatment, or role induction, as it is sometimes called. He introduces her to the therapy process, scheduling of sessions, between-session assignments, and so on.

# 8

# Develop an Accurate DSM Diagnosis

Because most health insurance companies, health maintenance organizations (HMOs), and clinics require a diagnosis based on *DSM* (*Diagnostic and Statistical Manual of Mental Disorders*) criteria, it is essential that mental health professionals are competent in making accurate and appropriate *DSM* diagnoses. The current version, *DSM–IV–TR* (American Psychiatric Association, 2000), has been designed for use across a variety of treatment settings, including inpatient, consultation-liaison, clinic, private practice, and primary care, and is the standard classification of mental disorders used by mental health professionals in the United States. For the purpose of making a *DSM* diagnosis, therapists-in-training should be familiar with the *DSM*'s diagnostic classification, diagnostic codes, diagnostic criteria sets, and a strategy for making a five-axes diagnosis. This chapter describes these *DSM* factors and the process of making a *DSM* diagnosis, and it illustrates this process with case examples.

## DSM–IV–TR

The *diagnostic classification* in the *DSM–IV–TR* is the list of nearly 300 mental disorders identified within 17 diagnostic categories. Making a *DSM* diagnosis involves selecting those disorders from the classification list that best reflect the symptoms of the individual being evaluated. Associated with each diagnostic label is a *diagnostic code*, which insurance companies, HMOs, clinics, and agencies utilize for data collection and billing purposes. For example, 301.83 is the diagnostic code for Borderline Personality Disorder. Each *DSM* disorder has a set of *diagnostic criteria* that specify what symptoms must be present and the time frame needed to qualify for a diagnosis (*inclusion criteria*), as well as those symptoms that cannot be present (*exclusion criteria*), in order for an individual to qualify for a particular diagnosis. These criteria distinguish the versions of *DSM–III* to the present from *DSM–I* and *DSM–II*, which had no criteria. Not surprisingly, these criteria greatly increase *diagnostic reliability*, that is, the likelihood that different clinicians assign the same diagnosis. Because these criteria provide a compact encapsulated description of each disorder, clinicians find the criteria to be clinically useful in making an accurate diagnosis.

Since *DSM–III* was published, a five-axes system of diagnosis has been adopted. It endeavors to account for the client's biological, psychological, and social functioning and overall adaptability to life's stressors.

The five axes are briefly described here.

*Axis I* is for reporting any clinical disorders, as well as other conditions that may be a focus of clinical attention.

*Axis II* is for specifying personality disorders and/or mental retardation.

*Axis III* specifies any general medical conditions that are relevant to understanding or managing of the Axis I disorder.

*Axis IV* is for reporting psychosocial and environmental factors that could affect the diagnosis, treatment, or prognosis of Axis I or II.

*Axis V* is for specifying the individual's overall level of functioning using the Global Assessment of Functioning (GAF) scale and the Global Assessment of Relationship Functioning (GARF) Scale, when applicable.

In short, these five axes provide a succinct summary of the biopsychosocial factors that influence an individual's symptoms and functioning.

## STRATEGY FOR DEVELOPING AN ACCURATE *DSM* DIAGNOSIS

There are no shortcuts to an accurate diagnosis, although the temptation is strong to "eyeball" a diagnosis. This means that the clinician considers the client's symptoms and quickly assigns a diagnosis that looks like it fits without reviewing the specific diagnostic criteria to ensure that it does. On the other hand, achieving an accurate *DSM* diagnosis involves a systematic strategy and process which is described in the following seven steps.

**Step 1:** Begin by focusing on Axis I, which deals with "symptom" disorders. Determine if your client is experiencing a mood disorder, anxiety disorder, developmental disorder, personality disorder, sexual disorder, substance abuse, or some other disorder. Table 8.1 lists these basic categories and gives a brief description of the most common diagnoses for each category. Narrow your basic criteria down to the three most likely categories.

**Step 2:** Make a list of the client's symptoms. Compare the client's symptoms to those of the diagnostic criteria you have narrowed.

**Step 3:** Make sure that the symptoms meet the *inclusion criteria* as well as *exclusion criteria* for the specific disorder you are attempting to diagnose.

**Step 4:** Code the disorder according to the diagnostic code in the *DSM–IV–TR*, and make sure you indicate any *specifiers*, for example, "in partial remission." Record your diagnosis and code for Axis I.

**Step 5:** Now shift focus to Axis II where personality disorders and mental retardation are coded.

**Step 6:** Begin by considering the essential feature of each personality disorder (Table 8.2). If the client manifests a specific essential feature, then proceed to review the specific criteria to determine if the client qualifies for that diagnosis. Then, record your diagnosis and code for Axis II.

**Step 7:** Finally, attend to Axis III, Axis IV, and Axis V and record the appropriate information to complete a five-axes diagnosis.

## ILLUSTRATION: DEVELOPING AN ACCURATE *DSM* DIAGNOSIS

### Case 1: Geri

Geri's depressive symptoms and increased social isolation are moderate to severe. At the time of the evaluation she meets six of the nine *DSM–IV–TR* criteria for clinical depression, called Major Depressive Disorder, Single Episode. These criteria are the following:

Depressed mood most of the day, nearly every day for more than 2 weeks (1)
Markedly diminished interest or pleasure—also called anhedonia (2)

**Table 8.1**   Essential Features of Common *DSM–IV–TR* Disorders

| | |
|---|---|
| Personality Disorders: A | Cluster of personality disorders characterized by odd or eccentric thinking and behavior |
| Personality Disorders: B | Cluster of personality disorders characterized by dramatic, emotional, or erratic behavior |
| Personality Disorders: C | Cluster of personality disorders characterized by anxious or fearful behavior |
| Cognitive Disorders | Clinically significant deficits in cognition that are markedly different from previous functioning |
| Delirium | Disturbance of consciousness and cognitive changes that develop within a short time frame |
| Dementia | Multiple cognitive deficits, including memory impairment |
| Psychotic Disorders | Significant dysfunctions in thought processes, speech, mood, motivation, and functioning |
| Schizophrenia | Prominent hallucinations, bizarre delusions, negative symptoms of disorganized speech and affect |
| Delusional Disorders | A prominent non-bizarre delusion not meeting the main criteria for a diagnosis of schizophrenia |
| Mood Disorders | Disorders with mood symptoms |
| Depression | Presence of either depressed mood or loss of interest and pleasure in daily life |
| Dysthymic Disorder | Chronic experience of depression for a period of at least 2 years without major depression |
| Bipolar Disorder | Manic or a hypomanic episode with problems with mood, functioning, grandiosity, and increased energy |
| Anxiety Disorders | Symptoms that are regarded as emerging from emotional conflict or biological sources |
| Panic Disorder | Sudden onset of physiological symptoms such as sweating, trembling, chest pain, and shortness of breath |
| Agoraphobia | Learned avoidance of events or activities that may trigger a panic attack |
| Generalized Anxiety Disorder | Excessive anxiety, worry, or apprehension about several matters |
| Posttraumatic Stress Disorder | Unwanted recollection or reexperiencing of a traumatic event with arousal symptoms |

**Table 8.1 (continued)**   Essential Features of Common *DSM–IV–TR* Disorders

| | |
|---|---|
| Dissociative Disorders | Symptoms of disturbance in self, memory, or awareness, e.g., Dissociative Identity Disorder |
| Somatoform Disorders | Physical symptom unexplained by a medical problem, substance abuse, or mental disorder |
| Childhood and Adolescence Disorders | Disorders that typically become manifest during childhood or adolescence |
| Attention Deficit Disorder | Pattern of inattention and/or hyperactivity/impulsivity, with some symptoms before the age of 7 |
| Autism | Delay or abnormal functioning before age 3 in social interaction, communication, and play |
| Asperger's Disorder | No delay in language acquisition and use and fewer repetitive motor behaviors than with Autism |
| Eating Disorders | Difficulties with too much, too little, or unhealthy food intake, and/or distorted body image |
| Bulimia Nervosa | Recurrent binge eating with loss of control over one's eating and compensation for overeating |
| Anorexia Nervosa | Refusal to maintain body weight at 85% of minimal normal body weight, with a fear of weight gain; distorted body image |
| Relational Disorders (V-Code) | Particular relational problems of clinical focus, e.g., parent–child, partner relational problems |

Weight loss of 10 pounds and appetite loss (3)
Insomnia with some early morning awakening (4)
Fatigue and low energy (6)
Diminished concentration(8)

Geri also meets four criteria of the seven criteria for Avoidant Personality Disorder:

She avoided the job promotion because of fear of criticism and disapproval (1). This is the essential or optimal feature for this personality disorder (see Table 2).
She showed restraint within intimate relationships because of fear of being teased and ridiculed (3).
She was preoccupied with being criticized and rejected in social situations (4).
She views herself as socially inept and personally unappealing (i.e., obese) and inferior to others (6).

**Table 8.2**  Essential Features of *DSM–IV–TR* Personality Disorders

| Personality Disorders | Essential Feature |
|---|---|
| Antisocial | Criminal, aggressive, impulsive, irresponsible behavior |
| Avoidant | Avoids work activities that involve significant interpersonal contact fearing criticism, disapproval or rejection |
| Borderline | Makes frantic efforts to avoid real or imagined abandonment |
| Dependent | Needs others to assume responsibility for most major areas of their life |
| Histrionic | Is uncomfortable in situations in which he or she is not the center of attention |
| Narcissistic | Has grandiose sense of self-importance |
| Obsessive-Compulsive | Shows perfectionism that interferes with task completion |
| Paranoid | Suspects, without sufficient basis, that others are exploiting, harming, or deceiving them |
| Schizoid | Neither desires nor enjoys close relationships, such as being part of a family |
| Schizotypal | Odd thinking and speech, and odd, eccentric, or peculiar behavior or appearance |

Given that this is her first episode of depression, that her level of functioning is moderate rather than severe (based on current and baseline GAF), and that probability of suicide is low, hospitalization is not deemed a necessity at this time.

### *DSM–IV–TR* Five-Axes Diagnosis

I. Major Depressive Disorder, Single Episode, Moderate (296.22) Occupational Problem (V62.2)
II. Avoidant Personality Disorder (301.82)
III. None
IV. Limited support system; job stressor
V. GAF: 54 now; 71 highest in past 12 months

## Case 2: Mr. G.

Mr. G. is a 40-year-old accountant who presents with complaints of loss of interest in his job, hobbies, and family over a period of 6 weeks. He acknowledges sadness, reduced appetite with a 12-pound weight loss, early morning awakening, fatigue, and recurrent thoughts of death, but he denies suicidal ideation. Two days before he noted these symptoms, he states that a job promotion did not materialize as he expected. The referral note from the human resources director is that Mr. G. has shown up for work but is characterized as exhibiting "somewhat lowered productivity" rather than his usual adequate level of productivity. Mr. G. describes himself as unusually serious, conservative, and slow to express affection. He also acknowledges having an excessive commitment to work and being rigid, stubborn, and controlling in social situations. He admits to perfectionistic tendencies that interfere with completing work assignments. His coworkers complain that he is unusually conscientious and inflexible about business ethics. The results of a recent medical examination, lab tests, and neurological studies indicate no abnormalities.

### *Axis I:* **Major Depressive Disorder, Single Episode 296.21**
Mr. G. meets all stated criteria for this diagnosis. Specifically, in terms of criterion A, he experiences five symptoms which were present for more than the 2-week minimum:

Sadness (1)
Loss of interest in his job, hobbies, and family (2)
A 12-pound weight loss and reduced appetite (3)
Fatigue (6)
Recurrent thoughts of death (9)

Because he is able to show up for work and perform with "somewhat lower productivity," his depression is characterized as "mild" and thus is coded as 296.21 rather than as 296.22, which would denote a moderate level of depression. (Cf. Axis V below for additional insight into this rating.)

### *Axis II:* **Obsessive-Compulsive Personality Disorder 301.4**
Mr. G. meets more than four criteria for this diagnosis:

Unusually conscientious and inflexible about business ethics (4)
Rigid, stubborn, and controlling in social situations (8)
Has an excessive commitment to work (3)
Shows perfectionistic tendencies that interfere with completing work assignments. (2) This is the essential or optimal feature for this personality disorder (see Table 8.2).

*Axis V:* **GAF of 65 now**
The rating of 65 reflects mild or "some difficulty." Mr. G. experiences mild difficulty occupationally and socially, rather than moderate or severe difficulty. It should be noted that Axis V must be consistent with the level of severity of the Major Depressive Disorder diagnosis. In this case, a severity rating of "mild " (296.21) is given, as only minor impairment ("somewhat lower productivity") was reported by the human resources director. This rating is consistent with a GAF of 65.

*DSM–IV–TR* **Five-Axes Diagnosis**
   I. Depressive Disorder 296.21
   II. Obsessive-Compulsive Disorder 301.6
   III. None
   IV. Occupational problems
   V. 65 now

## Case 3: Mrs. E.

Mrs. E. presents with extraordinary concern about the safety of her husband and young daughter. She rarely leaves them alone, and when at work, she telephones home every hour. She has lost one job because of this, and her husband has threatened to leave her if she does not get counseling. Six months ago, the symptoms, which have been present for years, became worse after her husband had a serious job-related accident. She describes recurrent worries in which dangerous events befall her family and she is not there to save them. She knows the thoughts are silly and that they come from her own mind rather than any real danger, but she cannot resist contacting her husband or daughter in some way to be certain they are safe. Her husband has arranged to lift the telephone receiver briefly, then hang up, which is usually sufficient to allay her fears for an hour or so. Until recently she had performed her job reasonably well when not distraught by her fears. For the past 2 months she has been absent three or four times a month and coworkers are complaining that they are getting tired of having to cover for her. She describes herself as nurturing, supportive, and a good friend. She does admit that making decisions is hard without the input of others, and she feels uncomfortable when alone.

Her husband reports that she is a pleaser and fears others' disapproval, and that she needs and expects others to take responsibility for most areas of her life. She is also somewhat conscientious and perfectionistic. There is no history of significant medical illness or substance abuse. She completed high school and works as a data entry clerk. Medical examination and lab tests show no abnormalities.

### *Axis I:* Obsessive-Compulsive Disorder 300.3

Mrs. E. meets criteria for this disorder in that she has both obsessions and compulsions.

With regard to diagnostic criteria A, she meets criteria (1) and (2) as she has recurrent worries in which dangerous events befall her family and she is not there to save them and this causes her marked distress; she meets criterion (3) as she attempts to suppress these thoughts with repetitive phone calls and criterion (4) as she knows the thoughts are "silly" thoughts that come from her own mind rather than that there is any real danger. With regard to diagnostic criteria B, she meets criterion (1) as she engages in repetitive telephone calls, and criterion (2) as this behavior reduces her distress.

### *Axis II:* Dependent Personality Disorder 301.6

Mrs. E meets more than four criteria for this diagnosis.

Difficulty making decisions without the input of others (1)
Uncomfortable when alone (6)
Pleaser who seldom disagrees with others and fears others' disapproval (3)
Expects others to take responsibility for most areas of her life (2). This is the essential or optimal feature for this personality disorder (see Table 8.2).

Obsessive-compulsive traits are also reported for Mrs. E. on Axis II. These include conscientiousness and perfectionism.

### *Axis V:* GAF of 55 now

Her job absence record (3–4 times a month) because of the exacerbation of her conditions and coworker complaints about having to cover for her reflect moderate impairment, and thus a GAF of 55.

*DSM–IV–TR* **Five-Axes Diagnosis**

   I. Obsessive-Compulsive Disorder 300.3
  II. Dependent personality disorder 301.6 with obsessive-compulsive traits
 III. None
 IV. Parental overprotection; occupational problems
  V. 55 now; 70 highest in the past year

## Case 4: Leslie

Leslie is a 22-year-old English major at a private university. During the initial evaluation she exhibits both shyness and uncomfortableness. Her chief complaint is of panic attacks, which she reports are sufficiently immobilizing that she limits her contact with others and prefers to remain in her dormitory room. With a new semester approaching, she wonders if she will be able to attend classes. The pattern is always the same in that suddenly she experiences her heart quicken, then she begins to sweat as the fear of an attack grows, then her heart begins to race faster and faster and she is overtaken by panic.

Leslie tries to work each day, takes care of necessary errands, and shops for food every week. Generally, she lets things accumulate and then tries to do them all at once, to get them over with. In the past, she occasionally enjoyed volunteer work at a botanical garden, but she has never held a real job. When asked about her social life, she has difficulty naming friends. Her fear "is that others won't like me if they really find out about the real me!" Although her words are deeply felt, she never makes eye contact with the interviewer. She concedes that although others may be capable of succeeding in the world, she desperately wants to be left alone. Even when she is just sitting in class, she has difficulty believing that others who are laughing are not making fun of her.

Leslie's developmental and social history provides a context for understanding her symptoms. She has been reminded many times that her birth was an accident, something unpleasant that her mother and father "had to go through." She cannot recall a time when she felt loved by her parents. "Not that they were neglectful," she quickly points out, "but I always felt like a burden to them." Life at home was without warmth or joy, with much time spent fantasizing alone in her room, something she still does today. Her parents are highly successful and had high expectations for her but were often excessively critical, even of the smallest mistakes. Because

**106**

of her shyness, she had to endure hours of merciless teasing from the other children, apparently the origin of a crippling self-consciousness that has followed her ever since childhood. Unable to defend herself, she withdrew socially, as if to become smaller and less noticeable to others.

When asked about relationships, Leslie refers to her only boyfriend, when she was a high school senior. She stated that "I was afraid to be myself or voice any kind of opinion of my own. I was afraid he would dump me." When asked about marriage, Leslie admits she has dreams of being accepted unconditionally but doubts that it will ever happen. Instead, she prefers to be alone, "where it's safe, where no one can see your faults, much less judge you or criticize you for them. If you keep with what you know," she says, "you at least don't have to worry about embarrassing yourself."

This client meets the criteria for the Axis I and an Axis II diagnosis.

### *Axis I:* Anxiety Disorder Not Otherwise Specified (NOS)

Primary among the features of the presentation of Anxiety Disorder NOS is that Leslie exhibits some clinically significant symptoms of anxiety but does not fulfill the criteria for any specific Anxiety Disorder or Adjustment Disorder with Anxiety symptoms.

She does exhibit accelerated heart rate and sweating when she experiences panic, but the diagnosis of Panic Disorder requires at least four panic-like symptoms that develop abruptly and reach a peak within 10 minutes. She does appear to be somewhat agoraphobic (e.g., preferring to stay in her dorm room), but she does not meet the *DSM* criteria for Agoraphobia.

For her to meet the criteria for Panic Disorder with Agoraphobia (300.21) she would need to meet full criteria for Panic Disorder as well as full criteria for Agoraphobia. Because she does not but has clinically significant anxiety symptoms, the diagnosis of Anxiety Disorder NOS (300.00) is an appropriate diagnosis for her.

### *Axis II:* Avoidant Personality Disorder

Leslie displays many of the features of Avoidant Personality Disorder.

She avoids occupational activities involving interpersonal contact (1) e.g., she has never held a real job because she fears that people will not like her or they will reject her. This is the essential or optimal feature for this personality disorder (Table 8.2).

She shows restraint with intimate relationships for fear of being shamed (3) and cites that with her only boyfriend, she was afraid to express her real self because she thought he would "dump" her.

She shows a preoccupation with being criticized or rejected in social situations, stating that she believes her classmates are laughing or making fun of her for no apparent reason (4).

She claims she has had a pattern since being teased in childhood of withdrawing to become smaller and less noticeable, demonstrating that she is inhibited in new social situations because of feelings of inadequacy (5).

In her statement regarding that if others found out about the "real me," they wouldn't like her, she exhibits a belief that she is personally unappealing (6).

Thus, Leslie meets five, more than the minimum of the four, criteria needed to fulfill the diagnostic analysis of Avoidant Personality Disorder.

### *Axis IV:* Occupational concerns. Relational concerns. Problems related to the social environment.

The main stressors Leslie faces are occupational, that is, being a university student who consistently feels uncomfortable in situations outside her dormitory room, and who also feels uncomfortable around other people. The first two concerns seem more related to her panic and anxiety symptoms (Axis I) while the third seems more related to avoidant personality (Axis II).

### *Axis V:* GAF of 63

Leslie appears to be experiencing mild symptoms and impairment. Although it is uncomfortable for her she continues in her university classes. She is also able to attend her counseling sessions.

### *DSM–IV–TR* Five-Axes Diagnosis

   I. Anxiety Disorder Not Otherwise Specified (300.00)
   II. Avoidant Personality Disorder (301.82)
   III. None
   IV. Occupational concerns. Relational concerns. Problems related to the social environment
   V. GAF = 63

# 9

# Develop an Effective Clinical Case Conceptualization

Case conceptualizations have become increasingly associated with effective, quality mental health practice. Basically, a case conceptualization is a method and process of summarizing seemingly diverse clinical information about a client into a brief, coherent statement or "map," which elucidates the client's basic pattern and which serves to guide the treatment process. The capacity to develop and utilize a case conceptualization is an essential clinical competency.

This chapter begins by describing case conceptualization and its functions, and then describes its four components: diagnostic formulation, clinical formulation, cultural formulation, and treatment formulation. The first two components are described and illustrated here, while cultural formulation is the focus of Chapter 10, and treatment formulation is the focus of Chapter 11. Next, protocols for developing diagnostic and clinical formulations are provided and illustrated. Then, the case of Geri serves to illustrate how a working case conceptualization can be derived from the initial interview. The commentary on the interview transcription demonstrates how a highly effective therapist "thinks" and "acts" in this process. Finally, case material illustrates various aspects of the case conceptualization process.

## CASE CONCEPTUALIZATION: DEFINITION AND FUNCTIONS

Case conceptualizations provide therapists with a coherent treatment strategy for planning and focusing treatment interventions in order to increase the likelihood of achieving treatment goals. While many therapists develop tentative conceptualizations to guide their practice, not all therapists explicitly articulate these conceptualizations. It should not be surprising that expert therapists develop better case conceptualizations than trainees and experienced therapists (Eells et al., 2005). There are a number of reasons for developing and articulating a case conceptualization, but the most compelling reason is that a conceptualization enables therapists to experience a sense of confidence in their work (Hill, 2005). Hill (2005) believes that this confidence is then communicated to the client, which strengthens the client's trust and the belief that the therapist has a credible plan, and that therapy can and will make a difference. In other words, an effective case conceptualization increases "clinician credibility" (Sue & Zane, 1987).

A case conceptualization can be formally defined as a clinical strategy for obtaining and organizing information about a client, explaining the client's situation and maladaptive patterns, guiding and focusing treatment, anticipating challenges and roadblocks, and preparing for successful termination. This definition highlights five interrelated functions of a case conceptualization when it is understood as a clinical strategy. These functions are described next.

### 1. Obtaining and Organizing

The case conceptualization process begins with the first client contact and formulating tentative hypotheses about the client's presentation, expectations, and dynamics. These hypotheses are continually tested out while performing an integrative assessment guided by a search for patterns—maladaptive patterns—in the client's current and past life with regard to precipitating, predisposing, and perpetuating factors.

### 2. Explaining

As the contours of the client's maladaptive pattern comes into focus and hypotheses are refined, diagnostic, clinical, and cultural formulations emerge. Within these formulations is a likely explanation of the factors that account for the client's reactions in the past, the present, and the

110

future without treatment. This explanation also provides a rationale for treatment that is tailored to the client's needs, expectations, culture, and personality dynamics.

### 3. Guiding and Focusing Treatment

Based on this explanation, a treatment formulation emerges, including strategies for specifying treatment targets and for focusing and implementing treatment.

### 4. Anticipating Obstacles and Challenges

The test of an effective case conceptualization is its viability in predicting the obstacles and challenges throughout the stages of therapy, particularly those involving resistance, ambivalence, alliance ruptures, and transference enactments.

### 5. Preparing for Termination

The case conceptualization also assists therapists in recognizing when the most important therapy goals and treatment targets have been addressed and in identifying when and how to prepare for termination (Cucciare & O'Donohue, 2008).

## CASE CONCEPTUALIZATION: FOUR COMPONENTS

A case conceptualization consists of four components: a diagnostic formulation, a clinical formulation, a cultural formulation, and a treatment formulation (Sperry, 2005a; Sperry, Blackwell, Gudeman, & Faulkner, 1992).

### Diagnostic Formulation

A diagnostic formulation is a descriptive statement about the nature and severity of the individual's psychiatric presentation. The diagnostic formulation aids the therapist in reaching three sets of diagnostic conclusions: whether the client's presentation is primarily psychotic, characterological, or neurotic; whether the client's presentation is primarily organic or psychogenic in etiology; and whether the client's presentation is so acute that it requires immediate intervention. In short, diagnostic formulations are descriptive, phenomenological, and cross-sectional in nature. They answer the "what" question, that is, "What happened?" For all practical purposes the diagnostic formulation lends itself to being specified with *DSM–IV–TR* criteria and nosology.

## Clinical Formulation

A clinical formulation, on the other hand, is more explanatory and longitudinal in nature and attempts to offer a rationale for the development and maintenance of symptoms and dysfunctional life patterns. Just as various theories of human behavior exist, so do various types of clinical formulations, such as dynamic, Adlerian, cognitive, behavioral, biological, experiential, family systems, and biopsychosocial. Clinical formulations answer the "why" question, that is, "Why did it happen?" In short, the clinical formulation articulates and integrates the intrapsychic, interpersonal, and systemic dynamics to provide a clinically meaningful explanation of the client's *pattern*—that is, the predictable style of thinking, feeling, acting, and coping in stressful circumstances—and a statement of the causality of their behavior. Not surprisingly, the clinical formulation is the central component in a case conceptualization and serves to link the diagnostic and treatment formulations.

## Cultural Formulation

A cultural formulation supports the clinical formulation and can inform treatment focus and the type of interventions chosen. The cultural formulation is a systematic analysis of cultural factors and dynamics that have been described in the "Social History and Cultural Factors" section of a clinical case report. It answers the "what role does culture play?" question. More specifically, the cultural formulation statement describes the client's cultural identity and level of acculturation. It may provide a cultural explanation of the client's condition as well as the impact of cultural factors on the client's personality and level of functioning. Furthermore, it addresses cultural elements that may impact the relationship between the individual and the therapist and whether cultural or culturally sensitive interventions are indicated (Committee on Cultural Psychiatry, 2002).

## Treatment Formulation

A treatment formulation follows from the diagnostic, clinical, and cultural formulation and serves as an explicit blueprint governing treatment interventions. Informed by the answers to "What happened?", "Why did it happen?", and "What role does culture play?", the answer to the "how" question, that is, " How can it be changed?" is the basis of the treatment formulation. A well-articulated treatment formulation provides treatment goals, a treatment plan, treatment interventions, and predictions about the course of treatment, obstacles, and its outcomes.

The most useful case conceptualizations focus on the unique dynamics, needs, contexts, and resources of the individual (Carlson, Sperry, & Lewis, 2005; Sperry et al., 2003). Different cognitive processes are operative for different parts of the case conceptualization. Assessment and diagnosis tend to rely more on deductive reasoning wherein clinical data are analyzed in relation to established criteria. For instance, a therapist uses deductive reasoning process (i.e., logic that proceeds from general to specific) in arriving at a specific *DSM* diagnosis. A diagnosis is established if and when an individual's depressive symptoms meet specific *DSM* diagnostic criteria. Clinical formulations, on the other hand, tend to rely more on an inductive reasoning process (i.e., logic that proceeds from specific to general). In this form of reasoning, the clinician seeks to synthesize various pieces of seemingly unrelated data about a client into a consistent pattern and explanation (Sperry, 2005b). Treatment formulations seem to require both forms of reasoning. Thus, clinicians who are more adept and experienced with inductive reasoning might find developing a clinical formulation easier and faster than those whose forte is deductive reasoning. Clinicians who are adept at both deductive and inductive reasoning tend to find the process of developing diagnostic, clinical, cultural, and treatment formulations pleasantly challenging as well as clinically useful.

## CASE CONCEPTUALIZATIONS: THERAPISTS VERSUS CLIENTS

Trainees are surprised to learn that clients have developed "case conceptualizations" of their own. Because clients are often aware of their conceptualization, therapists need to understand it, because the greater it differs from the therapist's conceptualization, the more likely treatment will be negatively impacted. This can be manifested in many ways: tardiness or no-shows for appointments, failure to do homework, or even premature termination. Accordingly, the therapist should elicit the client's case conceptualization, particularly the client's treatment expectations and explanatory model, which is the client's personal "explanation," and then negotiate a mutually agreeable one with their client (Sperry, 2005b).

## CASE CONCEPTUALIZATION MAP

This section describes a practical method for developing a case conceptualization. It is based on the premise that a case conceptualization is basically a "map" of the client's maladaptive pattern of perceiving and responding to others and an alternate pattern that is more adaptive. Thus, developing a case conceptualization involves pattern analysis. This analysis begins with understanding the "what" and "why" of the client's situation and culture in order to answer the "how" question, that is, treatment formulation considerations. This approach involves a detailed inquiry and understanding of patterns. Pattern reflects an individual's predictable and consistent style or manner of thinking, feeling, acting, and coping, and defending the self in stressful and nonstressful circumstances. Pattern analysis is the process of examining the interrelationship among four factors: presentation factors, precipitating factors, predisposing factors, perpetuating factors, and including relational response factors (Sperry, 2005a, 2005b; Sperry et al., 1992). The fifth factor, pattern, integrates these four factors. These factors were found to be common to most case conceptualizations (Eells et al., 2005; Kendjelic & Eells, 2007).

| | |
|---|---|
| **Presentation** | The client's characteristic response to precipitants. The type and severity of symptoms, history, course of illness, diagnosis, and individual, relational and systemic behaviors, including collusion, coalitions, communications, and level of well-being. |
| **Precipitants** | The triggers or stressors that activate the pattern resulting in the presentation. |
| **Predisposition** | All the intrapersonal, interpersonal, and systemic factors, including attachment style and trauma, which render a client vulnerable to maladaptive functioning. |

**114**

**Perpetuants**     Also referred to as maintaining factors, these are processes by
                    which a client's pattern is reinforced and confirmed by both the
                    client and the client's environment.
**Pattern**         An explanation of the client's characteristic way of perceiving,
**Explanation**     thinking, and responding, which is reflected in the client's
                    presentation or presenting symptoms or concern, as well as
                    related precipitants, predispositions, and perpetuants.

In other words, a client's pattern or predictable style of behavior and functioning reflects, and is reflected in, their characteristic presentation, precipitant, predispositions, and perpetuants.

While it may appear that predisposing factors such as traumatic events, maladaptive beliefs or schemas, defenses, personality style, or systems factors primarily "drive" one's thoughts, feelings, and actions, the contention is that both individual and systemic dynamics are a function of all four factors, and thus should be included in a pattern analysis. Because pattern analysis includes all these and associated individual and systemic dynamics, it provides a systematic and comprehensive basis for developing and articulating a clinical case conceptualization, particularly the clinical formulation component. The case conceptualization map consists of these factors and the links and interactions among them. Table 9.1 depicts this map.

**Table 9.1**   Case Conceptualization Map

| Pattern Factors | Clinical Formulation | Treatment Formulation and Targets |
|---|---|---|
| Precipitant | | |
| Predispositions | | |
| Perpetuants | | |
| Presentation | | |

**115**

**Table 9.2** Worksheet for Developing a Case Conceptualization

Directions: Write a phrase or sentence (or more) for each:

**Presentation:** Presenting difficulty, symptoms or conflict [for Diagnostic and Clinical Formulation statements]

**Precipitating Stressor:** Events/stressors that contribute to current symptoms or problem, aka, triggers [for Diagnostic and Clinical Formulation statements]

**Predisposing Factors:** Events in the past or other situations that increase vulnerability to the precipitating stress and the expression of symptoms [for Clinical Formulation statement]

**Perpetuating Factors:** Processes that maintain and reinforce the pattern

**Pattern–Explanation:** Builds on previous four components to offer a viable hypothesis or explanation of the presenting difficulty [for Clinical Formulation statement]

**Relational Issues:** Likely resistance, transference/countertransference, due to personality, culture, or gender considerations [for Treatment Formulation statement; see Chapter 11]

**Treatment-promoting and treatment-interfering patterns/dynamics or behaviors:** Possible impact of support system, past success at change efforts, etc.; and likelihood of interfering patterns/behaviors on treatment progress, such as tardiness, noncompliance, etc. [for Treatment Formulation statement; see Chapter 11]

In the following two sections, a set of guidelines are provided for developing diagnostic formulations and clinical formulations. Chapters 10 and 11 will similarly provide guidelines for developing cultural formulations and treatment formulations. In applying the following guidelines, some will find the worksheet in Table 9.2 useful.

## DEVELOPING A DIAGNOSTIC FORMULATION STATEMENT

Here are some guidelines for establishing a diagnostic formulation and formulation statement.

### 1. Identify the Presentation and Precipitants

Begin by listing the client's reason for seeking therapy or presenting problem as one or more symptoms or a brief phrase specifying the personal or interpersonal concern or area of impaired functioning. Then, identify the most likely one or more triggers or precipitant. Also, search for previous instances, in the developmental and social history, for similar presentations and precipitants.

For example, in the case of Geri the presentation list would read: "social isolation and depressive symptoms" and the precipitant statement would read: "impending job transfer and promotion."

## 2. Specify a Five-Axes *DSM* Diagnosis

Chapter 8 provides a detailed strategy for accomplishing this task. Complete the seven steps of the strategy and transfer that information in the five-axes *DSM* format, which specifies the diagnoses. For the case of Geri this would be

   I. Major Depressive Disorder, Single Episode, Moderate (296.22)
      Occupational Problem (V62.2)
  II. Avoidant Personality Disorder (301.82)
 III. None
 IV. Limited support system; job stressor
  V. GAF: 49 now; 65 highest in past 12 months

## 3. Specify the Link Between Presentation and Precipitants and Write a Diagnostic Formulation Statement

Identify a link between the presenting problem(s) and the trigger(s). Also look for a link between previous instances of similar presentations and precipitants. Then, draft a short statement connecting the presentation with precipitants.

For example, in the case of Geri the statement would read:

> Geri's increased social isolation and depressive symptoms appear to be her reaction to an impending job promotion and transfer out of a close-knit work group where she had been for 12 years. This is her first experience with clinical depression or any other diagnosable condition. In short, her presentation and initial evaluation were consistent with diagnoses of a Major Depressive Disorder and Avoidant Personality Disorder.

## DEVELOPING A CLINICAL FORMULATION STATEMENT

Here are some guidelines for developing a clinical formulation and clinical formulation statement.

### 1. Specify Operative Predisposing Factors

From the developmental, social, and health history, identify likely predisposing factors. Search for factors that, when activated or triggered by specific stressors or demands, will result in the presenting symptoms or problems. Also, check if these or similar predispositions were operative in other previous situations. Think of predispositions as biological, psychological, or social vulnerabilities. These could include specific automatic thoughts or core maladaptive beliefs and schemas. They might be biological vulnerabilities such as history of substance abuse/dependence or depression, or specific social or environmental factors such as drinking friends or living or working in a place hostile to immigrants. Then, write a brief statement summarizing these predisposing factors.

For example, in the case of Geri the statement would read: "Her reaction is understandable given her pattern of avoiding situations in which she might be criticized, rejected, and otherwise harmed, and in light of demanding, critical, and emotionally unavailable parents, and teasing and criticism of peers."

### 2. Specify Operative Perpetuating Factors

From the developmental, social, and health history, identify likely perpetuants or maintaining factors. Search for factors that reinforce predisposing factors and maintain the presenting symptoms or problems in the current situation. Also, check if these or similar perpetuants were operative in other previous situations. Commonly perpetuants serve to "protect" or "insulate" the client from symptoms, conflict, or the demands of others.

For example, individuals who are shy and sensitive may gravitate toward living alone because it reduces the likelihood that others will criticize or make interpersonal demands on them. Because the influence of these factors seem to overlap, at times it can be difficult to specify whether a factor is a predisposition or a perpetuant. These might include personal or social skill deficits, hostile work environment, living alone, negative responses of others, and so forth. Then, write a brief statement

118

summarizing these perpetuating factors. For example, in the case of Geri the statement would read: "This pattern is maintained by her shyness, living alone, and generalized social isolation."

## 3. Identify the Underlying Maladaptive Pattern

A pattern is an explanation that links and makes sense of the client's presentation, precipitants, predispositions, and perpetuants. A pattern can be situation specific or longitudinal. A situation-specific pattern is an explanation that is unique to the current situation only. On the other hand, a longitudinal pattern is an explanation that is common to the current as well as previous situations. In other words, it reflects a lifelong, and usually maladaptive, pattern. Such a pattern can be informed by a theoretical model such as psychodynamic or cognitive–behavioral therapy, or it can be clinical, meaning atheoretical. To identify the underlying maladaptive pattern, search for an explanation that meaningfully links the client's presentation, precipitants, predispositions, and perpetuants. Also, check if this or a similar pattern is operative in other previous situations. Then, draft a pattern statement.

For example, in the case of Geri, the statement would read:

> Based on her early life experiences she came to believe that life was demanding, that others were critical and harsh, and that she was inadequate. Therefore, she would socially isolate and conditionally relate to others. Given these maladaptive beliefs, her family history of depression, her lack of social skills, her tendency to "test" others' trustability, and the resulting lifelong pattern of conditionally relating to others, it is not unreasonable to conclude that her current depression and increased isolation were triggered by news of a job promotion, news that others would find uplifting rather than depressing.

## 4. Write an Integrative Clinical Formulation Statement

This integrative statement combines statements of the presentation, precipitants, predisposition, perpetuants, and pattern. Combine these statements into a composite statement.

For example, in the case of Geri the statement would read:

> Geri's increased social isolation and depressive symptoms (*presentation*) appear to be her reaction to an impending job promotion and transfer out of a close-knit work group where she had been for 12 years (*precipitant*).

**119**

Her reaction is understandable given her pattern of avoiding situations in which she might be criticized, rejected, and otherwise harmed, and in light of demanding, critical, and emotionally unavailable parents, and teasing and criticism of peers *(predisposition)*. This pattern is maintained by her shyness, living alone, and generalized social isolation *(perpetuant)*. Based on her early life experiences she came to believe that life was demanding, that others were critical and harsh, and that she was inadequate. Therefore, she would socially isolate and conditionally relate to others. Given these maladaptive beliefs, her family history of depression, her lack of social skills, her tendency to "test" others' trustability, and the resulting lifelong pattern of conditionally relating to others, it is not unreasonable to conclude that her current depression and increased isolation were triggered by news of a job promotion, news that others would find uplifting rather than depressing *(pattern)*. While presumably adaptive as a child, this pattern is not serving her well now.

## ILLUSTRATION: DERIVING A CASE CONCEPTUALIZATION FROM THE DIAGNOSTIC INTERVIEW

This section describes the way in which a highly effective therapist begins to develop a case conceptualization during an initial diagnostic interview. It demonstrates how such a therapist "thinks" and "acts." The case of Geri is used to describe and illustrate the process of developing a case conceptualization, particularly the clinical formulation.

This is the first contact between therapist and client, and the therapist's goal in this session is to develop a "working" case conceptualization during the course of the interview. Rather than being a "definitive" conceptualization of the case, a "working" case is a tentative understanding of the client and likely treatment plan based on available information that is subject to modification as additional information becomes available.

Geri R. is a 35-year-old single African American who is an administrative assistant at a manufacturing corporation. She was referred for therapy because of an extended absence from work. She complained of "being sad" and described a number of vegetative symptoms of depression. She lives alone, has never been in a long-term relationship or been married, and has worked at the same company since graduating from a local community college. This is her first experience with therapy. Segments of the transcript that follow are from the first session in which the therapist's plan was to begin developing a therapeutic relationship, to complete a diagnostic evaluation, and develop a working case conceptualization using the case conceptualization map. The running commentary reflects how this therapist thinks, that is, makes hypotheses and collects additional data to confirm or modify the working hypotheses.

*Th.:* I understand that Ms. Hicks, the director of human resources at your company referred you to me. What's your understanding of why we're meeting today?

*Cl.:* She wanted me to see you because I haven't been feeling too well lately.

*Th.:* In what way haven't you been feeling well?

*Cl.:* Over the past 2 weeks, I've been feeling pretty sad. And, I guess it's been affecting my work a lot. I've got no initiative, no desire to get involved with anything.

So far the *presentation* is known, or at least part of it. The therapist then focuses on identifying a *precipitant* or triggering event.

*Th.:* So this all started about 2 weeks ago?

*Cl.:* Yeah.

*Th.:* What was going on that time?

*Cl.:* Well, my supervisor said there was an opening for a senior administrative assistant in the vice president of sales' office. She said she recommended me for the job and that I should be ready to move to the executive suite in a week. (pause) The last thing I'd do is switch to another office and for someone I don't know. (exhales and sighs) Even if there's a promotion and raise that goes with it.

*Th.:* It sounds like that news deeply affected you.

*Cl.:* Yeah. It's like the bottom fell out of my world right then.

The therapist is momentarily taken back by what he hears. Whereas most people would be happy and energized upon receiving news of a promotion and raise, this client experiences just the opposite: She becomes depressed and immobilized. The obvious question is "why"? At this point there is a *presentation* (depression) and a *precipitant* (news of a job promotion). Understanding "why" she became depressed will become clearer as the therapist elicits the remaining pattern dimensions of *predispositions* and *perpetuants*. Apparently, moving to another office and working for a new boss are important factors for her. Geri is asked:

**121**

*Th.:*   What were you anticipating might happen if you started in the new job?

*Cl.:*   That I'd get some new boss who would be really demanding and critical.

*Th.:*   Demanding and critical?

*Cl.:*   Yeah. Complaining that I made typos or that I didn't get a report or letter just right. And being around someone I don't know.

*Th.:*   What would that be like?

*Cl.:*   Uncomfortable … even scary. I'd rather be around people I've known a long time and can trust.

*Th.:*   It sounds like being around supportive and noncritical people is important to you.

*Cl.:*   Yeah. It is.

*Th.:*   Even if it means giving up a promotion and a raise?

*Cl.:*   Feeling safe is worth more to me than more money or promotion to senior administrative assistant.

*Th.:*   Does that mean that you feel safe with the current boss?

*Cl.:*   Definitely. I've been working there for 16 years now and most of it for the same boss. I mean she's not a friend or anything like that, but she's fair and considerate. It just threw me for a loop when she told me about the promotion. Why is she letting me go? What's the point in getting rid of me? I work really hard and am loyal.

*Th.:*   I don't know the answer, but is it possible that she thought that you could use the extra money that comes with the promotion?

*Cl.:*   I suppose. But, I do like working in her department.

*Th.:*   I hear that. (pause) Is having friends at work important in your feeling safe?

*Cl.:*   Yeah.

*Th.:*   What's that like for you?

*Cl.:*   I have friends at work. Well, actually one for sure. Sally started about the same time I did. She's different than others. Kind, never a harsh word.

*Th.:*   You can count on her?

*Cl.:*   I sure can.

*Th.:*   How about the other secretaries and support staff?

*Cl.:*   They're pretty catty and gossipy. And they can tease, and I don't like that. I mean, I'm pretty thin-skinned.

*Th.:*   Have you done things socially with them?

*Cl.:*       Yes, I did. Well at least a time or two. Most of them just want to talk about men. And I don't like that kind of sharing. They want to get real close and find out everything about you. Secrets and all. I mean I really wanted to be at their parties, but it was so scary being around all those people. They're always ready to judge you before they know you. … I wouldn't know what to say to them. Whenever I opened my mouth I know I'd make a fool of myself. They were ready to laugh if I said anything.

*Th.:*       Did they actually laugh at you?

*Cl.:*       Well, no … but they could have.

*Th.:*       What would happen if they'd find out a little bit about you?

*Cl.:*       I feel that if they really got to know me they wouldn't like me … I don't have much to offer (long pause, head down).

At this point the therapist surmises that to feel safe, Geri needs to be around supportive and noncritical coworkers at work, at least her boss and friend, Sally. Presumably, Geri's promotion involves a transfer to a new office and a new boss and coworkers who will not be safe. Without ever meeting him, Geri assumes that her new boss will be demanding and critical, and Geri assumes that she will lose the only trusting and supportive friend at work, Sally, who will remain in her current job and department. So far, the therapist considers that *predispositions* involve her expectation that others will be critical, intrusive, and demanding. Avoiding such situations with social isolation and limited involvement not only provides Geri a sense of safety and insulation from social anxiety but also reinforces her beliefs about and expectations of others. These are *perpetuants* or factors that maintain her current, albeit problematic, *pattern*.

Thus, a tentative case conceptualization, more specifically the clinical formulation part of it, can be summarized.

Geri's increased social isolation and depressive symptoms (*presentation*) appear to be her reaction to an impending job promotion and transfer out of a close-knit work group where she had been for 16 years (*precipitant*). Her reaction is understandable given her pattern of avoiding situations in which she might be criticized, rejected, and otherwise harmed, and in light of demanding, critical, and emotionally unavailable parents, and teasing and criticism of peers (*predisposition*). This pattern is maintained by her shyness, living alone, and generalized social isolation (*perpetuant*).

At this point, it is not known whether this problematic pattern is situation specific or whether it is a long-standing maladaptive pattern. Eliciting

Geri's developmental history and dynamic should help in making this determination. Accordingly, later in the interview when the developmental history is taken, the following information is elicited.

*Th.:*  What was it like growing up in your family?

*Cl.:*  It wasn't good.

*Th.:*  How did your parents treat each other back then?

*Cl.:*  A lot of shouting, criticizing, and blaming. It was awful. It scared me so much ... I just wanted to get away from all that.

*Th.:*  You wanted to get away from them?

*Cl.:*  I needed to get away from them after they fought because they would come after me and get on my case.

*Th.:*  How did they get on your case?

*Cl.:*  They constantly told me that there was nothing I did that was right. My grades weren't good enough. My room wasn't clean enough. I was too fat and not athletic enough. If only I had combed my hair better, the boys would like me ... All that stuff ... I couldn't stand it (voice raised).

*Th.:*  What was your father like?

*Cl.:*  He was so strict. He always criticized and made fun of me. He wanted so much from me. I had to get straight As or else. One demand after another. Such high standards. I could never be good enough to be everything he wanted me to be. (pause) A lot of time, I felt like a failure. That I was worthless.

*Th.:*  And your mother. What was she like?

*Cl.:*  Well I remember feeling cared for in the beginning. I mean she's not real lovey-dovey but she took care of me. But after my brother was born, it was like she just wasn't there for me. She doted on him.

*Th.:*  What was it like being around your brother?

*Cl.:*  He was my parent's favorite. He treated me just like my father, teasing and criticizing me.

*Th.:*  He was 3 years younger than you?

*Cl.:*  Yeah. I had to take care of him. Babysit him. He used to tease me and call me names. The little brat. And so did his friends. We weren't close. My parents spoiled him rotten. He got whatever he wanted.

*Th.:*  How about the other kids in the neighborhood and at school?

*Cl.:*  They always teased and made fun of me. I was the fat girl who couldn't do anything right (pause) At school it was pretty much the same. I'd get so nervous trying to answer the teacher in class that I'd freeze up even when I knew the answer. It was awful.

*Th.:*  Geri, can you tell me your earliest recollection?

*Cl.:*  What is that?

*Th.:*  The earliest recollection is a person's first event or situation that they can recall happening. It is a one-time experience that occurred in the first few years of life.

*Cl.:*  (pause) Well I remember when my brother came home from the hospital after he was born.

*Th.:*  Can you tell me how old you were and the circumstances of his coming home?

*Cl.:*  I was about 4 years old or so. I remember my mother being gone for a while and not knowing where she went. I stayed at my grandma's house which I liked. But I was worried and nobody would tell me anything. Dad picked me up and took me home. Then I saw mom holding the baby and smiling and saying this was my new brother. Dad said this was the happiest day of his life. I guess I was whining and upset and asking all kinds of questions. Dad told me to be quiet and go outside because Mom and the baby needed to be alone. I ran outside crying and hiding in my tree fort where it was safe.

*Th.:*  What do you remember thinking?

*Cl.:*  That I was confused. Didn't they want me anymore now that there was this new baby?

*Th.:*  And what did you feel?

*Cl.:*  (pause) That I was frightened, and probably angry, too.

This recollection contains themes of rejection by "dethronement" (i.e., a previously favored older sibling is displaced by a younger one), themes of criticalness, inadequacy, and social isolation. These themes are consistent and confirmatory of her developmental history and Geri's view of herself, others, and her basic coping strategy of withdrawal and isolation.

*Th.:*  What does your brother do now?

*Cl.:*  He's a computer programmer. He's married and has two kids. I hardly even see him. We're not close.

*Th.:*  Is there anything else you can think of that helps describe what it was like growing up in your family?

*Cl.:*     Well, we were supposed to be "seen and not heard," and never
were we to "hang our dirty wash out in public." Like they
say today, we were supposed to "stuff our feelings." Also,
we were expected to work hard and achieve. My brother was
a lot better at that than I was. And, my parents got into some
knock-down-drag-out fights. That happened pretty often. No
outsiders would have guessed that they had marriage problems,
but their fighting scared me. I really thought they'd get divorced
and I'd end up in some foster home or something. I guess living
by myself now is a lot more tolerable than what it was like living
with my family when I was growing up.

Exploration of her developmental history and dynamics was quite
enlightening. Her early life experiences predictably formed her view of
self, view of the world and others, and her basic coping strategy. The
therapist summarized this information in the Case Conceptualization
Map, which is shown in Table 9.3.

The therapist concluded that Geri's current pattern reflected her overall
maladaptive pattern. This pattern can be either situational, that is, identified only in the current situation, or ongoing, that is, a lifelong pattern with
similar themes that have occurred in prior situations as well as in the current situation. Her *ongoing pattern* was described in the following terms.

Based on her early life experiences she came to believe that life
was demanding, that others were critical and harsh, and that she was
inadequate. Therefore, she would socially isolate and conditionally relate

**Table 9.3**   Case Conceptualization Map: Case of Geri R.

| Pattern Factors | Clinical Formulation |
| --- | --- |
| Precipitant | Offer of job promotion leads to perceived loss of safety and increased criticism and demands |
| Predispositions | Demanding, critical, and emotionally unavailable parents; anticipates teasing and criticism of peers |
| | *Self-view*: Sees herself as inadequate |
| | *World-view*: Others are critical and demanding |
| | *Strategy*: Stay safe and test others' trustability |
| Perpetuants | Generalized social isolation |
| | Living alone; shyness |
| Presentation | Depressive symptoms and social isolation |

to others. Given these maladaptive beliefs, her family history of depression, her lack of social skills, her tendency to "test" others' trustability, and the resulting lifelong pattern of conditionally relating to others, it is not unreasonable to conclude that her current depression and increased isolation were triggered by news of a job promotion, news that others would find uplifting rather than depressing.

After the session, the therapist reviewed the information from the Case Conceptualization Map and dictated a clinical case report of this initial evaluation. Here is the clinical formulation statement and case conceptualization section of that report.

> Geri's increased social isolation and depressive symptoms appear to be her reaction to an impending job promotion and transfer out of a close-knit work group where she had been for 16 years. Her reaction is understandable given her pattern of avoiding situations in which she might be criticized, rejected, and otherwise harmed, and in light of demanding, critical, and emotionally unavailable parents, and teasing and criticism of peers. This pattern is maintained by her shyness, living alone, and generalized social isolation. Based on her early life experiences she came to believe that life was demanding, that others were critical and harsh, and that she was inadequate. Therefore, she would socially isolate and conditionally relate to others. Given these maladaptive beliefs, her family history of depression, her lack of social skills, her tendency to "test" others' trustability, and the resulting lifelong pattern of conditionally relating to others, it is not unreasonable to conclude that her current depression and increased isolation were triggered by news of a job promotion, news that others would find uplifting rather than depressing. While presumably adaptive as a child, this pattern is not serving her well now.

## ILLUSTRATION: DIFFERING PREDISPOSITIONS FOR THE SAME CLINICAL PRESENTATION

Identifying predispositions is often a challenge for trainees. They struggle with whether to look for just psychological factors such as maladaptive schemas or whether to look for biological, social, and/or situational factors. They worry about whether there is only one predisposition or whether there are two or more that are operative. The following case material underscores the point that there can be widely different predispositions for the same clinical presentation. In the four cases that follow the presentation is the same: depressive symptoms, but the predisposing or causal factors differ significantly in each case.

*Andrew* is a 44-year-old married Caucasian male who presents with depressive features that he has experienced for a period of 3 weeks. The day before his symptoms were first noted, this staff accountant was passed over again for promotion to accounting supervisor. He is described as an unusually conscientious and hardworking employee, who has been observed criticizing coworkers for their lack of commitment. It appears that news of failure to receive a promotion triggered his *depressive symptoms.*

*Geri* is a 35-year-old single, African American female who works as an administrative assistant at a manufacturing corporation. She was referred for therapy because of extended absence from work, presumably because of depressed mood, markedly diminished interest, insomnia, difficulty concentrating, and increased social isolation. Prior to the onset of symptoms, she had learned of her promotion to a senior administrative assistant position, a position she had not wanted. It appears that news of her promotion triggered her *depressive symptoms* and increased social withdrawal.

*Myling* is a 23-year-old single, Asian American female who presented for treatment with complaints of depression and social isolation. She had recently withdrawn from law school because she felt excluded from a study group and was hurt by a rumor among white students that she and minorities were admitted only because of affirmative action. It appears that false rumors and exclusion triggered her *depressive symptoms* and increased social withdrawal.

*Luis* is a married 28-year-old Mexican male who was diagnosed with clinical depression by a physician in an inner-city health clinic. Luis had left his family in rural Mexico and emigrated to the United States to find full-time employment and send money to support his wife and two children. In the 10 weeks since his arrival, he had been unable to find work because of the economic downturn and inability to communicate in English. He experienced considerable stress attempting to survive in a large urban community with a culture so different from his village, while facing the prospects of being deported. It appears that failure to find a steady job and other immigration stresses triggered his *depressive symptoms.*

In the case of *Andrew* it appears that his obsessive-compulsive personality dynamics (later formally diagnosed as a personality disorder) essentially account for his experience of becoming depressed following his failure, for the second time, to secure the promotion. This case illustrates that *personality* was the main predisposing factor.

In the case of *Geri* it seems that she experienced depression rather than experiencing joy and exuberance, the typical expected response most people would have upon learning of a promotion and raise. Her response should alert the therapist that this is not a typical case, and that unique predisposing factors are needed to explain Geri's unusual response. The case was conceptualized in terms of the dynamics of Avoidant Personality Disorder and perceived social (working in a new environment without the only coworker that she come to trust, depend on, and feel comfortable with over the years) and interpersonal threats (working for a new boss she has never met but assumes will be critical and demanding). These factors explain both her increased social withdrawal and the dread experienced by her as clinical depression. This case illustrates that *personality, social, and interpersonal* factors were all operative as predisposing factors.

In the case of *Myling* it appears that feelings of rejection over racial remarks and excluding behavior by her white peers influenced her decision not to deal more directly with the situation and instead withdraw from school. She reports responding in a similar fashion in middle school when she was hit in the head with a rock during a racial confrontation between white and Hispanic female students even though she had tried to avoid being involved in it. A medical evaluation yielded the diagnosis of hypothyroidism, and thyroid replacement medication was begun. It was conceptualized that both cultural factors and dependent–avoidant personality dynamics were operative in these situations, that is, prior experiences with racism and nonassertiveness and social isolation. Her newly diagnosed medical condition may have expressed but also exacerbated her depressive symptoms. This case illustrates that *cultural, personality, and biological* factors were all operative as predisposing factors.

In the case of *Luis* a consultation with the clinic's Hispanic psychologist found no evidence of maladaptive beliefs or schemas or other psychological or interpersonal dynamics that could account for his clinical depression. He had never experienced depression or severe stress reactions before. This case illustrates that *social, cultural, and situational* factors were all operative as predisposing factors.

Some trainees have found the following worksheet (Table 9.4) to be helpful in considering which client and contextual factors are operative in a particular case. This worksheet would be useful in identifying the multiple predispositions in the cases of Andrew, Geri, Myling, and Luis. However, the worksheet can also be helpful in considering which class of factors are operative with regard to perpetuants, precipitants, and presentation.

**Table 9.4**   Clinical Formulation Worksheet

| Factors | Pre-dispositions | Precipitants | Perpetuants | Presentation |
|---|---|---|---|---|
| Personal | | | | |
| Relational | | | | |
| Situational | | | | |
| Social/ environmental | | | | |
| Cultural | | | | |

# 10

# *Develop an Effective Cultural Formulation*

The cultural formulation is the third of the four components of a case conceptualization. Given the prominent role that cultural beliefs, values, attitudes, and practices can play in the lives of clients, highly effective therapists are sensitive to, and routinely seek to learn, additional cultural information about their clients. Such information helps therapists better understand their clients' personal coping and social resources, as well as helping them explore the various cultural issues that contribute to clients' suffering and distress (Ridley & Kelly, 2007).

How effective are therapists and trainees in developing and using cultural formulations in their practice? In a study of practicing therapists, most believed that effective practice was aided by the use of cultural formulations. However, very few actually developed or used these formulations to guide their clinical practice (Hansen et al., 2006). Trainees seem to share a similar fate (Neufield et al., 2006). At a time when mental health professions are expected to be culturally sensitive and competent, developing this essential competency is not optional for trainees and therapists, it is mandatory. This chapter begins by briefly describing cultural formulations and two common models of cultural formulations. This is followed by detailed guidelines for developing such formulations. Next is a discussion of how therapists can proceed when there is no agreement with the client on the cultural formulation. Finally, the process of developing a cultural formulation is illustrated with three case examples.

## CULTURAL FORMULATION

A cultural formulation supports the clinical formulation and can inform treatment focus and the type of interventions chosen. The cultural formulation is a systematic review and analysis of cultural factors and dynamics that have been described in the "Social History and Cultural Factors" section of a clinical case report. It answers the "what role does culture play" question. More specifically, the cultural formulation statement describes the client's cultural identity and level of acculturation. It provides a cultural explanation of the client's condition as well as the impact of cultural factors on the client's personality and level of functioning. Furthermore, it addresses cultural elements that may impact the relationship between the individual and the therapist and whether cultural or culturally sensitive interventions are indicated (GAP Committee on Cultural Psychiatry, 2002). The decision about whether cultural interventions, culturally sensitive therapy, or culturally sensitive interventions should be implemented is complex and beyond the scope of this chapter. However, the topic is discussed in detail and illustrated in Chapter 16.

## TWO MODELS OF CULTURAL FORMULATIONS

There are two models of how cultural formulations are best developed. The first envisions cultural formulations, called multicultural case conceptualizations, in terms of two dimensions. The first dimension is the degree to which cultural elements contribute to the etiology of the client's presenting problem. The second dimension is the extent to which cultural elements are integrated in treatment, that is, the extent to which culturally sensitive interventions are indicated for effective treatment (Constantine & Ladany, 2000).

The second model envisions cultural formulations in terms of five dimensions. This model was developed by the Group for the Advancement of Psychiatry (GAP) Committee on Cultural Psychiatry. These dimensions are assessed and integrated into a formulation statement that guides treatment. The five dimensions are the client's cultural identity, the client's cultural explanation of illness, the client's psychosocial environment, the cultural elements likely to influence the relationship between client and therapist, and the cultural elements likely to be operative in the treatment process (GAP Committee on Cultural Psychiatry, 2002). Although both models are clinically useful, developing a formulation around the five dimensions is easier and more straightforward, particularly for trainees. For that reason the GAP model informs the guidelines and the case illustrations in this chapter.

## DEVELOPING A CULTURAL FORMULATION

Here are some guidelines for developing a cultural formulation and a cultural formulation statement.

### 1. Identify the Client's Cultural Identity and Level of Acculturation

The cultural formulation begins to take shape during the diagnostic assessment. As part of the "Social and Cultural History" of that assessment, the therapist presumably elicited information on the client's cultural identity (i.e., sense of being defined by membership in a cultural or ethnic group), as well as the client's level of acculturation (i.e., the extent of adaptation to the dominant, mainstream culture). Draft a sentence describing these elements.

For instance, in the case of Geri, the statement would read: "Geri identifies herself as a middle-class African American but with few ties to her ethnic roots, and it appears that Geri and her parents are highly acculturated."

### 2. Identify the Client's Cultural Explanations of Illness and Expectations

Clients' explanation of the reason they believe they are experiencing their problem or concern is very revealing, as are the words and idioms they use to express their distress (Bhui & Bhugra, 2004). Therapists should routinely elicit an explanatory model, that is, clients' beliefs regarding the cause of their suffering, disease, or impairment, such as "nerves," possessing spirits, somatic complaints, inexplicable misfortune, testing or punishment from God, and so on. In addition, their expectations and preferences for treatment and, if indicated, past experiences of healing in their culture should also be elicited. Draft a sentence describing these elements.

For instance, in the case of Geri, the statement would read: "She believes that her depression is the result of stresses at work and a 'chemical imbalance' in her brain."

### 3. Identify the Cultural Elements in the Client's Psychosocial Environment

The client's psychosocial environment includes both stressors as well as supports related to the patient's cultural background. It also includes cultural beliefs and practices that help the individual cope with such psychosocial stressors. Furthermore, the client's personality dynamics interact with cultural dynamics. Draft a sentence describing these elements.

For example, in the case of Geri, the statement would read: "There are no obvious indications of prejudice or conflicting cultural expectations or other cultural factors. Instead, it appears Geri's personality dynamics are significantly operative in her current clinical presentation."

### 4. Identify Cultural Elements Likely to Be Operative in the Therapeutic Relationship

Awareness of the client's cultural beliefs and practices allows the therapist to accommodate such beliefs in the case conceptualization. These include the way the client relates to others, ease or difficulty in communicating, the potential for transference enactment, gender and age of the therapist, and the need for referral when cultural questions extend beyond the therapist's expertise. Draft a sentence or more describing these elements.

For instance, in the case of Geri, the statement would read:

> Gender dynamics could impact the therapeutic relationship between Geri and her African American male therapist, given her strained relationship with her father and limited involvement with men ever since. However, it is not anticipated that other cultural dynamics will negatively impact the therapeutic relationship. Given her shyness and avoidant style, it may take a while for her to become comfortable and engaged in group therapy, but it is less likely that cultural factors will be operative in a Caucasian female–led group of middle-aged women of different ethnic backgrounds.

## 5. Identify Cultural Elements Likely to Be Operative in the Treatment Process

The treatment process includes assessment, diagnosis, interventions, and termination. The culturally sensitive therapist will identify the extent to which cultural elements are operative and tailor treatment accordingly. By assessing the interaction of cultural elements with the influence of biological factors, personality dynamics, and situational factors, the therapist can plan and implement cultural interventions or culturally sensitive interventions. Draft one or more sentences describing these elements.

For example, in the case of Geri, the statement would read:

> Overall, it appears that Geri's avoidant personality dynamics are more operative than cultural factors in her current clinical presentation, and it does not appear that cultural factors will negatively impact or interfere with therapy process or outcomes. Furthermore, treatment progress does not seem dependent on cultural or even culturally sensitive interventions.

## 6. Write an Integrative Cultural Formulation Statement

This integrative statement combines sentences of the five previous elements. Combine these sentences into a paragraph.

In the case of Geri, the statement would read:

> Geri identifies herself as a middle-class African American but with few ties to her ethnic roots, and it appears that Geri and her parents are highly acculturated. She believes that her depression is the result of stresses at work and a "chemical imbalance" in her brain. There are no obvious indications of prejudice or conflicting cultural expectations or other cultural factors. Instead, it appears Geri's personality dynamics are significantly operative in her current clinical presentation. Gender dynamics could impact the therapeutic relationship between Geri and her African American male therapist, given her strained relationship with her father and limited involvement with men ever since. However, it is not anticipated that other cultural dynamics will negatively impact the therapeutic relationship. Given her shyness and avoidant style, it may take a while for her to become comfortable and engaged in group therapy, but it is less likely that cultural factors will be operative in a Caucasian female–led group of middle-aged women of different ethnic backgrounds. Overall, it appears that Geri's avoidant personality dynamics are more operative than cultural factors in her current clinical presentation, and it does not appear that cultural factors will negatively

impact or interfere with therapy process or outcomes. Furthermore, at this time, treatment progress does not seem dependent on cultural or even culturally sensitive interventions.

## ILLUSTRATIONS OF CULTURAL FORMULATIONS

Three cases that illustrate the process of developing cultural formulations are presented in this section. The first involves a fourth-generation African American female with work-related issues, the second is a first-generation Irish American whose cultural issues involve addictions and religion, and the third is a second-generation Mexican American female with conflict between family and career. The last case asks the reader to develop a cultural formulation.

### Case 1: Geri

You will recall that Geri is a 35-year-old female administrative assistant who experienced a 3-week onset of depressed mood and increased social isolation following word that she was to be promoted and transferred out of a relatively close-knit work team where she had worked for 16 years. She has only one close friend and a relative whom she can trust. She lives alone and has never been in a long-term relationship or married. She has worked at the same company since graduating from a local junior college. She is a fourth-generation African American, and she and her parents appear to be highly acculturated. Her grandparents migrated to the Midwest from Mississippi in the late 1930s. Although she occasionally attends an annual Black pride festival in the summer, she is not otherwise active in the Black community, nor are her parents. She has not become close to the two other African Americans in her office because, she says, "All they want to do is talk about men which I'm not into." Although she was reared as a Baptist, she no longer considers herself to be religious. She identifies herself as heterosexual and describes herself and her parents as middle class in values and orientation. Based on this and other cultural information elicited from the client, the following cultural formulation was developed.

### Cultural Formulation Statement

Geri identifies herself as a middle-class African American but with few ties to her ethnic roots, and it appears that Geri and her parents are highly acculturated. She believes that her depression is the result of stresses at work and a "chemical imbalance" in her brain. There are no obvious indications of prejudice or conflicting cultural expectations or other cultural factors. Instead, it appears Geri's personality dynamics are significantly operative in her current clinical presentation. Gender dynamics could impact the therapeutic relationship between Geri and her African American male therapist, given her strained relationship with her father and limited involvement with men. However, it is not anticipated that other cultural dynamics will negatively impact the therapeutic relationship. Given her shyness and avoidant style, it may take a while for her to become comfortable and engaged in group therapy, but it is less likely that cultural factors will be operative in a Caucasian female–led group of middle-aged women of different ethnic backgrounds. Overall, it appears that Geri's avoidant personality dynamics are more operative than cultural factors in her current clinical presentation, and it does not appear that cultural factors will negatively impact or interfere with therapy process or outcomes. Furthermore, treatment progress does not seem dependent on cultural or even culturally sensitive interventions.

**Case Commentary**
This cultural formulation statement summarizes considerable information about this client on five key dimensions. It provides the basis for making several decisions concerning treatment issues, including the potential influence of the gender and ethnicity of the therapist and the consideration of the advisability of utilizing culturally sensitive treatment.

## Case 2: James T.

James T. is a 33-year-old single male who is employed at an electronic store, where he services computers and small electronic devices. He is first-generation Irish American Catholic who was referred for counseling to the Catholic Charities Counseling Center by his parish priest. He presents for treatment complaining of relationship problems, inability to control guilt feelings about pornography, and confusion about preferring masturbating with pornography to sexual relations with his girlfriend of 3 years. James's father died when James was 15 and subsequently functioned as a parent to his two younger sisters. Reportedly James began masturbating when his teenage sisters would walk around the house in their underwear. Although he considers himself an alcoholic, James has maintained sobriety for the past year.

After completing an initial diagnostic evaluation, James's assigned therapist developed an integrative case conceptualization that included the cultural formulation statement in the following paragraph. The therapist is a 59-year-old, married European American male. He is an elder in the Anglican Church and had been a detective with the city police department before he retired because of a service-related disability. Two years ago he completed a Psy.D. in clinical psychology and went on to finish postdoctoral internship training at the Catholic Charities Counseling Center, after which he was hired there as a staff psychologist.

**Cultural Formulation Statement**
James's cultural identity is that of a first-generation Irish American who is a practicing Catholic. He is a member of same parish in which he was baptized as a young boy. He grew up with strict Catholic upbringing; his religious beliefs are essentially the same and he maintains many of the same religious practices from his youth. He believes that his sexual guilt is the result of his family and religious upbringing and has negatively influenced his intimate relationship with women. He regularly meets with a parish priest who provides spiritual guidance as his confessor and believes that the priest has helped him. James considers his parish to be a source of strength; with his priest's urging and support, he has been somewhat successful in reducing his drinking but not his use of pornography. The parish life is also a stressor in that he is continually exposed to revelations of sexual misconduct in his diocese by priest pedophiles. Needless to say, this has reinforced his ambivalence about the Church. In terms of coping strategies, James's involvement with Alcoholics Anonymous (AA) meetings and his AA sponsor, along with the encouragement of his priest, seem to account for his current sobriety; at the same time his image of God is negative and he perceives negative life events as God's punishment. James stated that working with an older married male clinician who was not Roman Catholic would be important to him. "There'd be less spiritual baggage since we come from different faith traditions." He believes he can talk freely about his various concerns with the clinician as he has done with the parish priest. Although James experienced his alcoholic father as abusive, demanding, and emotionally unavailable while he was alive, it appears that he could easily identify the therapist as competent and a concerned father figure; perhaps similar to

the way James has identified with the parish priest and his AA sponsor, who are approximately the same age as the therapist. Countertransference reactions such as judgmental statements and impatience at slow or limited progress will likely strain the therapeutic alliance. James is likely to respond to relationally oriented dynamic therapy that is sensitive to his conflicting feelings about God and his biological father.

## Case Commentary

This formulation statement is quite informative and guides the therapist in considering various therapeutic alliance and treatment planning considerations, including predictions of likely obstacles to treatment progress.

# Case 3: Maria

Maria is a 17-year-old second-generation Mexican American female who was referred for a psychological evaluation by her parents, who are concerned with Maria's mood shifts in the past 2 to 3 months and concerned about her alcohol use. Maria described her basic concern as a conflict between going away to college in the fall and staying home to attend to her mother, who is terminally ill. Whereas her parents want her to stay home, her boyfriend and friends—all European Americans—are encouraging her to go to college. She reports being pulled in two different directions and "stuck in the middle" and feeling "down" and "pressured" regarding this decision. She also feels guilty that she may fail to measure up to being a "good daughter" and may lose her parents' acceptance and approval. Her family is extremely important to her and she says she has an "obligation to my parents." Yet she also wants to expand her horizons; however, "if I stay with my family my whole life, I'll be a failure. ... I'll have wasted all my potential." She has tried to talk with her parents but they seem unable to understand her. She's conflicted, yet she does not want to "disappoint" or "make the wrong decision—I'll regret it forever." Although she admitted to a single episode of alcohol use to make her feel better, she denies any other alcohol and substance use.

Maria is the youngest of four children: two older brothers who are college graduates and an older sister who did not finish high school and has a history of drug usage and has minimal contact with the family. Her parents emigrated from Mexico some 25 years ago, although her extended family remains in Mexico. Her parents live in a middle-class, largely Mexican community in a large, diverse metropolitan area, where they own a small dry cleaners and lead "traditional Mexican American lives." Reportedly, they unfairly compare Maria to her sister and believe that Maria will end up just like her sister. But while they are overly strict with her, Maria believes "it is because they care." Maria was not taught to speak Spanish because her parents had a difficult time when they arrived in the United States and did not want their children to experience similar anti-immigrant discrimination. She believes her problems are due to a "lack of faith in God," and she says that she prays every day to be "delivered from darkness." She is convinced that her parents don't understand that adolescents in America have much more independence than their Mexican counterparts. Maria's mother's illness has also affected her father, who is worried that without a caretaker—like Maria—she will not live long.

### Learning Activity: Cultural Formulation Statement
Write a cultural formulation statement for this case. Use the following questions to structure your statement.

1. What is Maria's cultural identity and level of acculturation? Her parent's?
2. What is her explanation of her illness and her expectation for how it should be treated?
3. To what extent are Maria's conflict and symptoms a function of cultural factors, personality factors, or both?
4. The mental health counselor is a 30-year-old married Caucasian female. To what extent can gender and culture factors influence the therapeutic relationship with Maria and counseling outcomes?
5. What indication, if any, is there for culturally sensitive interventions?

# 11

# *Plan Treatment Interventions and Predict Obstacles to Their Implementation*

One of the characteristics of a highly effective case conceptualization is coherence among its components. In my experience, if a lack of coherence or consistency is noted in a case conceptualization, it is most likely to be between the clinical formulation and the treatment formulation components. One of the fortunate and unfortunate effects of managed care is the standardization of treatment plans (Jongsma, 2006). The fortunate effect is that treatment plans today are likely to specify particular treatment targets with particular interventions and sometimes even a plan to monitor progress. The unfortunate effect is the extent to which many trainees and practicing therapists have uncritically adopted this standardized treatment mind-set. The result is there is a remarkable similarity in treatment plans. It is not unusual to review several charts of clients in the same clinical setting and find that most of the treatment plans are surprisingly similar. In my role as a consultant to various mental health clinics, I might pull and review 20 charts in a particular clinic. Among those charts there might be 12 clients with the *DSM* diagnosis of major depression. In reviewing the clinical case reports, sometimes called initial evaluation reports, I would turn to the treatment plan section and often would find an almost identical treatment plan for at least 10 of the cases. The plan would usually include medication evaluation and monitoring combined with Cognitive-Behavioral Therapy keyed to the treatment objectives of symptom reduction, behavioral activation, and return to baseline functioning. Needless to say, therapists may have to undergo some unlearning to become reasonably effective with treatment and intervention planning.

The fourth component of the case conceptualization is the treatment formulation and, in many ways, it should be one of the easier components to develop. This chapter provides a strategy for deriving the treatment formulation and intervention planning from the other components. To set the stage for this, a brief discussion of treatment formulation begins the chapter, followed by an even briefer discussion of establishing a treatment focus and anticipating likely obstacles and challenges to treatment. Next is a description of a strategy and guidelines for developing a treatment formulation and statement. Then a brief description of treatment tailoring is provided. Finally, this strategy is illustrated with case material.

## COMPONENTS OF THE TREATMENT FORMULATION AND PLAN

A treatment formulation follows from a diagnostic, clinical, and cultural formulation and serves as an explicit blueprint governing treatment interventions. Informed by the answers to "What happened?", "What role does culture play?", and "Why did it happen?", the answer to the "how" question, that is, " How can it be changed?" is the basis of treatment formulation. Based on this explanation, a treatment formulation emerges, including strategies for specifying treatment goals and targets and for focusing and implementing treatment and strategies. Of these components, treatment goals, treatment focus, and predictions about obstacles to implementing the plan are critically important.

### Treatment Goal and Focus

The treatment focus serves as a guide or action plan for the therapist to achieve the treatment goal. The treatment focus derives from the treatment goals and the theoretical orientation that informs the therapist's work. For example, in a case in which the treatment goal was to change certain maladaptive beliefs and the therapist's orientation was Cognitive-Behavioral Therapy, the focus of treatment would be to analyze and process situations in which those specific maladaptive beliefs are operative. Since establishing and maintaining such a focus is so important it is the subject of Chapters 13 and 14.

## Predicting Obstacles and Challenges

Anticipating obstacles and challenges to the implementation of the treatment plan is indispensable in achieving treatment success. The test of an effective case conceptualization is its viability in predicting the obstacles and challenges throughout the stages of therapy, particularly those involving resistance, ambivalence, and transference enactments. Chapter 17 continues this discussion of treatment interfering factors.

## DEVELOPING A TREATMENT FORMULATION

Developing and drafting a treatment formulation is rather straightforward since it is a logical extension of the diagnostic, clinical, and cultural formulations. Just as a clinical formulation can be structured around the Case Conceptualization Map, the treatment formulation can be likewise structured. In many instances, the treatment target and objective will be the opposite of the given factor in the clinical formulation. For example, in the case of Geri the perpetuants noted in the clinical formulation are: increased social isolation, living alone, and shyness at work.

Accordingly, reasonable treatment targets in the treatment formulation would be reduce social isolation and increase a supportive social network on and off the job. Table 11.1 shows the Case Conceptualization Map adapted for intervention planning.

## GUIDELINES FOR DEVELOPING A
## TREATMENT FORMULATION

Here are some guidelines for developing a treatment formulation and a treatment formulation statement.

**Table 11.1**  Case Conceptualization Map and Intervention Planning

| Pattern Factors | Clinical Formulation and Targets | Treatment Formulation and Targets |
|---|---|---|
| Precipitants | | |
| Predisposition | | |
| Perpetuants | | |
| Presentation | | |

## 1. Review the Case Conceptualization Map

The first decision involves choosing an initial treatment mode: inpatient, intensive outpatient, partial hospitalization, residential, or outpatient treatment. If there is any indication of self-harm or harm of others, these must be addressed immediately. Then, proceed to review any biological aspects in any of the factors, including the predisposing factors. For instance, if caffeine, nicotine, or xanthine use seems to be triggering or exacerbating the client's condition and symptoms, reduce or remove them. If a medical evaluation or a medication evaluation is indicated, consider making an appropriate referral, arrangements for collaboration, or both. Evaluate the extent to which social–environmental predisposing factors are operative that are beyond the ken of therapeutic influence and consider options. If relational or family factors are operative, consider couples or family consultation or therapy. If the client's treatment expectations are potentially problematic or readiness is not at the action stage, address these and other related matters.

## 2. Consider Addressing Presentation and Precipitating Factors as the Initial Mode of Treatment

It may well be that symptomatic distress, conflict resolution, or other presentation might be directly reversed by eliminating the precipitating stressor or trigger. When this is not possible or sufficiently effective, response prevention techniques might reduce or stop the presentation, be it symptom, conflict, or impaired functioning. Presumably, resolution will occur. If, however, there is a reoccurrence, it may suggest that there is an ongoing maladaptive pattern that was not identified. If so, proceed to the third guideline.

## 3. Specify Treatment Targets That Reflect Treatment Goals and Specify a Treatment Focus

Specifying *treatment targets* related to operative predisposing and perpetuating factors is a common way of proceeding in therapy, perhaps in most therapies when there is no immediate change from eliminating triggers or when blocking responses is not sustainable. Thus, decisions about selecting interpretive, reframing, restructuring, or desensitization strategies are typically based on client receptivity and capacity to respond to an intervention in addition to considerations such as client resources, need, dynamics, explanatory model, and expectations. The *treatment focus* serves as a guide or action plan for the therapist to achieve the treatment goal. Typically, it is based on a conceptual map informed by the therapist's theoretical orientation. For example, in the interpersonally oriented dynamic therapies, the focus is usually the client's maladaptive interpersonal style or pattern, whereas in cognitive–behavioral therapies, the focus is usually maladaptive thinking and behaviors.

## 4. Consider How Interventions Might Be Tailored and Sequenced

Decisions about tailoring and sequencing are important and cannot be left to chance. Accordingly, consider how factors such as severity, level of functioning, level of acculturation, skill sets, and personality dynamics could foster or impede specific interventions. Also, consider client expectations. Decisions about sequencing are based on several factors, such as access to specific treatment resources, success in achieving a particular treatment goal, or situation-specific considerations. For example, if pattern is determined to be situation specific, begin by addressing precipitating factors and consider other factors only if there is little or no response.

### 5. Anticipate Potential Obstacles and Challenges to Treatment

Review the client's story, including the developmental and social history, looking for potential obstacles specifically related to the therapeutic alliance, personality dynamics, or the stage of therapy, and, in general, to treatment progress. Typically, these will involve resistances, ambivalence, transference enactments, and alliance ruptures, but they could include predictions of difficulty with certain treatment modalities or even termination. Foreknowledge of such potential obstacles allows the therapist time to plan how these challenges will be met if and when they arise.

### 6. Write an Integrative Treatment Formulation Statement

This statement incorporates the psychological and social treatment goals and interventions, and biological goals and interventions, if applicable.

## PREDICTING CHALLENGES AND OBSTACLES

One of the last sections of the treatment formulation should address possible roadblocks or other challenges to the therapeutic alliance and to the process and outcomes of treatment. The therapist would consider how personality could possibly influence both process and outcome. For example, clients with a passive–aggressive pattern or a high level of reactance might demonstrate ambivalence or resistance when certain expectations are communicated. Also considered would be the client's early relational conflict or trauma and the likelihood of transference enactments. That a client has not experienced previous success in making even a small personal change suggests that his or her proneness to failure will likely be operative in therapy unless these dynamics are directly addressed. Furthermore, a client with social avoidance might summarily reject involvement in group-oriented treatment, just as a client who has difficulty saying good-bye or has experienced unexpected loss of significant others will likely find termination most difficult.

## ILLUSTRATION OF TREATMENT FORMULATION

Two cases illustrate how a treatment formulation is developed and what the resulting treatment formulation statement looks like.

## Case 1: Geri

**Treatment Formulation and Plan**

Given that this is Geri's first episode of depression, that her current GAF score is 54, and her baseline GAF is around 71, the degree of severity of the depression would likely be considered "moderate" rather than "severe." Since the probability of suicide is low (a conclusion supported by Geri's denial of any suicide ideation as well as religious prohibition), hospitalization is not deemed a necessity at this time. Rather treatment could be initiated on an outpatient basis.

In terms of readiness for treatment, Geri agreed she was moderately depressed and was willing to collaborate with a combined treatment involving both therapy and medication. When offered an appointment with the clinic's psychiatric consultant for medication evaluation, she refused saying she was uncomfortable with someone she didn't know. She did agree to meet with her personal physician, Dr. Winston, for such an evaluation later this week. If medication is indicated, Dr. Winston would monitor it, and the clinic's psychiatrist agreed to consult with him as needed. Individual outpatient therapy will begin immediately with this counseling intern and will be time-limited psychotherapy. Because Geri does not appear to be particularly psychologically minded and has moderate skill deficits in assertive communication, trust, and friendships, she will likely require a more problem-focused, here-and-now psychotherapy. It was also discussed and mutually agreed that a skill-oriented psychoeducation group was the treatment of choice for helping her to increase relational and friendship skills and decrease her social isolation.

Treatment goals include reducing depressive symptoms, increasing interpersonal and friendship skills, and returning to work and establishing a supportive social network there. The treatment focus will be threefold: (a) reduction of her depressive symptoms and social isolation with medication, social skills training, and behavioral activation strategies; (b) cognitive restructuring of her interfering beliefs of self, others, and the world, as well as her coping strategy of shyness, rejection sensitivity, distrust, and isolation from others; and (c) collaboration with her work supervisor and the human resources director to accommodate her return to a more tolerable work environment. Treatment will be sequenced with cognitive–behavioral therapy, beginning immediately. Later, group

**147**

therapy with a psychoeducational emphasis will be added to help her improve her assertive communication, trust, and friendship skills.

Some obstacles and challenges to treatment can be anticipated. Given her avoidant personality structure, ambivalent resistance is likely. It can be anticipated that she will have difficulty discussing personal matters with therapists and that she will "test" and provoke therapists (both individual and group) into criticizing her for changing or canceling appointments at the last minute or being late, and that she will procrastinate, avoid feelings, and otherwise test the therapist's trustability. Once trust in the therapist has been achieved, she is likely to cling to the therapist and treatment; thus termination may be difficult unless her social support system outside therapy is increased. Furthermore, it is expected that she will have difficulty with self-disclosure in the group therapy setting. Transference enactment is another consideration. Given the extent of parental and peer criticism and teasing, it is anticipated that any perceived impatience and verbal or nonverbal indications of criticalness by the therapist will activate early transference.

Geri has agreed to an initial treatment of eight 45-minute individual sessions combining medication and brief cognitive–analytical psychotherapy with the sessions focused on symptom reduction and returning to work. With Geri's signed consent, her job supervisor will be contacted about the necessity of a familiar, trusting social support in order for Geri to return to work. Aware that her pattern of avoidance would make entry into and continuation with group work difficult, the plan is for the individual sessions to serve as a transition into group.

## Case Commentary

This case illustrates a treatment formulation and intervention plan with a high level of consistency among the diagnostic, clinical, and cultural formulations and the treatment plan (see Chapter 12, in which a complete clinical case report for the case of Geri contains these four formulation statements). The treatment formulation also articulates treatment goals and focus, as well as the intervention strategy, which detailed how the treatment would unfold. Finally, it anticipates a number of potential obstacles to the implementation of the plan and how these obstacles would be proactively addressed. Table 11.2 summarizes the treatment goals and targets as they relate to the case conceptualization.

**Table 11.2** Case Conceptualization Map in Intervention Planning for the Case of Geri

| Pattern Factors | Treatment Goals and Targets |
| --- | --- |
| Precipitants | Increase safety of work situation so that job transfer or promotion is tolerable |
| Predisposition | Modify interfering beliefs: self-view— inadequate, world is viewed as less critical and demanding; there is less need for strategy of shyness/distrust and social isolation |
| Perpetuants | Reduce isolative lifestyle and increase supportive social network on and off the job |
| Presentation | Reduce depressive symptom and social isolation |

## Case 2: Jack

Jack is a 13-year-old Caucasian male who has displayed extreme angry outbursts and disrespect toward his mother and stepfather for the past 4 months. This has included physically threatening his mother on two occasions that involved police intervention. He is now in a short-term residential treatment program, and his counselor there suggested that Jack might benefit from anger management and family counseling and made those referrals. Although Jack appeared to be engaged in individual counseling focused on anger management training, it seemed to have little impact on his behavior. Similarly, family counseling sessions seemed to be having little or no effect. The mother, upset with this lack of progress and fearful that Jack will become more violent, wants her son committed to a long-term residential treatment program.

The school district psychologist referred Jack for a consultation to a psychiatrist who specializes in child, adolescent, and family issues. A comprehensive evaluation elucidated the operative pattern wherein the primary precipitant for Jack's threatening behavior is his mother's behavior. Essentially, she searches his room looking for drugs and when she finds musical scores that Jack composed she tears them up. An argument ensues when Jack finds his torn music, and the mother exclaims, "I don't want you to turn out like your brother," and Jack attacks her. Jack's brother is a rock musician who is in state prison for selling and distributing cocaine. Jack wants to be a lead guitarist and write music like his brother. The stepfather sides with the mother in denigrating Jack's music writing efforts and refuses to pay for private music lessons. Otherwise, Jack is relatively respectful to his parents and other adults, is doing relatively well in school, and has no record of other acting-out behaviors toward peers or school staff. The consultant notes that the precipitant is situation specific, as is Jack's acting-out behavior. At this point it has not generalized and it appeared that anger management-based therapy seemed to be a misguided intervention. The second part of the consultant's report is included here.

### Diagnostic Evaluation and Clinical Formulation

Axis I:   Adjustment Disorder with Mixed Disturbances of Mood and Conduct (309.4)
Parent–Child Relational Problems (V61.20)
Axis II:  No Diagnosis (V71.09)
Axis III: None
Axis IV:  Family Conflict
Axis V:   GAF 62; GARF 52

Jack's acting out occurs as a response to his mother's and stepfather's provocations. Jack perceives that he is being treated unfairly, and presumably this reflects his belief that life is unfair and that he must be on guard and aggressively look out for his own needs and safety, lest he be hurt or harmed further. Accordingly, he reacts by becoming disrespectful, angry, and physically threatening and menacing especially when the musical compositions he has spent hours writing are destroyed. He seems convinced that since his mother remarried and moved away from Jack's father that she no longer cares for Jack. This is demonstrated by the lack of meaningful, positive time she spends with him, and that the only time she gives him any consideration is when she violates his privacy and criticizes him and his brother. This serves to reconfirm his belief in the "unfairness" of his mother and stepfather. On the other hand, Jack responds appropriately to the expectations and corrections offered by teachers and program staff, presumably because their style of communication and discipline is perceived by him to be firm but fair. Remarkably, his outbursts have been selective: including only his mother and stepfather. Interestingly, despite the occasional taunts of older adolescents in school and in the neighborhood, Jack has been able to control his anger, suggestive of the circumscribed nature of his schema and beliefs. That the behavior is situation

150

specific at the present and has not generalized to all or most situations is a positive prognostic indicator.

In terms of family dynamics, it appears that the family's narrative, championed largely by the mother, is one of a constant, heroic struggle. In this narrative or story line, family members are achievement oriented and show their caring and concern for others by defending against forces that are perceived as threatening family integrity, loyalty, and cohesion. The struggle is everything, even if the cost in relationships is high. The overriding belief is that the mother upholds standards for achievement and morality and others must be high achievers, loyal and obedient, or risk extrusion; for example, the father was extruded via divorce and the mother wants Jack committed to the residential treatment program.

**Treatment Formulation**
Based on this clinical formulation, the following short-term and long-term treatment goals can be specified. Given that Jack's outbursts are relationally specific (i.e., to his mother and stepfather) and have not generalized, a conservative treatment strategy would be to focus on the short-term goal of reducing provocation and parental overreaction. This would involve a few sessions with parents in which they are coached to reduce and eliminate "triggering" Jack's outbursts. A therapist would work with them to find ways of engaging Jack in a less provocative and more nurturing but firm manner. Presumably, without such triggers their relationship would be more like those that Jack experiences in school and the residential program. If this proved effective, no further individual or family treatment would be needed. If it was not sufficiently effective, a long-term goal would be to address the unfair schema in focused individual sessions and the heroic struggle family story in family sessions. Coming from the narrative therapy tradition, re-storying involves reflecting on the influence of particular events and relationships in a family's life and focusing on previously unexamined or unemphasized aspects of those experiences. The resulting story includes pieces of meaning and understanding that are new or different and that allow for a positive shift in the original family narrative. In this case, re-storying involved a bit less emphasis on the achievement, obedience, and loyalty and more on relaxing and recognizing each other's uniqueness.

**Table 11.3**   Treatment Plan for the Case of Jack

| Pattern Factors | Formulation/Treatment Targets | Interventions/Sequence |
| --- | --- | --- |
| Precipitant: | Parental provocation | 1. Parental coaching |
| Predisposition: | Jack's unfairness schema/family | 3. Schema modification and re-storying heroic narrative |
| Presentation: | Jack's angry outburst/disrespect | 4. Anger management if necessary |
| | Parent's overreaction | 2. Parental coaching |

**Case Commentary**

Table 11.3 summarizes the treatment plan—including treatment targets, interventions, and the sequencing of interventions—for the case of Jack. Note that the numbering represents the order in which interventions are sequenced; that is, parental coaching is first and second, while schema work and re-storying are third, and so on. Jack's prognosis remains quite good even without individual therapy, given that the parents are able to better modulate their communication and discipline style. If Jack's mother is unable to modulate her triggering behavior, family therapy or even individual sessions with her would be indicated. A reasonable therapeutic marker of success of these goals and interventions would be for Jack to "graduate" from the short-term residential program and return home.

# 12

# *Draft an Integrative Clinical Case Report*

A clinical case report is a clinical document that describes the results of the diagnostic assessment of a client and specifies a plan of treatment consistent with the presenting problem and the case conceptualization. An *integrative* clinical case report is a clinical case report that is internally consistent, formulation-based, cogent, and coherent. Preparing a report that is internally consistent, formulation-based, cogent, and coherent is an essential competency that trainees and therapists can find considerably challenging. The clinical case report is not simply a document containing the facts of the case or a summary of all the data collected in the diagnostic assessment interview. In my view, it is more like a legal brief, which makes the case for a specific diagnosis, a specific case conceptualization, and a specific treatment plan. Rather than being a nontheoretical description of a client's life and concerns, the clinical case report should be a theoretically informed *explanation* and tailored treatment prescription. Furthermore, the report should be internally consistent, meaning that the diagnostic formulation and *DSM* diagnoses should directly reflect the presenting problem and be directly addressed in the treatment goals and focus specified in the treatment formulation. Finally, a clinical case report should be a compelling portrait of the client: present (presenting problem, etc.), past (developmental history, etc.), and future (treatment plan, etc.). The portrait description should be sufficiently compelling and detailed that other clinicians could pick the client out of a line-up. For all practical purposes, such a report reflects the professional's capacity to "think like a therapist."

I have had considerable experience as a consultant in reviewing case files, which include clinical case reports, at several clinics. Three deficits stood out in such reviews. First, there was a lack of consistency between sections of the clinical case reports; for example, the treatment plan often did not address and match the client's presenting condition. Second, case conceptualizations were omitted entirely or if there was a "clinical impression" section, it seldom offered a compelling explanation of the client's dynamics. Third, treatment plans were seldom tailored to the client's needs and personality. Instead the plans tended to be very general, often recommending "cognitive restructuring" or "CBT" (cognitive–behavioral therapy) for conditions and clients for whom these interventions may not have been indicated. In short, few were integrative clinical case reports.

Occasionally, however, I would review clinical case reports that were internally consistent, formulation-based, cogent, and coherent. These integrative clinical case reports were presumably written by individuals who "thought" like master therapists. However, one does not need to be a master therapist to prepare such integrative reports. In fact, if trainees are provided an integrative framework for developing such reports and are also exposed to examples of integrative clinical case reports, they begin thinking like highly effective therapists and, in time, learn to prepare internally consistent, formulation-based, cogent, and coherent clinical case reports. This chapter provides such a framework, or map, for developing such integrative reports. It then illustrates this framework with an integrative clinical case report. Finally, it offers an evaluation tool that trainees may find useful in reviewing their reports.

## INTEGRATIVE CLINICAL CASE REPORT MAP

The following 11 categories provide a framework, or map, for preparing the clinical case report. The reader may recognize that the first six categories are the same as the first six categories of the Diagnostic Assessment Interview Map of Chapter 7.

1. *Presenting problem and context:* Describe presenting symptoms, diminished functioning, and/or concern; address the "why now" question; specify the link between precipitant(s) and presentation; reflect the clinician's awareness of client's personality dynamics on interview process.
2. *Mental status:* Specify appearance, orientation, language, and intelligence; mood and affect; perceptual and cognitive status; memory; harm potential to self and others; insight; and judgment.
3. *Developmental history:* Report information on parent–child, sibling, and parent–parent relationships; family values; self-management; and relational capacity and functioning.
4. *Social history and cultural dynamics:* Describe school and job performance; social and intimate relationships; acculturation; ethnic and gender identity.
5. *Health history and health behaviors:* Describe health status, medical treatment; any previous individual or family therapy; response to medications; substance use or abuse.
6. *Client resources:* Includes previous change efforts, level of readiness and motivation for change, and social support system.
7. *Diagnostic formulation:* Provide a succinct statement that adequately addresses the "what" question; refer to specific *DSM* criteria for Axes I and II indicated in narrative (optional).
8. *DSM–IV–TR diagnosis:* Specify a five-axes diagnosis that accurately reflects the presentation; 5-digit codes are present and appropriate.
9. *Clinical formulation:* Adequately link presentation, precipitant, perpetuants, and predisposing factors in a convincing explanation of "why" the client thinks, feels, and acts (maladaptive pattern) as he or she does in terms of CBT, dynamic, or other theoretical approach.
10. *Cultural formulation:* Identify level of acculturation, ethnic and gender identification (if relevant); link presentation to culture versus psychological factors; anticipate impact of cultural factors on treatment process.
11. *Treatment formulation:* Specify a treatment plan consistent with clinical formulation; specify a treatment focus and treatment goals and corresponding treatment interventions; articulate a treatment strategy; specify culturally sensitive interventions, if indicated; predict likely obstacles (resistance, transference, alliance ruptures, ambivalence) and other challenges that might arise over the phases of treatment.

## ILLUSTRATION OF AN INTEGRATIVE
## CLINICAL CASE REPORT

In previous chapters you have followed the case of Geri R. from the diagnostic interview through the case conceptualization process. You have observed how the therapist conducted the interview and developed the case conceptualization with its four components: diagnostic formulation and *DSM* diagnosis, clinical formulation, cultural formulation, and treatment formulation. The clinical case report that follows simply links each of these four components to a succinct description of the results of the first six categories of the Diagnostic Assessment Interview Map.

**NOTE:** The reader may find that the following report is quite detailed in some sections such as the diagnostic formulation. For example, in the diagnostic formulation category (number 7 in the previous list of 11 categories)—and reported in the case example that follows—indicating specific *DSM* criteria for Axis I and Axis II diagnoses in the case report narrative is optional. This means that while providing this degree of detail has proven helpful to trainees in their graduate training, these data are not routinely expected in the reports of practicing therapists.

### Presenting Problem and Context

Geri R. is a 35-year-old single, never married, female administrative assistant who was referred for an initial evaluation following a 3-week onset of depressed mood. Other symptoms included loss of energy, markedly diminished interest, insomnia, difficulty concentrating, and increasing social isolation. She had not shown up for work for 4 days, and this prompted the mental health referral. Cutbacks at her office led to her being transferred out of a relatively close-knit work team, where she had been for 16 years and had been an administrative assistant for 6 years, to a senior administrative assistant position for the new vice president of sales in the adjoining executive annex building. It is noteworthy that Geri showed up late for the initial evaluation, explaining that she "couldn't find the address" although this clinic is six blocks from her home. She indicated that she had come for the evaluation only at the insistence of the director of human resources, and, although she admitted she felt awful, she was not convinced that she really had a problem that needed psychological treatment. Her explanation was that she was "just dragging because I went back to work too soon after having the flu," and that was the reason she had taken sick days. Self-disclosure was clearly difficult for her. However, she did admit that her job transfer was a significant loss and tentatively agreed that it might have triggered her depressive symptoms and social isolation. During the course of the interview, Geri's long-standing sensitivity to criticism became increasingly evident. Accordingly, as the formulation of avoidant personality style emerged, the evaluator endeavored to be particularly gentle and supportive both verbally and nonverbally.

## Mental Status

The client appears her stated age and is appropriately dressed and groomed. She is oriented to person, place, and time and is cooperative with the evaluation. Her intelligence, language skills, and ability to think abstractly appeared to be above average, consistent with her having earned an associate's degree. Her mood is moderately depressed, while her affect is slightly constricted but appropriate to the situation. No obvious perceptual or cognitive deficits were noted. Her immediate, short-term, and long-term memory appeared to be intact. She denied current suicidal and homicidal ideation, intentionality, or plan. She admitted having occasional thoughts that she might be better off dead but dismisses them, stating "I'd never do it because it's against my religious beliefs." Her insight into her current situation is fair, and her judgment is adequate to good.

## Developmental History and Dynamics

A review of the family system indicates that Geri is the older of two siblings. Her brother Jaime is 4 years younger, is married with two children, and reportedly is happily employed as a computer programmer for a pharmaceutical manufacturer. Both parents are alive and relatively healthy. Geri describes her father as emotionally distant but demanding. He had worked as a senior accountant until the firm he had been with for 28 years downsized and forced him into early retirement 3 years ago. His "drinking problem" has been denied by the family, as they are active Baptists. Two years ago the parents relocated to a retirement village in Arizona. Geri's mother never worked outside the home. Family values included hard work, social conformity, and obedience.

Geri believes she was most like her mother but has had a somewhat distant relationship with her, both as a child and now. She remembers being "fussed over" by a maternal aunt, until the aunt died when Geri was 7 years old. Geri believes her brother was the favorite of both her parents. She recalls having had few friends while growing up, and the one and only best friend she had ever had had moved away when Geri was 8 years old. She painfully recalls being ridiculed by others for being somewhat obese and "clumsy" in junior and senior high school. She did not date in high school or in college, although she admits to "sleeping with a guy once; I don't know how it happened." She admitted that the prospect of intimate sharing of herself now is absolutely overwhelming.

Her earliest childhood memory, when she was 4, was seeing her infant brother for the first time. She recalls her parents had just returned from the hospital. Geri had been frightened staying with her aunt and not knowing where her mother had gone. Her mother lovingly placed her baby brother in the Geri's old crib, while Geri's father said that the birth was the happiest day of his life. Geri was told to stop whining and asking questions about the baby and to go outside to play or she would be punished. She remembers running outside crying and hiding in her tree fort until it got dark. She felt frightened and confused. Geri described intense feelings of humiliation and rejection following the birth of her younger brother.

A second childhood memory is reported when she was about 7 years old. Geri recalls answering her friend's question about why Geri's father wasn't at church the day before. She said it was because he had drunk too much the night before. Geri's mother overheard this and spanked her for being a bad girl and "airing the family laundry in public." Geri ran to her bedroom crying and feeling unloved and hurt for being unjustly punished for answering her friend's question. In short, it appears she experienced her parent's harsh treatment of her after her brother's birth as the nullification of the sense of specialness and nurturance that she had previously enjoyed from her parents.

## Social History and Cultural Dynamics

Geri lives alone in a condominium near her office. She reports having only one older female coworker whom she can trust (but Geri's promotion threatens to change that) as well as a paternal aunt whom she talks to by phone but seldom visits because she lives in an out-of-state nursing home. Geri reports she has never been in a long-term relationship or married. She has worked at the same company since graduating from a local, junior college. Culturally, Geri is a fourth-generation African American, and she and her parents appear to be highly acculturated. Her grandparents migrated to the Midwest from Mississippi in the late 1930s. Although she attends an annual Black pride festival every summer, she is not otherwise active in the Black community; neither are her parents. There are two other African Americans in her office, but she has not become close to either of them saying, "All they want to do is talk about men, which I'm not into." Although she was reared as a Baptist, she no longer considers herself to be religious. She identifies herself as heterosexual and describes herself and her parents as middle class in values and orientation.

## Health History and Health Behaviors

She denies having previous psychological or substance-related problems or treatment, but a maternal aunt probably was treated for depression. Because the aunt died at an early age and Geri does not know the cause, suicide is a possibility. Health behaviors include daily exercise and a reasonable diet. She denies the use of alcohol or tobacco but drinks several cups of coffee a day, which leave her somewhat jittery and appear to fragment and reduce the depth of her sleep. She also reports taking a multiple vitamin daily but denies the use of any prescription or over-the-counter medications or any mineral herbal supplements. Her last physical exam was about a year ago, and she has not seen a physician in at least 6 months.

## Client Resources and Treatment

This client brings the following resources to therapy. Her level of readiness for treatment appears to be between the contemplative and the preparation stage of change. She is intelligent, is loyal to her employer and has worked at the same job for 16 years, which suggests she can sustain commitments. She has maintained contact with a paternal aunt, has one coworker she trusts, and cares for her pet, a responsive small dog. However, her shyness and rather limited social support system are deficits that will need to be addressed in this therapy.

159

## Diagnostic Formulation

Geri meets six of the nine *DSM–IV* criteria for Major Depressive Disorder, Single Episode, Moderate Severity (296.22). The criteria met include (1) depressed mood most of the day, nearly every day for more than 2 weeks; (2) markedly diminished interest or pleasure (called *anhedonia*); (3) weight loss of 10 pounds and appetite loss; (4) insomnia, with some early morning awakening; (5) fatigue and low energy; and (6) diminished concentration. She does not meet criteria for recurrent suicidal ideation or excessive or inappropriate guilt. Geri also meets four criteria of the seven criteria for Avoidant Personality Disorder: (1) She avoided the job promotion because of fear of criticism and disapproval; (2) she showed restraint within intimate relationships because of fear of being teased and ridiculed; (3) she was preoccupied with being criticized and rejected in social situations; and (4) she views herself as socially inept and personally unappealing (i.e., obese) and inferior to others. In short, Geri's history and initial evaluation are consistent with a major depressive episode. In addition, she meets criteria for Avoidant Personality Disorder.

### *DSM–IV–TR* Five-Axes Diagnosis

 I. Major Depressive Disorder, Single Episode, Moderate (296.22)
    Occupational Problem (V62.2)
 II. Avoidant Personality Disorder (301.82)
 III. None
 IV. Limited support system; job stressor
 V. GAF 54 (at time of initial evaluation); 71 (highest in past 12 months)

## Clinical Formulation

Geri's increased social isolation and depressive symptoms seem to be her reaction to the news of an impending job transfer and promotion, given her history of avoiding situations in which she might be criticized, rejected, and otherwise harmed. Her reaction and predisposition can be understood in light of demanding, critical, and emotionally unavailable parents, strong parental injunctions against making personal and family disclosure to others, and the teasing and criticism of peers. Thus, she came to believe that life was demanding, others were critical and harsh, that she was inadequate, and that it was necessary to socially isolate and conditionally relate to others. Given these maladaptive beliefs, her biological vulnerability for depression, her lack of social skills, her tendency to "test" others' trustability, and the resulting life-long pattern of conditionally relating to others, it is not unreasonable to conclude that her current depression and increased isolation were triggered by news of a job promotion, news that others would find uplifting rather than depressing. Although presumably this pattern was adaptive as a child, it appears to be quite maladaptive now and may negatively impact the treatment process, at least initially.

## Cultural Formulation

Geri identifies herself as a middle-class African American with few ties to her ethnic roots, and it appears that Geri and her parents are highly acculturated. She believes that her depression is the result of stresses at work and a "chemical imbalance" in her brain. There are no obvious indications of prejudice or conflicting cultural expectations or other cultural factors. Instead, it appears Geri's personality dynamics are significantly operative in her current clinical presentation. Gender dynamics could impact the therapeutic relationship between Geri and her African American male therapist, given her strained relationship with her father and limited involvement with men. However, it is not anticipated that other cultural dynamics will negatively impact the therapeutic relationship. Given her shyness and avoidant style, it may take a while for her to become comfortable and engaged in group therapy, but it is less likely that cultural factors will be operative in a Caucasian female–led group of middle aged women of different ethnic backgrounds. Overall, it appears that Geri's avoidant personality dynamics are more operative than cultural factors in her current clinical presentation, and it does not appear that cultural factors will negatively impact or interfere with therapy process or outcomes. Furthermore, at this time treatment progress does not seem dependent on cultural or even culturally sensitive interventions.

## Treatment Formulation and Plan

Given that this is her first episode, that her current GAF is 54, and her baseline GAF is around 71, the degree of severity of the depression would likely be considered "moderate" rather than "severe." Since the probability of suicide is low (a conclusion reached in light of Geri's denial of any suicide ideation as well as religious prohibition), hospitalization is

161

not deemed a necessity at this time. Rather treatment could be initiated on an outpatient basis.

In terms of readiness for treatment, Geri agreed she was moderately depressed and was willing to collaborate with a combined treatment involving both therapy and medication. When offered an appointment with the clinic's psychiatric consultant for medication evaluation, she refused, saying she was uncomfortable with someone she didn't know. She did agree to meet with her personal physician, Dr. Winston, for such an evaluation later this week. If medication is indicated, Dr. Winston would monitor it, and the clinic's psychiatrist agreed to consult with him as needed. Individual outpatient therapy will begin immediately with this counseling intern and will be time-limited psychotherapy. Because Geri does not appear to be particularly psychologically minded and has moderate skill deficits in assertive communication, trust, and friendship skills, she will likely require a more problem-focused, here-and-now psychotherapy. It was also discussed and mutually agreed that a skill-oriented psychoeducation group was the treatment of choice for helping her to increase relational and friendship skills and decrease her social isolation.

Treatment goals include reducing depressive symptoms, increasing interpersonal and friendship skills, and returning to work and establishing a supportive social network there. The treatment focus will be threefold: (a) reduction of her depressive symptoms and social isolation with medication, social skills training, and behavioral activation strategies; (b) cognitive restructuring of her interfering beliefs of self, others, and the world, as well as her coping strategy of shyness, rejection sensitivity, distrust, and isolation from others; and (c) collaboration with her work supervisor and the human resources director to accommodate her return to a more tolerable work environment. Treatment will be sequenced with CBT beginning immediately. Later, group therapy with a psychoeducational emphasis will be added to help her improve her assertive communication, trust, and friendship skills.

Some obstacles and challenges to treatment can be anticipated. Given her avoidant personality structure, ambivalent resistance is likely. It can be anticipated that she will have difficulty discussing personal matters with therapists, and that she will "test" and provoke therapists (both individual and group) into criticizing her for changing or canceling appointments at the last minute or being late, and that she will procrastinate, avoid feelings, and otherwise test the therapist's trustability. Once trust in the therapist has been achieved, she is likely to cling to the therapist and treatment;

thus termination may be difficult unless her social support system outside therapy is increased. Furthermore, it is expected that she will have difficulty with self-disclosure in the group therapy setting. Transference enactment is another consideration. Given the extent of parental and peer criticism and teasing, it is anticipated that any perceived impatience and verbal or nonverbal indications of criticalness by the therapist will activate early transference.

Geri has agreed to an initial treatment of eight 45-minute individual sessions combining medication and brief cognitive–analytical psychotherapy with the sessions focused on symptom reduction and returning to work. With Geri's signed consent, her job supervisor will be contacted about the necessity of a familiar, trusting social support in order for Geri to return to work. Aware that her pattern of avoidance would make entry into and continuation with group work difficult, the plan is for the individual sessions to serve as a transition into group.

# 13

# *Establish a Treatment Focus*

A precise case conceptualization permits a therapist to establish a specific focus for treatment intervention. Establishing such a treatment focus is analogous to switching from a floodlight, which illuminates an entire parking lot, to a spotlight, which illuminates one car within that parking lot. This treatment focus serves as a guide, or action plan, for the therapist to achieve the treatment goal. Consequently, focused treatment increases the likelihood of better treatment outcomes. "There is now a convincing body of empirical evidence indicating that therapist ability to track a problem focus consistently is associated with positive treatment outcomes" (Binder, 2004, p. 23).

This chapter begins with a brief discussion of the necessity of having a treatment focus and a method of specifying such a focus. This is followed by illustrations of how a focus treatment was established in three cases. A closing comment reflects on how master therapists focus treatment.

## NECESSITY OF TREATMENT FOCUS

Why is a treatment focus necessary? For many years, therapists have been trained to give undivided attention to the client's words, feelings, body language, and concerns. Clinical lore has encouraged and supported this view of practice with the dictum "follow the client's lead," which means that the clinician should provide a nondirective and nonevaluative environment, show interest and respond empathically to whatever the client wants to talk about, and refrain from giving advice. This viewpoint is more attuned to the open-ended, long-term approach to therapy of yesterday than it is to the accountability-based, time-limited therapy that third-party payers are currently willing to authorize. Today more than ever, the expectation is that therapists must focus treatment. Accordingly, therapists must also learn selective attention or else be overwhelmed by the multiple therapeutic rabbits that could be chased. Treatment focus not only provides direction to treatment, it also "serves as a stabilizing force in planning and practicing therapy in that it discourages a change of course with every shift in the wind" (Perry, Cooper, & Michels, 1987, p. 543).

## ESTABLISHING A TREATMENT FOCUS

How does a therapist establish or specify a treatment focus? The treatment focus is identified in the process of developing a case conceptualization, and the basic theme of the case conceptualization further specifies the focus. Not surprisingly, because the case conceptualization is based on a conceptual map reflecting a theoretical orientation, the focus of treatment is also likely to be informed by the therapist's theoretical orientation. For example, in the interpersonally oriented dynamic therapies, the focus is usually the client's maladaptive interpersonal style or pattern. In the cognitive–behavioral therapies the focus is typically maladaptive thinking and behaviors. Table 13.1 provides a concise listing of basic treatment focus and basic treatment goals associated with the most common therapeutic approaches. Note that Cognitive Behavioral Analysis System of Psychotherapy (CBASP) is a form of CBT (McCullough, 2000). The following three cases illustrate how a treatment focus is established within different theoretical orientations.

### Specifying a Treatment Focus in Dynamic Therapy

Louis J. is a divorced 47-year-old Caucasian male who sought therapy because of a work-related issue: He was distressed over the criticalness and lack of support of his supervisor and coworkers. He was particularly concerned that his job was in jeopardy because of his attitude toward his boss and coworkers. In his personal and social life he was quite isolated.

**Table 13.1** Treatment Focus and Goals in Common Psychotherapeutic Approaches

| Psychotherapeutic Approach | Basic Goal | Treatment Focus |
|---|---|---|
| Cognitive–behavioral therapy | Change maladaptive beliefs and behaviors | Analyze and process situations involving specific maladaptive beliefs and behaviors |
| Cognitive–behavioral analysis system of psychotherapy | Find alternate thoughts and behaviors to achieve desired outcomes | Analyze and remediate thoughts and behaviors in terms of actual and desired outcomes |
| Time-limited dynamic therapy | Experience insight and corrective interpersonal experiences | Analyze and interpret troublesome interpersonal relationships and plan corrective experiences |
| Solution-focused therapy | Facilitate the smallest changes needed for better functioning | Find exceptions and implement solutions |
| Emotionally focused psychotherapy | Modify emotional responsivity, schemas, and self-narrative to live a more vital and adaptive life | Analyze and process client's core pain |
| Adlerian psychotherapy | Increase social interest and modify faulty convictions | Analyze and change faulty lifestyle convictions and basic mistakes |

Divorced for some 19 years, he rarely had contact with his grown children. He prides himself on taking care of himself and being successful despite "all the crap I've endured over the years." He was the oldest of three siblings, all of whom he describes as "take charge people." His father would ridicule Louis and his two younger sisters if they tried to enlist any emotional support from either parent. His mother was emotionally withholding and withdrawn. Both parents wanted their children to be self-sufficient and demanded that each child solve his or her own problems. They offered no guidance about career and educational decisions.

From a time-limited dynamic therapy orientation, the following *case conceptualization* was developed: Louis' basic desire was that significant others would understand and support him. But because of early life experiences he expected others would only mock and reject him if he revealed this desire. Thus, he would typically misinterpret the efforts of others as critical and intrusive. Accordingly, he responded to others by being irritable and emotionally withdrawn. As a result he believed and felt himself to be defective and worthless, and so he socially isolates from others and is self-sufficient.

From this case conceptualization the following primary theme (number 1) and secondary themes (numbers 2 and 3) were specified as the *treatment focus*:

1. Self-sufficiency is his main problem: It results from expecting those at work to be unsupportive, which he interprets as being critical and intrusive, to which he responds with irritability, withdrawal, and increased self-sufficiency.
2. He views himself as defective and worthless.
3. He transposes his expectations of his family onto his work relations.

**Case Commentary**

Therapy proceeded by analyzing and processing various workplace situations in terms of the primary theme of self-sufficiency and the recurrent pattern of how his expectations and behaviors actually elicited the response of others that were so distressing to him. As Louis began to understand how this maladaptive pattern led to increasing distress and isolation, he collaborated diligently with the therapist to revise this pattern. Furthermore, as he became aware of the parallels between his job difficulties and his early child experiences and self-view (*secondary themes*), his work situation improved and he became more eager to examine the social isolation in his personal life.

## Specifying a Treatment Focus in Cognitive–Behavioral Therapy

Carl A. is a 28-year-old third-generation Filipino male who, until recently, had been a high school science teacher. He presented for therapy with symptoms associated with social anxiety disorder: primarily feeling anxious around others, including students, teachers, and administrators at his school. He became so nervous in class that he found it increasingly difficult to give short lectures or even give students instructions on doing lab experiments. A week ago he went on a medical leave from his job 2 days after the beginning of the new school year, and his physician referred him for Cognitive–Behavioral Therapy because Carl was unable to tolerate medication for the anxiety.

He is the only son of moderately acculturated Filipino parents who are college professors in the sciences. He notes that his family was close although not particularly affectionate, and that he had an uneventful childhood. Because his parents moved when one or the other received a faculty promotion (which was often), he did not have a best friend, at least for more than a year at a time. He reports experiencing low levels of anxiety around others from elementary school on. However, he excelled throughout high school in science and won a 4-year National Science Foundation college scholarship to prepare for a career in teaching science. His parents were excited about his award and encouraged him to pursue a career in the sciences. He received his B.S. degree in physics and began teaching in a public high school. Although he enjoyed science, he felt somewhat uncomfortable around students. However, because the science program at the school was largely discovery based, he worked largely with students on an individual basis, as lab experiments were the center of the program. This changed at the beginning of this school year when the superintendent changed the science curriculum to a more traditional one in which lab assignments were secondary to teacher lectures. A few days after the beginning of the school year, Carl experienced high levels of anxiety and difficulty breathing.

The following *case conceptualization* was developed: Carl's core belief is that others will reject or even abandon him when he makes mistakes. He is terrified of this outcome and so he engages in avoidance behavior. However, given that Carl sets exceedingly high standards for himself, it is not unreasonable to assume that he will make mistakes. Given that he associates making mistakes with rejection and abandonment, his beliefs contribute to his symptoms of social anxiety and his avoidance behaviors. Unfortunately, such avoidance behaviors have the effect of preventing Carl from learning that his beliefs are inaccurate as well as exaggerated, and that the consequences of making mistakes are far less drastic than Carl predicts. Unfortunately, because his predictions of making mistakes and being rejected do not occur, Carl mistakenly credits his avoidance behaviors as the safeguard; this only reinforced those maladaptive behaviors.

From this case conceptualization, the following maladaptive beliefs and behaviors were specified as the *treatment focus*:

1. Carl believes that making mistakes leads to rejection or abandonment by others.
2. Having overly high standards greatly increases the likelihood that Carl will make mistakes.
3. Carl's avoidance behaviors are self-reinforcing and hinder recognition of the inaccuracy of these beliefs.

**Case Commentary**
The initial treatment focus with Carl was on the behavioral side of cognitive–behavioral therapy, specifically the downside of Carl's avoidance behavior. He came to understand that by safeguarding himself with social isolation, to the extent that he had, had inadvertently resulted in intense feelings of loneliness. Carl was willing to take part in behavioral experiments designed to increase his social contact in circumstances with minimal or no risk of making mistakes. Instead of experiencing rejection or abandonment, he experienced enjoyment and some degree of acceptance by others. As the process of therapy evolved, the focus shifted more to the cognitive dimensions (numbers 1 and 2).

## Specifying a Treatment Focus in Integrative Therapy

Rod is a 32-year-old Caucasian married male who works as a computer programmer in the development lab of a small but cutting-edge software company. He was referred to therapy by his employer's human resources director because of increasing anxiety and worry, decreased energy, and insomnia. He relates the onset of his symptoms to the recent diagnosis of multiple sclerosis in his wife, Jenny. She had been experiencing increasingly debilitating but vague symptoms for the past 2 of their 6 years of marriage. Two months ago she temporarily lost her sight, and 3 weeks ago she woke up and could not walk. She was given the diagnosis of rapidly progressive multiple sclerosis and now uses a wheelchair to get around. Because her job as a women's sports consultant requires considerable mobility and air travel, she has not returned to her job and has applied for workers' compensation. Rod has been devastated by the diagnosis, in large part because he relies so much on his wife. He reports that he has taken to calling his mother at least twice a day since Jenny has been incapacitated.

He is the youngest of three siblings and grew up in a family that valued hard work and masculinity. He was asthmatic as a child and so became quite attached to his mother, who would regularly take him for medical appointments and to the emergency room when he was symptomatic. She was caring, acquiescent, and avoided conflict in all matters. His father was a tyrant who would explode emotionally when he didn't get his way. Rod was his favorite and, like his father, was successful but self-absorbed. From his father's perspective, Rod was beyond reproach and got special attention, gifts, and dispensations that neither of his sisters received.

Rod excelled in school and graduated from college with a degree in computer science at the age of 23 and has been employed as a programmer ever since then. He has two close male friends and is an avid sports fan. He met his wife in college where she was a standout player on the women's basketball team. He describes her as very supportive and fun to be with "except when she starts making demands on me."

The following *case conceptualization* was developed: Rod believes that the universe should revolve around him and insists that life should be exciting and that others should meet his needs at all times. He relies on others, particularly women, to take care of him. He also believes that men are superior to women and that because he is hardworking and successful, others, particularly women, will make no demands or challenge him. Premature processing of grandiosity and entitlement themes in therapy are likely to engender resistance.

From this case conceptualization the following mistaken or interfering beliefs and attitudes were specified as the *treatment focus*:

1. His self-view is one of grandiosity and entitlement.
2. He believes men are superior and expects that women will care for but not challenge him.
3. Becoming emotionally upset and demanding are basic problem-solving and conflict resolution strategies.

### Case Commentary

Therapy proceeded by processing Rod's symptoms and concerns in terms of these three interfering beliefs, although at the beginning of therapy the focus was primarily on numbers 2 and 3. He was particularly intrigued that acting upset and being demanding were problem-solving strategies. In time he recognized that whereas these strategies worked for his father and for Rod earlier in his life, they didn't work very now well, particularly since Jenny has been wheelchair bound. He balked at the belief that women are inferior and that they should take care of him without challenging him. Because she was now unable to care for him, Rod experienced cognitive dissonance with this belief.

The notion that negotiation solved problems and resolved conflicts as a result of both parties relinquishing one or more demands was difficult for him to comprehend, at least initially. After all, he had role-modeled his father's demanding, nonnegotiating style in which neither he nor his father relinquished anything. That meant demanding and emotionally haranguing others until he got what he wanted. In time he was able to accept the therapist's coaching in finding other, more adaptive problem-solving and conflict resolution strategies based on negotiation.

As Rod became more proficient in these alternative strategies, he was more receptive to discussing and processing his narcissistic features of grandiosity and entitlement. Had these features (number 1) been the initial focus of therapy, the prediction was that resistance would have quickly been engendered. As treatment evolved Rod was able to moderate his self-view and became more accepting of his wife's illness and the necessity to meet (at least some of) her needs.

## CLOSING COMMENT: MASTER THERAPISTS AND TREATMENT FOCUS

The preceding cases illustrated how a treatment focus can be established and is influenced by the therapist's theoretical orientation. In this closing comment, the question is posed: How do master therapists focus treatment? A study addressing this question compared master therapists with a cognitive–behavioral orientation with master therapists with a psychodynamic–interpersonal (e.g., time-limited dynamic therapy) orientation (Goldfried, Raue, & Castonguay, 1998). As previous research has shown, master therapists function relatively similarly irrespective of their espoused theoretical orientations (Blatt, Sanislow, Zuroff, & Pilkonis, 1996; Fiedler, 1950; Skovholt & Jennings, 2004). The current study found that the treatment focus in both groups of master therapists involved a greater focus on clients' ability to observe themselves in an objective way, their evaluation of their self-worth, their expectations about the future, and their thoughts, their emotions, and their functioning. Master therapists of both orientations were also more likely to encourage clients to view things more realistically and to highlight how a specific thought, feeling, intention, or action was part of a larger theme. In addition, they pointed out how clients were interfering with therapeutic progress (Goldfried et al., 1998).

# 14

# *Maintain the Treatment Focus*

Research is beginning to support the clinical observation that treatment outcomes are significantly improved when therapists maintain a treatment focus (Binder, 2004). However, maintaining that focus is not as easy as it may sound. After all, the lives of clients are complex and changing, and it is to be expected that they will want to discuss and process recent issues and concerns that arise between sessions. Oftentimes, these concerns are not directly related to the focus of treatment. The challenge is for therapists to "track" a treatment focus along "with flexibly modifying the content as new information arises and digressing from the initial focus as circumstances dictate" (Binder, 2004, p. 100). This chapter briefly discusses the value and challenge of maintaining a focus for treatment. Then it provides a case example and extended transcription of how a therapist seeks to "stay on track" with a very articulate client who easily and quickly shifts the focus to other issues and concerns.

## THE CLINICAL VALUE OF
## MAINTAINING THE TREATMENT FOCUS

The primary reason for staying on track is that treatment is more likely to achieve the specified treatment goals than if the focus is lost. However, staying on track is a considerable challenge for therapists given that clients have a tendency to shift, consciously or unconsciously, the focus of discussion to a less threatening or less demanding topic or concern. Accordingly, treatment can easily be slowed or derailed when the therapeutic momentum strays from the primary treatment focus. In such situations, therapists face a number of "decision points" in any session in which they can choose various ways of responding to their client. The choice they make directly affects whether the treatment focus is maintained or not.

## THE CHALLENGE OF
## MAINTAINING THE TREATMENT FOCUS

Staying on track can be a significant challenge, particularly for trainees and beginning therapists. Often because of inexperience and limited familiarity with refocusing strategies, beginning therapists tend to respond to client shifts with empathic statements or clarifying questions that may take the session in a direction different from that of the primary treatment focus. It is only as therapists become aware of such shifts, or "decision points," that they can attempt to reestablish the primary focus of treatment.

The reality is that clients do chase "therapeutic rabbits" and that the therapist's role often involves discouraging "a change of course with every shift in the wind" (Perry et al., 1987). Typically, clients shift away from the focus because they are overwhelmed with a new life stressor and feel compelled to process that situation and reduce their distress. Other times, clients are hesitant to keep on track because resolving a problem or conflict means that they would have to face difficult relationships or responsibilities in their lives for which symptoms or conflicts have safeguarded them from facing. Or, they may want to change but are ambivalent. With supervision and experience therapists learn to discern the various reasons clients divert from the treatment focus. Chapter 17 describes some of these treatment-interfering behaviors and offers specific strategies for refocusing treatment when ambivalence and resistance are operative.

## ILLUSTRATION: TRACKING TREATMENT FOCUS

The following case illustrates how a therapist consistently and effectively maintains and tracks a treatment focus. It is inspired by Carlson (2006). The extended case transcription and commentary illustrate four decision points in which the therapist weighs various therapeutic options.

The reader will note that the therapist endeavors to closely maintain or track the treatment focus themes of choice and empowerment. These particular themes present an ironic challenge for the therapist. On the one hand, the therapist wants and needs to foster and promote choice and empowerment by giving the client opportunities to make choices within the session. On the other hand, sessions are only 50 minutes and there are only a limited number of sessions. Accordingly, the therapist's challenge is to delicately keep the treatment process on track by limiting, reframing, or refocusing the client's attempts to shift to another topic or a less salient therapeutic theme before time runs out and therapy is over. Sometimes these decision points involve deciding whether to stay with the treatment focus when the client shifts the conversation in another direction, *or* to go along with the client, at least for a short time. Other times, the decision involves more options.

## Case Illustration: Veneta

Veneta is a 32-year-old divorced female who seeks therapy for feeling overwhelmed with personal, family, and workplace demands. She experiences anxious depression and experiences occasional insomnia. She is a highly acculturated, third-generation Cuban American who is employed as a beautician and has a 12-year-old daughter. The assessment reveals that the client's issues and need to please others are primarily driven by personality and not by culture. A contract is agreed upon for 10 sessions of individual psychotherapy. In the first session the therapist conceptualizes the case in terms of a pattern of meeting others' expectations out of a need to please others while disregarding her own needs, that is, the "pleasing servant" theme. The goals of therapy were for Veneta to become empowered and centered and to develop more adaptive relationships with her parents, her husband, and her children. The treatment focus was on choice and empowerment. The second and third sessions focused largely on Veneta's relationship with her mother, who relegated child rearing to the grandmother. Because Veneta's primary treatment expectation was to establish a healthy relationship with her mother, it was agreed that she would talk to her mother, saying that she wanted her mother to function like a mother from henceforth.

Veneta came to the fourth session noticeably dysphoric and indicated that she had been "down and depressed all week." Ruminating about difficulties had exacerbated her distress and interrupted her sleep. Because she was unable to control this rumination, the therapist spent about 5 minutes teaching her controlled breathing and practicing it with good outcomes. About halfway through the session Veneta said:

*Cl.:*    I just have to say again that I got so depressed this week. I've had some big setbacks. Just thinking about what comes next gets me down.

**Decision Point 1:** Because the triggers (i.e., predisposing and maintaining factors) for her anxious depression were discussed earlier in the session and controlled breathing was offered to reduce rumination and distress, the therapist could go back to further discussion of *clinical* aspects of depression, *or* the therapist could maintain the treatment focus on the "pleasing servant" dynamic. The therapist chose to maintain the treatment focus and emphasize *dynamic* aspects of Veneta's depressive feelings and other issues that might arise related to the theme of choice and self-empowerment.

*Th.:*    Sounds like the depressed feelings result from your thinking. Your depression comes from those thoughts. So, the kind of thoughts you choose to think will make the difference between feeling depressed and not feeling depressed.

*Cl.:*    But those depressing thoughts can be overwhelming.

*Th.:*    That's why it's helpful to develop ways of getting control over those thoughts. When that happens it's important to engage in non-depressing activities. Like the activities we talked about last week.

*Cl.:*    When I get those depressed thoughts I don't want to do anything. When I'm depressed the whole world seems to stop. I don't want to put on makeup. I don't want to get off the couch. I don't want to do the dishes.

*Th.:*    Do you think those are choices?

*Cl.:*    Yes, it's a choice. (nervous laugh) I choose to do that.

*Th.:*    What do you suppose the purpose is in "choosing" depression?

*Cl.:*    Maybe it's a way of not feeling or not confronting what I need to do. It's a way of procrastinating. It's an excuse really.

*Th.:*    So the purpose of depression for you is avoidance?

*Cl.:*    (smiles) Yeah. That's one way I don't do what I want to do.

*Th.:*    Uhm-hmm.

*Cl.:*   Because this is really difficult for me to do. (pause) I was think-
        ing about what we had talked about before. I got down on myself
        because I chose to be passive instead of being assertive in this
        particular situation. So, it was at an emotional cost to me again.
*Th.:*   Uhm-hmm.
*Cl.:*   I know I don't have to be mean to people but just being assertive
        and telling people how I feel is hard. I'm just afraid of it. And, so
        becoming more assertive is what I've been thinking about.
*Th.:*   And so you're afraid of being assertive—so far.

**Decision Point 2:** The therapist recognizes that Veneta is beginning
to talk about another issue and that to shift the focus to another theme
(i.e., assertiveness) could derail the treatment focus, even if temporarily.
Recognizing assertiveness is related to empowerment, the therapist considers how to proceed. Because the treatment focus is on empowering
the client and helping her to make decisions rather than be a "pleasing
servant" to others, the therapist reiterated "so far"—a therapeutic device
he initiated in the first session by which she could take some responsibility for anticipating that she could and would be more empowered at
a future point in time, rather than hopelessly reenacting her "pleasing
servant" pattern. Then the therapist shifted back to the primary focus.

*Cl.:*   Yeah, so far.
*Th.:*   Have you found yourself adding the qualifier "so far" in the
        past few days?
*Cl.:*   Yes. A few times. But I mostly focused on the negative aspects of
        not doing what I wanted to do.
*Th.:*   It seems that you're using depression as fear of avoiding things you
        need to do. I'm adding "fear" to what you said. Is that accurate?
*Cl.:*   That's accurate.
*Th.:*   Then what you do is negative: You don't do anything and feel
        guilty about it. (pause) Can you give yourself permission not to
        do anything and as a result not feel badly about yourself?
*Cl.:*   I guess. (wringing hands) But when I think back about what I'm
        most afraid of, it's being assertive. It's what I fear most. I don't
        know why. It's like someone has to push me out of an airplane
        to do it.
*Th.:*   I hear you. But I'm not sure why you do that, because it seems
        when you do that it creates a lot of pain for you.

179

*Cl.:*    Oh, it does.

*Th.:*    And I'm not sure what it is about the pain you like. And if you're not going to do something, why not play music (she's an accomplished musician) or do something else you like. Instead of laying on the couch, call a friend and go out to a movie or go shopping. And, give yourself permission not to do housework.

*Cl.:*    It would be a better choice.

*Th.:*    It would be a less depressing choice. It's one thing to have the problem not doing what you wanted to accomplish, and it's another to feel bad and depressed about that. It'd be much better to give yourself permission not to do a task, and feel good about the break you're giving yourself.

*Cl.:*    But I'm not depressed if I have company and others are over at my place. But, I'm a loner and don't have many friends. I need to make friends, but I'm afraid.

**Decision Point 3:** Here the focus could have shifted to Veneta's lack of friends, and the therapist could have commiserated with her or engaged her in an assignment to find a friend or work on friendship skills training. Instead, the therapist maintained the primary treatment focus.

*Th.:*    But the purpose of the fear is not to do the task. So, I suggested you can give yourself permission not to do anything.

*Cl.:*    You know I don't have depression too often. But I'm beginning to see that it comes up because most of my life I've avoided most issues instead of facing them.

*Th.:*    I think I see it a little differently. It seems you've been good at making yourself miserable. But I'm not sure that it's primarily because of avoidance. After all, you've graduated from college, raised a daughter by yourself, hold down a full-time job, and take care of your aging father and grandmother; you also ended an abusive marriage.

*Cl.:*    Yeah, but I don't take care of myself. I do make myself miserable.

*Th.:*    What do you suppose is the purpose for making yourself miserable?

*Cl.:*    I don't know. (pause) Even as a child I was kind of melancholic. I didn't let myself be happy-go-lucky because I was afraid if I was too happy I'd get distracted and miss doing something I was supposed to do, like turn in a paper on time. And bad things would happen. So I didn't let myself get too happy.

**Decision Point 4:** Here the therapist could take several tracks: empathize with the client's bind, explore childhood melancholy, or stay on track and focus on further processing the "pleasing servant" dynamics.

*Th.:*  Well, it seems like you have had considerable practice in meeting others' needs at the expense of making yourself miserable.

*Cl.:*  Yeah. But, I if I do something for me, then I might not be doing something for somebody else.

*Th.:*  So if you do something for yourself, other people might be disappointed. And, what will others do to you if they are disappointed?

*Cl.:*  I don't know. Maybe tell me that I'm selfish or something.

*Th.:*  So if they said, "Why don't you do that for me?" what would you say?

*Cl.:*  Ooh! I'm not sure what to say.

*Th.:*  But you're taking care of yourself. (pause) Won't taking care of yourself just get you in trouble with others?

*Cl.:*  (pause) Sometimes I think it would be nice if someone would take care of me. But I would probably feel weird about it, and not accept it. I'm not even good at accepting compliments.

*Th.:*  You're not very good at accepting compliments. So far.

*Cl.:*  Yeah. So far (smiles and laughs). (pause) I hope it's not too corny, but I've been thinking of putting up little Post-its around my house to remind me of all the things I've accomplished, instead of thinking about all things that I'm not doing or avoiding.

*Th.:*  It's a choice you have: putting up little notes to yourself that acknowledge what you've done versus ruminating about your failings.

*Cl.:*  I could say it in my head, but I think I need to make it public so I can see those accomplishments often. Then maybe later I can just think about it.

*Th.:*  You're proposing a course of action that could break an old pattern. It sounds like a positive action and worth a try. Now, what's an example of what you would write on the Post-its?

*Cl.:*  One would be "You're a wonderful mother." "I'm a really good musician." Stuff like that.

*Th.:*  Those written reminders can be very important. And, that goes back to choice. If we choose to think of what went wrong, then we feel bad. If we choose to think of what went right, then we feel good.

181

*Cl.:*  And that happens to me every day, because I may overlook one small thing, like with my daughter, and then I feel really bad about myself. (pause) But it's tough right now thinking about all these things. It can get me down. But I know I'm going to have to move on and progress if I'm going to heal inside. It's difficult, just stewing over it.

*Th.:*  Well, it's a choice. It's a choice to stew. (client laughs) But I'm not sure why you're choosing to stew, when you have other choices. It doesn't particularly help you.

*Cl.:*  No, it doesn't.

*Th.:*  You can avoid doing something and not stew, if you want to. The reality is that you create two problems: You avoid doing a task, and then you feel bad about. The solution is simple: Eliminate the second problem. Maybe you could choose to do something else that would make you feel better about the situation and yourself.

*Cl.:*  (laughs) You're very convincing.

*Th.:*  I don't know if I'm convincing, but it might be a way to break that pattern. It means coming up with alternatives that don't bring on these bad thoughts and feelings.

The session wraps up. The therapist gives the client an assignment to practice controlled breathing before sleep and when needed throughout the day. An appointment for a subsequent session is made.

**Case Commentary**
The therapist was very effective in keeping the focus on track. To some extent the client's attempts to shift was to avoid dealing with her core dynamics of pleasing and putting others' needs first. Thus, it was easy for her, being so articulate, to shift away to safer topics. Interestingly, when she was redirected back, she rather easily was able to process those core dynamics.

# 15

# *Modify Maladaptive Cognitions, Behaviors, Affects, and Interpersonal Relations*

Strategies for facilitating change have evolved from the four basic elements of human functioning: cognitions, behaviors, emotions, and relations. Historically, therapeutic approaches have emphasized one element, for example, cognitions in cognitive therapy, behavior in behavior therapy, emotions in emotionally focused therapy, and relations in interpersonal and systemic therapies.

Today, therapeutic approaches are much more integrative and inclusive and change strategies are often organized by treatment targets: cognitive, behavioral, emotional, and relational. These treatment targets were once viewed as separate entities, but they are actually mutually influential and intersect with each other. If one element changes, the other elements usually—but not always—follow suit (Beitman & Yue, 1999). This chapter begins with an overview of the four main therapeutic strategies: cognitive, behavioral, emotion-focused, and relational. Then it provides extended transcriptions of sessions in which these strategies are illustrated.

**Table 15.1**   Intervention Types and Specific Strategies

| Type | Specific Strategies |
| --- | --- |
| Cognitive and behavioral strategies | Cognitive restructuring |
| | Cognitive–behavioral replacement |
| | Exposure |
| | Behavioral rehearsal |
| | Stress reduction and relaxation |
| | Social skills training |
| Emotion-focused strategies | Empathic exploration |
| | Emotion evocation and evocative responding |
| | Emotional schema restructuring |
| | Focusing |
| Relational strategies | Identifying maladaptive interpersonal patterns |
| | Interpersonal cognitive restructuring and cognitive–behavioral replacement |
| | Restructuring interactions |
| | Corrective emotional and interpersonal experiences |

## THERAPEUTIC STRATEGIES FOR MODIFYING COGNITIONS, BEHAVIORS, EMOTIONS, AND RELATIONSHIPS

Table 15.1 lists common therapeutic change strategies for the basic elements of human functioning. These include cognitions, behaviors, emotions, and relationships. Note that cognitive and behavioral have been combined, reflective of the cognitive behavioral therapies.

## ILLUSTRATIONS OF COGNITIVE, BEHAVIORAL, EMOTIONAL, AND RELATIONAL STRATEGIES

Following are three cases that illustrate the four basic clinical strategies. The first case is inspired by Driscoll, Cukrowicz, Reardon, and Joiner (2004) and Leahy (2003) and illustrates both cognitive and behavioral strategies with a distressed individual. The second case is inspired by Smith and Greenberg (2007) and illustrates the emotionally focused strategies with a distressed individual. The third case is inspired by Driscoll et al. (2004) and illustrates the interpersonal cognitive restructuring and cognitive–behavioral replacement strategy with a distressed couple.

## Case 1: Cognitive and Behavioral Strategies

Jason is an 18-year-old, single, male college student with debilitating social anxiety. Whereas he can tolerate most solitary and family activities, he experiences considerable anxiety in situations that involve "outsiders," by which he means those he does not know well, such as those in his classes, his dormitory and in other social situations. Being around others has been difficult since childhood, but the difficulty has increased since he has been away from home and in college. Because he was homeschooled by his mother, he has had minimal contact with others until recently. He was accepted and began his first semester of college at a large state university 2 hours from his home. He became increasingly anxious during new student orientation and sought help at the university counseling center. In the first session after a short diagnostic interview the therapist introduced cognitive–behavioral therapy, including the steps and process of the cognitive–behavioral analysis system of psychotherapy; Jason agreed to perform an "experiment" before the next session in which he was to make eye contact with someone in a store in which he had already been and presumably would shop at in the future. The transcription that follows picks up near the beginning of the second session.

### Cognitive and Behavior Replacement Strategy

Th.:     So you did follow up on the assignment to make eye contact and greet someone you've not met before. Great! Could you tell me about it?

Cl.:     Yeah. I went to the university bookstore the other day, and when I was going through the checkout line, I said hello to the cashier and asked her how she was doing.

Th.:     What were your interpretations or thoughts when you were in that situation?

Cl.:     I was thinking: "I'm not normal because I am here alone."

Th.:     Were there other thoughts?

*Cl.:*   Yeah. (pause) My other thought was: "I'm a loser."

*Th.:*   And what was your SUDS [Subjective Units of Distress Scale—a self-rated measure of perceived anxiety] level then?

*Cl.:*   It was about 80 or so.

*Th.:*   Okay. So your interpretations in this situation were "I'm not normal because I am here alone" and "I'm a loser," and your SUDS rating associated with these thoughts was 80. In a little while, we can focus on these interpretations. But for now, what were your behaviors in that situation?

*Cl.:*   While I was trying to talk, I kept my head down the entire time and looked at the floor or nothing at all, except when I looked at the cashier and made eye contact.

*Th.:*   What else did you do?

*Cl.:*   I just pretty much kept my head down and did not talk to anyone except for when I asked the cashier how she was doing. So I said "hi" and asked her how she was doing. It probably was barely audible.

*Th.:*   Did the cashier respond?

*Cl.:*   Yes. She said she was doing fine. But then I couldn't think of anything else to say, so I looked down and didn't say anything else.

*Th.:*   So your behaviors in this situation were to keep your head down and look at the floor and not to talk to anyone except when you greeted the cashier.

*Cl.:*   Yes.

*Th.:*   What outcome did you expect?

*Cl.:*   To go to the bookstore and pick up a couple of items without any stress.

*Th.:*   And what actually happened?

*Cl.:*   I got a book and some pens, but my SUDS was about 80 or so. I did make some eye contact with the cashier and ask her how she was doing.

*Th.:*   Did you achieve what you were hoping to?

*Cl.:*   Sort of. I was able to make eye contact with the cashier and speak to her, but I wasn't able to talk to anyone else or even look at anyone else and I still experienced a lot of stress.

*Th.:*   It sounds like you may have actually had two desired outcomes. One was to get your bookstore items without experiencing any stress. But it also seems like a second one was to be to make eye contact and greet that person. Do you think that is true?

*Cl.:*   Yeah. I was able to look at the cashier and ask her how she was doing. But I still experienced a lot of anxiety while in the bookstore and I couldn't think of anything else to say to her.

*Th.:*   Good. Would you like to look at this situation again and see if we can make some sense of it and how it might have turned out differently?

*Cl.:*   Sure.

*Th.:*   Okay, then, let's go back through your interpretations to see which ones were helpful and hurtful to you in getting your expected outcome of making eye contact with someone and greeting the person, while tolerating any anxiety. Your first interpretation was "I am not normal because I am here alone." Do you think that thought was helpful or hurtful to you in this situation?

*Cl.:*   Hurtful.

*Th.:*   Why?

*Cl.:*   Because I kept my head down and didn't speak to anyone because they would look at me and think I was weird because I was alone and because I was talking to them.

*Th.:*   Can you think of any thoughts, then, that you could replace the hurtful thought with that would be helpful to you in this situation?

*Cl.:*   I am normal.

*Th.:*   Good. How do you think that would have helped you?

*Cl.:*   Well, if I kept telling myself that I was normal and was not weird for being there alone, and that it's okay to feel anxious, I may have been more likely to have kept my head up and made eye contact with someone. I probably would have been more likely to say hello to someone.

*Th.:*   Your second interpretation was "I'm a loser." Was that thought helpful or hurtful to you in this situation?

*Cl.:*   Hurtful.

*Th.:*   How was it hurtful?

*Cl.:*   Because it made me even more out of place and feel bad about myself. Like I can't even go to a store and make small talk with a clerk and other people. (pause) I have that thought a lot.

*Th.:*   That thought makes it really hard to feel good about yourself. (It does) What alternate thought would be helpful to you in this situation?

*Cl.:*   Well, if I could tell myself that I am a regular person doing the best I can. I am a worthwhile person and not a loser even though

**187**

|||
|---|---|
||I have shortcomings. It sounds strange saying that, but that's how I would like to think of myself.|
|*Th.:*|I agree. I experience you as a worthwhile person. (client smiles) How would thinking of yourself as a worthwhile person who happens to have some shortcomings be helpful to you?|
|*Cl.:*|It would help me have more self-confidence. It would make it easier for me to hold my head up and talk to people.|
|*Th.:*|So telling yourself that "I am normal and I am not weird for being here alone or feeling anxious" and "I am a worthwhile person who happens to have some shortcomings" would have made it easier for you to feel more confident about yourself, keep your head up, make eye contact with others, and to talk to others?|
|*Cl.:*|Yes. I believe it really would.|
|*Th.:*|It seems, though, that in this situation you were able to do that. You made eye contact with the checkout cashier and greeted her.|
|*Cl.:*|But I still felt a lot of anxiety, which really bothered me, and that made it harder to look up.|
|*Th.:*|Do you think that your replacement thoughts would have made you feel less anxious, then, or help you accept the anxiety you felt?|
|*Cl.:*|Probably. It would have been a lot easier for me.|
|*Th.:*|So your interpretation "I am not normal because I am here alone" and "I'm a loser" were hurtful to you because you didn't feel confident and you kept your head down and did not speak to anyone while you were in the bookstore, except when you spoke to the cashier, and then you still experienced a lot of anxiety, which made you feel more uncomfortable. If you replaced those interpretations with "I am normal and I am not weird for being here alone, and it's okay to feel anxious" and "I'm a worthwhile person," you would have experienced less anxiety. Or, you would have been more accepting of the anxiety. And, just as important, you would have been more likely to keep your head up and speak to others. (pause) Is that right?|
|*Cl.:*|Yes.|
|*Th.:*|Then let's move on to your behaviors. One of your behaviors in this situation was to keep your head down the entire time, except when you made eye contact with the cashier. Do you think this was helpful or hurtful to you in achieving your desired outcome?|

*Cl.:*   Hurtful. I probably would have been more likely to make eye contact with other people and maybe even say hi if I didn't look down the entire time.

*Th.:*   But you were able to make eye contact and speak to the cashier. How was it hurtful, then?

*Cl.:*   While I was looking at the ground, I just kept thinking about how I wasn't normal and that I just wanted to leave.

*Th.:*   So keeping your head down actually made you think more negatively?

*Cl.:*   Yes. If I had my head up and looked at other people, I might have been distracted and not thought those things over and over again.

*Th.:*   Then, what behavior would have been helpful to you in this situation?

*Cl.:*   To keep my head up. I probably wouldn't have thought negatively as much and would have been more likely to make eye contact with others and to even speak to others in the bookstore.

*Th.:*   So in this situation, if you had thought to yourself "I am normal and I am not weird for being here alone, and it's okay to feel anxiety" instead of "I am not normal because I am here alone, and I shouldn't feel anxiety," and if you had kept your head up instead of looking at the ground the entire time, you would have been more likely to achieve your desired outcome, which was to make eye contact and greet someone while feeling less anxiety and better tolerating the anxiety you did feel. Is that accurate?

*Cl.:*   Yes. It is.

## Cognitive Restructuring Strategy

*Th.:*   So, Jason, you said you have the thought "I am a loser." You say you have that thought a lot.

*Cl.:*   Yes. I am a loser. People don't like to be around me.

*Th.:*   And if people don't like to be around me then what would happen ... ?

*Cl.:*   Life would have no meaning.

*Th.:*   OK. So not being able to easily connect with others has important meanings to you. It means that you are a loser, that people don't like to be around you, and that life has no meaning.

*Cl.:*   Pretty much.

*Th.:*  We all have "automatic thoughts." They are thoughts that come to us spontaneously and we believe them to be true. They are often associated with feeling sad, anxious, or angry. It appears that your automatic thoughts include "I'm a loser" and "People don't like to be around me." How do you define "loser"?

*Cl.:*  Well, it's someone who has nothing to offer. Someone who can't connect with others.

*Th.:*  OK. So when you're alone and feeling really anxious, how much do you believe this belief on a scale from 0% to 100%, with 100% meaning that you believe it with absolute certainty.

*Cl.:*  I'd say about 95%.

*Th.:*  And how anxious do you feel, from 0% to 100%, when you have this thought?

*Cl.:*  About 99%.

*Th.:*  All right. Now let's look at the evidence. What is the evidence "for" and "against" the belief that you are a loser. Let's begin with evidence "for." So, what are the grounds for your belief "I am a loser"?

*Cl.:*  The main evidence is that I don't really have any friends. I'm alone, and I've never been this anxious in my life. (pause) That pretty much says it.

*Th.:*  OK. What's the evidence that you are *not* a loser?

*Cl.:*  (pause) Well, I'm a pretty good student. I'm a good writer; I just got an essay accepted in the university magazine. My parents and family care about me a lot. But I don't see them very often since the campus is 2 hours from them.

*Th.:*  If you had to weigh out the evidence against the idea that you are a loser, would it be 50–50, 60–40, 80–20, or what?

*Cl.:*  I'd say the evidence is 70% I am not a loser.

*Th.:*  What do your parents and family think of you?

*Cl.:*  They think I'm a good guy. They would probably say I am loyal and kind, once you get to know me.

*Th.:*  Would they think you're a loser?

*Cl.:*  Probably not a loser, but someone who is very shy and anxious.

*Th.:*  Might they see you more accurately than you see yourself?

*Cl.:*  Probably.

*Th.:*  Let's go back to the evidence you gave for the belief that you are a loser. You said: "I don't really have any friends. I'm alone, and I've never been this anxious in my life." If you had to weigh the evidence that you are a loser, would it be 50–50, 60–40, 80–20, or what?

Cl.: I'd say that the evidence is about 20% to 25% that I'm a loser.

Th.: Does thinking about this issue in a larger context make you feel any differently?

Cl.: I guess I feel less hopeless and less anxious.

Th.: It seems that you have the belief that unless people want to be around you and even be your friends now, it proves that you are a "loser."

Cl.: (pause) That's the way it seems.

Th.: Let's look at what the advantages and the disadvantages of this belief are for you.

Cl.: I guess the only advantage I can think of is that I don't put myself in situations where others can make fun of me or criticize me.

Th.: What about the disadvantages?

Cl.: (laughs nervously) Just the opposite. I'm so insulated from others that it's almost impossible to connect with and become friends with others.

Th.: All right. So, if you didn't believe that you were a loser, how would you be better off?

Cl.: I'd be more connected to others. I'd probably find a few people around here that I could really trust.

Th.: Weighing the advantages and disadvantages, what would the percentages be?

Cl.: It would be about 20–80. Far more disadvantages.

Th.: If you would get more connected to others what do you suppose would happen?

Cl.: I'd probably feel better about myself. But I would probably be really anxious, too.

Th.: On a scale from 0% to 100%, where 100% represents the best you can ever imagine feeling and 0% is the worst, how would you feel if you could connect up with some people on campus you could trust?

Cl.: Probably about 60%.

Th.: If you felt better making those connections, what does that say about the belief that you are loser?

Cl.: It means it's not true. But it has a big price to pay for it.

*Th.:*    Are you saying that you would rather be safe and alone with no anxiety or that you would be willing to take the risk of having some anxiety while connecting up with some trusting friends?

*Cl.:*    Connecting with others would be better.

*Th.:*    How about if we do a role-play. I'll be your negative thoughts and you challenge me. Is that all right with you?

*Cl.:*    OK.

*Th.:*    (as negative) Being safe is the most important thing in life.

*Cl.:*    That's not true. The safer I am the more alone and worthless I feel.

*Th.:*    When you're safe you're not anxious.

*Cl.:*    But the price of being safe is too high. I need to connect with people even though it makes me anxious.

*Th.:*    You can't handle anxiety. You'll just have more panic attacks and people won't want to being around someone who is weird.

*Cl.:*    That's just not true. Just last week I made eye contact and talked to a cashier in the bookstore without having a panic attack. She seemed interested in talking to me.

*Th.:*    But, you've said that you are a loser and others don't want to be around you.

*Cl.:*    That's not true either. I'm a worthwhile person. I have a lot of things to offer others. I'm kind, loyal, smart, and sensitive.

*Th.:*    OK. How do you feel now?

*Cl.:*    I'm feeling a lot better and more confident.

*Th.:*    What if you knew someone who was very anxious about connecting with others here on campus? What advice would you give him?

*Cl.:*    I'd tell him to take the risk and go ahead and approach someone who seems caring. There is nothing to be gained by being so afraid and a lot more to lose.

*Th.:*    Great. Let's think of some things you could do to help yourself over the next week. (pause) What risk would you be willing to take to approach someone who seems caring?

In a subsequent session the treatment focus remains the same, although a different situation is analyzed.

*Th.:*    So when you were waiting for the new class to begin and you tried to talk to someone you didn't know, you got pretty anxious. Your SUDS was about 85, and you were thinking that the student you were trying to talk with would see that you were anxious and would think that you were a loser. Then, you concluded that you would never be able to meet and talk with anyone else. Is that correct?

*Cl.:*  Yes, that's exactly right.

*Th.:*  That sure seems to be putting a lot at stake on just one conversation.

*Cl.:*  Yeah. Because if I can't even have a conversation with someone, how am I ever going to meet anybody?

*Th.:*  That follows. (pause) But, it also follows that if other people had those same beliefs about conversations, they would probably feel really terrible if a conversation didn't go well.

*Cl.:*  Yes.

*Th.:*  So let's look at this a little closer. The first thought you had is that if you feel anxious then you will not be able to have a conversation. Let's evaluate this thought.

*Cl.:*  Sure.

*Th.:*  So, on a scale of 0% to 100% how much do you believe this particular thought?

*Cl.:*  Oh, I don't know, probably about 95% or so.

*Th.:*  All right. And what is your basis for thinking this thought is true?

*Cl.:*  Well, it's something I just know. Because every time I get anxious talking with someone I don't know, I'm not able to think of anything else.

*Th.:*  All right. So now let's look at what we have for evidence of this. (pause) Think back to our first appointment together. Were you anxious coming to that appointment?

*Cl.:*  Oh, yes.

*Th.:*  So before coming to my office and meeting me for the first time, how would you rate your anxiety on the SUDS scale?

*Cl.:*  It was very high. I didn't know what to expect, and I wasn't sure if you would like me or not. And, I guess I was thinking that my problems were so weird that you would think I was a loser.

*Th.:*  So, your anxiety was very high. What was your SUDS level?

*Cl.:*  About 85.

*Th.:*  So it was almost as high as it could possibly be.

*Cl.:*  Definitely.

*Th.:*  And after our therapy session began, you were able to tell me about your difficulties. In other words, you were able to have a conversation with me.

| | |
|---|---|
| *Cl.:* | Well, yes. |
| *Th.:* | Were you very anxious—around 85 or so—the whole time? |
| *Cl.:* | I was definitely off the chart at the beginning, but my anxiety seemed to lessen as we kept talking. |
| *Th.:* | It lessened. (Yeah.) How low did it go? |
| *Cl.:* | Maybe to 50 or so. |
| *Th.:* | Great, that's an important observation you just made. Even though you were very anxious, you were still able to answer my questions and even ask some of your own. In other words, *you were able to have a conversation when you were anxious.* |
| *Cl.:* | Yeah. I guess I did. |
| *Th.:* | Just as important is to remember that even though your anxiety was high at the start, it decreased as the conversation continued. |

**Case Commentary**

This case illustrates how the cognitive restructuring strategy and the cognitive–behavioral replacement strategy were successfully utilized with a client with a relatively complex presentation involving both a symptom disorder and personality disorder. It is noteworthy that symptom monitoring, that is, SUDS levels, was combined with monitoring of the strength of the client's beliefs.

## Case 2: Emotionally Focused Interventions

Jesse is a 47-year-old married Caucasian father of two adult sons. He has worked as an auto mechanic since he was 18. His wife had given him an ultimatum to do something about his "hair trigger anger" or she would divorce him. Jesse admitted that anger had been a problem since his youth and he was concerned about its effect on his family. Although he had never hit them, he regularly yelled and demeaned them with caustic words. Somewhat reluctantly, he agreed to seek professional help. Initially, he sought help in an anger management group but because it had not helped much, he took a referral for an individual therapy.

The developmental history revealed that Jesse was the older of two sons and that his father would become verbally and emotionally abusive to all family members when stressed about nearly anything, but particularly work and money issues. His mother was emotionally distant and did little in those early years to shield her sons from her husband's wrath. It appears that Jesse had not resolved angry and sad feelings toward his father from whom he never felt love. Therapy was provided for 14 weekly 1-hour sessions.

In their first session, the therapist observed that as Jesse talked about past angry and rageful experiences, he would become tearful and lose hope. With the therapist's help, the client was able to recognize that this pattern was increasingly interfering with his life and straining his relationship with his wife and sons, who no longer wanted to spend time with Jesse. It was mutually agreed that the goal of therapy would be to transform this maladaptive emotional pattern to one that was more adaptive. The assessment revealed three main "voices" that reflected Jesse's self: a "sensitive" and hopeless voice, which would be transformed into one of tenderness and compassion; a "strong" voice that would lash out at the "father," which would be transformed to nurturing and protective voice, and which—along with the "sensitive" voice—could be assertive and forgiving; and an internalized "father" voice of anger and abusiveness, which would be transformed to being remorseful and loving. In short, the hope was that therapy would break this maladaptive pattern such that Jesse would have more emotional response options.

Early in the second session, the therapist guides the client to a new experience of compassion for his "sensitive" voice:

*Th.:* If you could give him a voice, what would he say to you about what he needs? (pause) He must have been so scared and felt so alone ...

*Cl.:* He feels so alone and he's got no one to turn to. (pause) It's like no one loves him the way he needs to be loved.

*Th.:* So be that boy now. (pause) "I feel so alone. I really want someone to love me."

*Cl.:* (sobs)

Later, Jesse's "stronger" voice unleashes anger toward the "father" voice:

*Cl.:* "You repulse me so much."

*Th.:* OK. So, what are you feeling right now?

*Cl.:* I'm angry. I want to hit him. ... I want to kick the shit out of him.

Moments later, Jesse shows recognition of his maladaptive pattern. He describes a recent situation with his wife.

*Cl.:* After that I felt sad because I had been so angry. The pattern doesn't stop, it just goes on.

*Th.:* It's good that you can recognize the pattern. Your anger has a trigger point, it just doesn't come out of nowhere. Let's go back and look at the sequence of anger followed by sadness. (pause) You're tearing. ... What's going on right now ?

*Cl.:* Well. It's the anger. ... I don't know where it started or how to control it. It's so frustrating.

The therapist helps Jesse to imagine his father's presence vividly so he can reexperience the anger and then explore it:

*Th.:* Now, imagine your father. Picture him in a specific situation. Do you have an image of him? (Yes.) Now, tell him what you are most angry about ... So what are you experiencing Jesse?

*Cl.:* I have this image of him. He's right in my face. I'm angry.

*Th.:* What is he doing?

*Cl.:* Yelling.

*Th.:* Yelling. What is he yelling about?

*Cl.:* (pause) It's not clear.

*Th.:* He's in your face and making you angry. (pause) What do you want to say to him?

*Cl.:* Nothing. I want to punch him in the face! (laughs)

*Th.:* Now, put words to your actions. Is it something like "Dad, just get out of my face?"

*Cl.:* "Screw off." (smiles)

*Th.:* What are you feeling right now? I know it is hard to confront him.

*Cl.:* It was hard. (pause) Things never ended well when he was like that.

*Th.:* Is it possible that you were scared of what he might do?

*Cl.:* Yeah. I probably was. He could demolish anyone in his path. Especially when he would lose control.

*Th.:* What's going on right now?

*Cl.:* I'm so frustrated (pause) Things don't get resolved.

*Th.:* One thing we're trying to do is to get some resolution to all of what has gone on between you and your father. He can't change who he is. But, you have the option of changing your own reaction to him. (pause) Even though he's not alive, he still influences your life right now.

*Cl.:* That's for sure.

*Th.:* What do you want to say to him about his effect on you?

*Cl.:*      "I hate it, Dad. (pause) It would be different, though, if I had some hint that you cared about me."

*Th.:*      That's what makes it so hard. You don't feel that he cared about you at all.

*Cl.:*      In all those fights with him, I don't think he cared. (pause) And, if there's no caring, there can't be any resolution (tearful).

*Th.:*      That really hurts.

*Cl.:*      (crying)

*Th.:*      You feel so uncared for. (pause) Now, you're left feeling worthless and not good enough.

*Cl.:*      (nods) That's the worst of it.

*Th.:*      Yes. (pause) Now try and give that part words. Verbalizing experiences helps deepen their meaning.

To help the "sensitive" voice verbalize, the therapist modeled giving that voice words, asking Jesse to be aware of his bodily experience. Then, the therapist models how another voice could respond with compassion. Prompting the "sensitive" voice, the therapist says:

*Th.:*      He tries to pretend that nothing was wrong, but that's not true. You're hurting. A part of you feels broken inside. It's just so hard to believe that you are safe and OK. Can you try to give that part words? What would it say? "I feel so … " (pause).

*Cl.:*      I need to be loved. I deserve it. (pause) I shouldn't have to ask for it.

*Th.:*      A child shouldn't have to ask for love.

*Cl.:*      It should just be there.

*Th.:*      Yeah. "And I really suffered because it wasn't there." Now. Tell him what it was like for you. What it is still like for you.

*Cl.:*      The absolute pits.

The "stronger" voice had indicated that he was furious with the "father" for having withheld nurturing and was indignant at this injustice. He reports having dreamed that he was assertive toward the "father":

*Cl.:*      I had a dream about my father. (laughs) Never had one that I can recall. (pause) We were face-to-face arguing, and I told him that I had had enough, and that I wasn't going to take it from him anymore. He said: "You shouldn't talk to me like that. You should be respectful of your elders." Then, I said that I had earned the right to stand up to his hurtful ways (laughs).

*Th.:*     You earned it.
*Cl.:*     Yeah, I did. (pause)
*Th.:*     What did your response to him in the dream feel like? Strong? Justified?
*Cl.:*     Yes. Justified. That we were like equals, that I wasn't a little kid anymore who couldn't stand up for myself.

Even though the client was not yet able to forgive the "father," his attitude toward his father had softened. The "father" voice responds to this change;

*Th.:*     I want you to try being the father for now. OK? (OK.) (pause) Jesse says: "I can't forgive you for not caring for me enough." How do you feel when you hear that?
*Cl.:*     I feel really sad that you are hurting so much. And that it was my fault.
*Th.:*     So, what it is that you want Jesse to know?
*C:*       That I really do love him. (pause) Even if I didn't show it.
*Th.:*     Can you say it to him directly?
*Cl.:*     I'll try. (pause) "I love you, Jesse … I'm really sorry that I caused so much pain for you." (tearful)

The voice of the "father" has softened into compassion, and accepts responsibility:

*Cl.:*     "I guess I was damaged growing up that made it hard to demonstrate care for others. (pause) I just couldn't seem to take care of anyone else but myself."

The "father" voice expresses love for the client and affirms him as well. The therapist facilitates a deepening of the experiencing:

*Cl.:*     "I want you to know that I really cared about you, and was so proud of what you made of your life. But I was just incapable of showing that caring."
*Th.:*     Good. Now tell him what you were particularly proud of.
*Cl.:*     "I guess I was proud of your sports awards … your grades in school. (pause) Maybe you could have done even more if I had been more supportive."

The "stronger" voice responded and reflected his ongoing indignation, saying:

*Cl.:*     "Well, it's nice to hear all that, but it's kind of late to be recognizing that now. How could you have been so clueless for so long?"

The therapist guides the client to stay with the "sensitive" voice that was receiving the nurturing it needed:

*Th.:*     How does it feel when a part of you hears: "I was proud of you, and I did love you, and I'm sorry, and I was just so damaged that I really couldn't show you the way I felt about you" when another part of you has wanted to hear all of that throughout your whole life.

*Cl.:*     Well, it would have been really good to hear that throughout my life. It would have gone a long way. It would have been affirming to hear that when things were going so well.

*Th.:*     Right. So, how are you feeling right now?

The client's response suggests that the "sensitive" voice has experienced the nurturing:

*Cl.:*     Well, I feel a sense of calm and contentment.

The "sensitive" voice was now able to address the "father" voice directly:

*Cl.:*     "It seems like you had it bad growing up, too. That you felt damaged by it. And, it doesn't seem like you got much from your parents and others throughout your life."

*Th.:*     Can you tell him how that you realize the impact that he's had on you, and then think, "A lot of things have negatively impacted him, too."

*Cl.:*     "Looking back, I can see that there were a lot of problems in your family background. Things that didn't bring out the best in you. Maybe it was your anger toward your parents that was reflected onto the rest of us, because you were afraid of them, but then you turned your anger on us."

Jesse reexperienced the memory of his father's anger and rage, and feels the pain of it:

*Th.:*     Yes. So you look sad now. (pause) Where is it coming from?

*Cl.:*     Well, I am feeling sad. But, I can't forgive him. It's not that easy.

The therapist then endeavors to facilitate closure without forgiveness. The "sensitive" voice indicates he would like to say "good-bye" to any need for

**199**

the "father" voice's love and approval and to his influence on his life. He continues by saying:

Cl.:     I'm going to have to let go of my need for that love from you that I can't ever have.

Th.:     Where do you sense that coming from inside your body? It seems to be an empty feeling or hole.

Cl.:     When I say those things I get tension in my chest (touches rib cage). (pause) It was always ... so hard for me to express that I needed anything from him because I fought it for so long.

The therapist responds empathically after which the "sensitive" voice spontaneously switches to identifying his goal:

Cl.:     I want to be different from him and be able to show affection and express my needs. I don't want to be defensive all the time and have that closed-up feeling.

Th.:     To move forward in your life, it is important to recognize how you want to be and how you don't want to be. Because your father is not in your life anymore, the question is "What do I need from myself to get on with my life?"

Later in the session as the "sensitive" voice found the image of the "father" too threatening, the therapist facilitates a switch in the client to the "stronger" voice, who could stand up to the "father":

Th.:     Try to really see him as the man you are now, and not as a little boy. As you look at him, tell him: "I'm not going to let you hurt me anymore."

Cl.:     I'll try. "I'm not letting you hurt me anymore. I've had enough. It's all over now."

Th.:     What is it that you want him to know?

Cl.:     When I see him, I was experiencing myself as I am now. That's something I've never done before.

While the "stronger" voice could be confrontive and menacing, he now had a more realistic perspective of the "father," and chose to respond differently:

Cl.:     (pause) I see him as much smaller now. In a way, I'd almost like to rough him up a bit.

200

*Th.:*    OK. So, tell him: "You look so pathetic now, when I look you in the eye."

*Cl.:*    Yeah, I think he is pretty pathetic, because of what he's done to me, to us, to himself.

*Th.:*    He's not as big and powerful as he seemed to you back then. Tell him how you see him now.

*Cl.:*    Well, I see him now as a loser. He's thrown everything away that is important, and he's ended up with nothing. He has no family and no real friends.

*Th.:*    OK. It sounds like, in a way, that you feel sad for him?

*Cl.:*    Yeah, I guess I do feel sad about it.

*Th.:*    So, it's sadness at the loss, the regret of what will never be. (pause) What are you feeling, Jesse?

*Cl.:*    That this nothing guy has caused me so much aggravation. I wonder why?

The client's "stronger" voice now perceives that he was not a helpless recipient of the father's abuse, but had control:

*Cl.:*    Why have I let this happen? It's pretty sad that I let him have so much influence on my life.

The therapist acknowledges this new realization and moves to facilitate closure. The "stronger" voice's new sense of control tempers his indignation. Thus, as Jesse faces the "father," he began to disentangle himself from that influence.

*Cl.:*    I guess all I really want is for him to know that I don't need him.

*Th.:*    You don't need him. Can you tell him?

*Cl.:*    Absolutely. "I don't need you. I don't need anything from you. (pause) I'm a better man than you."

*Th.:*    You've survived despite all that has happened

*Cl.:*    That's right. "I've done a lot without you. I've done something in life. I have got a family that cares about me. I've done it, and you haven't been a part of it."

The "stronger" voice expresses sadness "for both of us ... that it couldn't have been better." The client responds to this from the "father" voice.

*Th.:*    So, what is your response? You say it's sad for both of you.

*Cl.:*    "Well, as an old man, I can see that I missed out on a lot that could have been different. Your children, my grandchildren, and all that could have been. It could have been a great life. But, as I look at what I have done with my life, I feel like I wasted it."

Th.:    There is the sadness of not knowing him, not knowing him and his kids.

Cl.:    "I wasn't there for all the normal things parents are there for. What a loss. I missed out on everything that was really important."

The therapist then guides the "father" voice to facilitate the saying good-bye:

Th.:    So what would you say to him now? He seems to be bidding good-bye. It's as if he's saying, "This is in the past and I needed a lot from you but I didn't get it. It's affected my life, and I've suffered."

Cl.:    "I'm a loser, and don't let me affect you anymore. You don't need my approval for anything anymore."

The "father" voice then expresses sadness:

Cl.:    "I feel pretty sad for me. I've really blown it and I'm sad for the mess I've made."

The "father" voice has acknowledged responsibility, and the therapist guides him to stay with and elaborate the feelings. In time the "father" said: "I didn't let myself care for anybody or myself either" and "I am sorry for not showing that I care for you. I cared but I couldn't show it at the time, and I'm sorry." The therapist reflects back this distinction between love and the inability to show it. He guides the "father" to speak directly to his "son":

Th.:    Try to convince him that you mean that.

Cl.:    "I know it is hard to believe, but I was not able to show love and caring. There was just too much of …

Th.:    Try to express it now so he can believe you.

Cl.:    " I love you. I really do."

Th.:    What do you love about him?

Cl.:    He is a good son.

Th.:    Can you tell him that?

Cl.:    Yes. "You're a good son. (pause) You're my son, and I care about you. (pause) I always loved you but I didn't show it. (pause) What a mistake." Then the "father" begs for forgiveness.

Th.:    Good. So what would you like to hear from him?

Cl.:    "I really hope he will forgive me." (tearful)

*Th.:*     You want forgiveness. (pause) Can you ask, Jesse for that forgiveness?

*Cl.:*     (pause) "Can you forgive me?" (tearful) "I hope you can see it in your heart to forgive me, but I won't blame you if you didn't. (pause) I know you have a lot of anger and resentment."

The client responds to the "father" voice, with the "stronger" voice.

*Cl.:*     Well, I suppose I could forgive him because I know he meant it.

*Th.:*     All right. So can you tell him?

*Cl.:*     "Well … it really helps to understand that it wasn't my fault. It was also helpful to hear you acknowledging your role in all this. Most of all it helps to hear that you did love me (pause) and that you were willing to make things right after all these years."

At this point, the client was able to forgive the "father":

*Cl.:*     So … I can forgive. I can forgive him under those circumstances.

*Th.:*     What else do you want him to know? What's left in your heart that you want to say to him before you can say "I forgive you."

*Cl.:*     Nothing more, I guess. Really. I mean, he's really had it worse in many ways. It seems like a bigger loss for him because I've got something and he's got nothing. So, now I can say it: "I forgive you."

*Th.:*     Can you say good-bye now?

*Cl.:*     (pause) "Good-bye."

Though emotionally drained, the client indicates that his experience of being in the "father" voice was genuine, and he accepts that voice as part of himself:

*Cl.:*     I know this is about the pain and forgiving, but the way it came up, was something. I mean it was in the back of my mind since it came up so naturally. That's a good sign.

## Case Commentary

The client came to appreciate that focusing on the flawed humanity of the "father" facilitated his own healing. By the end of therapy, the client had incorporated the loving transformed "father" into his self, and his assertive "stronger" voice had developed into a nurturer and protector of the "sensitive" voice. About 5 weeks later, the client reported feeling calmer, having more control over his anger, and was beginning to identify underlying causes of his reactions to others so that he could respond more appropriately.

## Case 3: Relational Interventions

Carol and Tom were married for 6 years and had been experiencing relational difficulties for nearly 2 years during which time Carol was experiencing chronic fatigue and depression. The couple's hopes and plans for starting a family seemed to all but disappear as her illness appeared to take center stage in their lives. Most of the time she had little energy to do even routine chores, and it soon became clear that the demands of rotating shifts as an emergency room nurse were exacerbating her condition. On the advice of her physician, she reduced her hours from 40 to 10 hours a week. Nevertheless, there were days when she felt energetic enough to think she was feeling her old self again and would set out to take on tasks she had easily accomplished in the past. Inevitably, she would overdo it and exacerbate her condition. Although relational discord had occurred occasionally before the diagnosis, it predictably had increased as Carol's symptoms worsened and were exacerbated by various demands in the home. They were referred to a therapist for couples work by Carol's physician after trials of three antidepressants showed little or no improvement.

During the initial evaluation, the therapist identified their commitment to the marriage, ineffective relational patterns, and treatment expectations. Both wanted to remain in the relationship. Ineffective communication and unresolved arguments left both feeling upset, with Carol assuming the pursuer role and Tom the distancer role. Tom's expectation for therapy was that Carol would be more verbally responsive and specify her needs. Carol's expectation was that she would regain her energy and that Tom would be more emotionally engaged in the relationship and acknowledge her contributions to their life together. In collaboration with the couple, the therapist established a treatment focus on supporting and revitalizing the relationship in the context of conjoint sessions. This case is inspired by Driscoll et al. (2004). What follows is a transcription from the beginning of the third session. (C. = Carol; T. = Tom)

*Th.:*     It's good to see the two of you again. How have things been this past week?

*T.:*       (Silence). ... Carol, as usual, seems to be waiting for me to take the lead. But I would really like it if she would respond to your question.

*Th.:*     I hear you, Tom. You don't feel that the responsibility for responding should be yours alone, and you wish that Carol would take the initiative sometimes.

*C.:*      Sure, I'll start off. Well, what happened is that Tom came home from work, and he was in a bad mood. Maybe, he had a bad day at the office. Whatever it was, he was grousing about dinner. Earlier I had decided not to cook and hoped that we might go out for a change. After all, I had a little more energy than usual that day, which doesn't happen too often. I had spent 3 hours cleaning the house that afternoon, and I was starting to drag and I was just too tired to cook dinner. He told me he was hungry and tired and wondered why dinner wasn't ready.

*Th.:*     What did this mean to you? What were your interpretations of the situation?

*C.:*      Well, I thought that when I'm not feeling well that I shouldn't have to cook a meal. But, I also knew from past experience that I can't presume that we'd go out to eat unless I first asked him.

*Th.:*     What other thoughts or interpretations did you have?

*C.:*      I also thought that he seldom appreciates the housework I do when I'm feeling well or really badly. I guess I also was thinking that he was angry at me for not being more considerate of the hard day he had at the office. This made me feel guilty. So, I apologized for not being considerate and started to put together a quick meal. But, I let him know by the tone of my voice that I was upset and I started tearing up, just on the verge of crying.

*Th.:*     What actually happened?

*C.:*      Tom became frustrated that I was upset, and we got in an argument. He had no idea what was happening inside me. We ended up ordering take-out and ignored each other the rest of the evening.

*Th.:*     What did you expect to happen?

*C.:*      I wanted him to hug and kiss me when he got home, and then I wanted to relax and go to our favorite restaurant. I really wanted some acknowledgment of the work I did around the house and the pain I endured in the process. I hoped that we could enjoy dinner out and relax after a long day.

*Th.:*     Did you get what you expected?

| | |
|---|---|
| C.: | I clearly didn't get what I wanted. |
| Th.: | Tom, please tell us your version of the story. |
| T.: | All right. Well, I walked through the door, and Carol was lying on the couch watching TV. There was nothing in the kitchen for dinner like there usually is, so I asked her when we were going to eat. She got all upset and started apologizing and crying. For the life of me I couldn't understand why she was so upset. After I picked up our food order, she told me that she had really wanted to go out to a restaurant. Then we started arguing. |
| Th.: | So what were your interpretations of that situation? |
| T.: | I thought that she was getting upset at me for no reason. When I finally figured out that she wanted to go to dinner, I couldn't understand why she didn't just tell me that she was tired and in pain. You know, even though we've been married 6 years I still can't read her mind. |
| Th.: | What other thoughts or interpretations did you have? |
| T.: | It was that I didn't need her picking a fight for no reason, especially after I had such a long and hard day at work. So I went and picked up some take-out and sat on the couch to watch the evening news. My tone of voice may have been a little gruff, but I wasn't upset with her at first. I guess I didn't say much to her the rest of the evening because I was in a bad mood after having an awful day at work. |
| Th.: | What did you want to happen when you got home that night? |
| T.: | I just wanted to come home after a hard day at the office, have a good meal, and take it easy for the rest of the evening. It didn't really matter to me if we ate out or ate at home. Instead, I arrived home, got into an argument with my wife, and went to sleep frustrated and angry. |
| Th.: | Did you get what you wanted? |
| T.: | Absolutely not. |
| Th.: | It seems that both of you wanted to spend a relaxing evening together. What I also heard is that Carol wanted you to appreciate the work she did around the house especially when she was so tired. And, Tom expected Carol to tell him directly her idea about dinner, whether it was to eat at home or go out. |

*T.:* Absolutely. She never tells me what she wants. Instead, she gets upset and leaves me clueless. I would not have objected to going out to eat, but I didn't know what she wanted.

*C.:* Well, you were so irritable and gruff that I assumed you were mad at me for not having dinner ready the minute you got home. You didn't even notice that I was exhausted from spending half the day cleaning. You know that doing that usually makes me even more fatigued.

*Th.:* It's clear that you are both still feeling frustrated with the way things turned out. I'd like to process this situation with you, with the hope of coming up with some alternate interpretations for it. Are you agreeable to that? (Both nod affirmatively.) (pause) Tom, you wanted to come home, have dinner with Carol, and settle in for the night, is that right?

*T.:* Yes, but I also wanted her to tell me she wasn't feeling well and that she wanted to go to a restaurant, rather than getting her feelings hurt for no reason.

*Th.:* Let's take a closer look at these interpretations. First, you thought or concluded that she was upset again for no reason. Did that interpretation help you or hurt you in terms of getting what you wanted?

*T.:* (pause) Well, I guess it hurt me. I assumed she was being unreasonable and nonresponsive and that just made me angry.

*Th.:* What might be another interpretation that would have helped you get what you wanted?

*T.:* Maybe I could have concluded that she was upset and probably had a reason for it, which means I should try to find out what's wrong. (pause) That would have helped me because I wouldn't have become so angry and maybe we could have talked calmly about things rather than argue.

*Th.:* Okay. Let's look at your second interpretation. You said that you didn't appreciate her picking a fight with you for no reason. Did this interpretation help or hurt you in getting what you wanted?

*T.:* That one really hurt me because, I assumed again that she was the one who was being unreasonable and that I had nothing to do with it. I guess I was being selfish because I was irritable and angry about my bad day at the office. Maybe if I had been more sensitive and observant of her fatigue—and the clean house—I wouldn't have hurt her feelings. That would have prevented the argument.

*Th.:*      In terms of your behaviors, you said that your tone of voice was unpleasant when you got home. Is that correct? (Yes.) Did that behavior help or hurt in getting what you wanted?

*T.:*      Looking back, it sure didn't seem to help. (pause) I think I follow what you're getting at. I guess it hurt me because it probably made her think that I was angry with her.

*Th.:*      What other behavior might have helped you get what you wanted?

*T.:*      I probably should have made it clear that I wasn't upset with her as soon as I got home, instead of the way I treated her.

*Th.:*      Good. You also said that you picked up some take-out and then ignored her for the rest of the evening. Did that behavior help or hurt in getting what you wanted?

*T.:*      It really didn't help because it hurt her feelings even more, which made everything worse. If I hadn't been so stubborn and talked to her about it, we might have resolved it within a few minutes instead of ruining the whole evening.

*Th.:*      Would changing this behavior have also helped you achieve your other expectation, which was for her to tell you what she wanted from you?

*T.:*      That's interesting. Maybe it would have helped. (pause) But it seems like that would really depend on her. So, it probably wouldn't be a realistic expectation.

*Th.:*      I can understand that you want her to feel comfortable telling you what she wanted, but it may be an unrealistic goal for you because it relies on her behavior, which, as you know, is beyond your control. Can you think of a related but more realistic expectation?

*T.:*      Sure. I guess it would be that I wouldn't dump my own bad mood on her. That would probably make it much easier for her to tell me what she needs and wants.

*Th.:*      That follows. I could anticipate that the alternatives you came up with might help you achieve this.

*T.:*      Yeah, I can too.

*Th.:*      Okay, Carol let's look more closely at how you experienced this same situation. You wanted to go out to dinner with Tom and then spend a nice evening together. You also said that you wanted him to acknowledge your pain when you exert yourself cleaning the house. Is this right?

*C.:*      Yes, it is.

*Th.:*     The first interpretation you gave was that you shouldn't have to cook dinner when you are not feeling well and that you should know better than to plan to go out to dinner without first asking Tom. Did this thought help you or hurt in terms of getting what you want?

*C.:*     (pause) Well, I still believe that others shouldn't expect someone who is sick to assume all her responsibilities. But, I guess it did hurt me because I didn't make it clear that I was too sick to cook and wanted to go out to dinner.

*Th.:*     What would be another interpretation that might have helped you get what you wanted?

*C.:*     I guess a better interpretation would have been that he won't know I'm too sick to cook and want to go out to eat unless I tell him how I'm feeling.

*Th.:*     So how would telling him exactly what you wanted have helped get what you wanted?

*C.:*     Well, because my words would make it clear what I wanted. That would be a lot better than hoping that Tom would accurately interpret my lying on the couch looking totally exhausted as me wanting to go out to dinner.

*Th.:*     Fine. Your second interpretation was that Tom didn't appreciate all the time and energy that went into cleaning the house. Is that accurate?

*C.:*     Hmm. Again, this one hurt me because I ended up feeling so bad and upset.

*Th.:*     What would be another interpretation that could have gotten you what you wanted?

*C.:*     I could have thought that he just walked in the door and probably didn't have a chance to even notice the cleaning that I had done or my pain and fatigue. Then, I would not have been upset, and maybe he wouldn't have gotten so frustrated and we could have had a nicer evening together.

*Th.:*     Will this new interpretation help you with your expectation, which was for him to acknowledge your work around the house?

*C.:*     Well, it might, but I can't really make him say anything no matter what I do. So maybe it's not a realistic interpretation.

*Th.:*     I agree, you can't control anyone else's behavior. Can you think of an alternate interpretation?

C.: I suppose I could have thought that he won't know that I'm not feeling well and am tired unless I tell him. And, then say that I'd like to go out to a restaurant.

Th.: That sounds reasonable. Your second interpretation was to assume that he was angry with you. Did this help or hurt you in terms of getting what you wanted?

C.: Well, it definitely hurt because my own feelings were hurt when I thought he was angry. If I had just thought that he might have had a bad day and his irritability and moodiness had nothing to do with me, I probably wouldn't have gotten so upset.

Th.: Sounds good. Hopefully, these new interpretations might help you.

C.: Yes, they might, assuming I can actually do it.

Th.: I hear your concern. (pause) Now, let's look at some of your behaviors. You said that you immediately apologized to him for not being a good wife and then began trying to quickly put together a meal. Did that help or hurt you in getting what you wanted?

C.: I know what I did wasn't helpful because it only made him more upset with me because he had absolutely no idea why I was upset. It would have been much better if I had just told him that I understood that he had a tough day at work and that I wanted to go out for dinner.

Th.: You also noted that you let him know you were upset by your tone of voice and that you were on the verge of crying. Did this help or hurt get what you hoped for?

C.: It hurt because he usually ignores me when I act like this. I should have just told him about my pain and fatigue. Then we probably could have resolved things much sooner.

Th.: Wonderful! You've both done some really good work today. What are each of you thinking right now?

C.: Well, it's clear that we both make assumptions about the other instead of just talking. And, it seems to lead to discord rather than harmony.

T.: I agree. It seems we are so accustomed to fighting with each other that we expect negative reactions and emotions from each other when what we really want to do is have a relaxing time together.

Th.: Was working through this situation helpful?

*T.:*    Definitely. I now see how I contributed to the argument and that blaming her was off the mark and made things worse.

*C.:*    It was helpful to realize that my being submissive and non-assertive can actually hurt our relationship. I've been this way in the past, assuming that being submissive would reduce the chance of us fighting. But, it actually promotes discord.

*Th.:*   A real irony. (pause) Is what you've learned today applicable to other situations?

*T.:*    It sure makes me more aware of how I come across to her. I've got to find other ways to let her know about things that get to me at work without taking it out on her and hurting her feelings. She might even feel more comfortable asserting herself with me then.

*C.:*    It's becoming clearer to me that if I could be a bit more assertive and tell Tom what my needs are and how my energy level is, we would probably get along much better.

*Th.:*   Well, we've done a lot this session. And, it seems like things are going in the direction you hoped they would.

**Case Commentary**

The application of this clinical strategy, a modification of the cognitive–behavioral replacement strategy for couples, facilitated a shift in how this couple perceived each other and related to each other. The therapist was an effective agent of change because he assisted the partners in focusing on achieving desired outcomes. He came across to each partner as caring, helpful, and trustworthy, but not as directive, evaluative, or partial, as he formed a coalition rather than side with either partner.

# 16

# *Plan and Implement Culturally Sensitive Treatment*

A basic assumption of effective practice is that therapists will consider the use of culturally sensitive treatment with culturally diverse clients. The question is how does a therapists decide if, when, and how to utilize a cultural intervention, a culturally sensitive therapy, or a culturally sensitive intervention, instead of a conventional Western intervention, such as cognitive–behavioral therapy (CBT)? Unfortunately, graduate coursework and the professional literature provide little clarity and few specific guidelines for answering this question. If textbooks on treating culturally diverse clients address the issue at all it is only indirectly (Paniagua, 2005). Nevertheless, this essential competency is becoming increasingly important in everyday practice. This chapter addresses this basic question directly. It begins by briefly distinguishing cultural intervention, culturally sensitive therapy, and culturally sensitive intervention. Then it provides general guidelines for making such decisions. Finally, the chapter provides illustrations of various forms of interventions when cultural factors are operative.

## CULTURAL INTERVENTION, CULTURALLY SENSITIVE THERAPY, OR CULTURALLY SENSITIVE INTERVENTION

This section briefly defines and distinguishes three different ways of providing culturally sensitive treatment. These include cultural intervention, culturally sensitive therapy, and culturally sensitive intervention.

## Cultural Intervention

A cultural intervention is an intervention or healing method or activity that is consistent with the client's belief system regarding healing. Examples include the use of talking or healing circles, the use of prayer or exorcism, or the involvement of traditional healers from that client's culture. For a mainstream culture therapist, the use of cultural interventions may necessitate collaboration with, or referral to, an expert. However, it may also be possible for a mainstream culture therapist to begin the treatment process by focusing on core cultural values, such as *respito* and *personalismo*, in an effort to increase "clinician credibility" and collaboration.

## Culturally Sensitive Therapy

Culturally sensitive therapy, also referred to as culturally centered therapy, is defined as a psychotherapeutic intervention that addresses the cultural characteristics of diverse clients, that is, beliefs, customs, attitudes, and socioeconomic and historical context (La Roche & Christopher, 2008). Because they utilize traditional healing methods and pathways, such approaches are appealing to certain clients. An example of a culturally sensitive therapy is *cuento* therapy. This therapy addresses culturally relevant variables such as *familismo* and *personalismo* through the use of folk tales (*cuentos*) and is used with Puerto Rican children. *Morita* therapy is another example of a culturally sensitive therapy. It originated in Japan and is now used throughout the world for a wide range of disorders ranging from shyness to schizophrenia (Li & He, 2008). Although these and other culturally sensitive therapies are effective and find favor with ethnic clients, an obvious shortcoming is that there are relatively few therapists who are competent to practice these approaches in the United States. It has also been noted that culturally sensitive therapies seem to be less effective with more highly acculturated individuals, who might not resonate with approaches that utilize traditional healing pathways (Cardemil, 2008). In other words, culturally sensitive therapies may work better with clients with lower levels of acculturation.

## Culturally Sensitive Intervention

A culturally sensitive intervention is a conventional Western intervention that has been adapted or modified to be responsive to the cultural characteristics of a particular client. CBT interventions are not only the most often utilized interventions, but are most often modified to be culturally sensitive (Hayes & Iwanasa, 2006). One author refers to this process as "making CBT more culturally responsive" (Hayes, 2006, p. 8). An increasing number of journal articles, book chapters, and books (Hayes & Iwanasa, 2006) address adapting CBT, and a few other treatment approaches, for culturally sensitive practice. A special issue of *Cognitive and Behavioral Practice* (vol. 13, issue 4) in 2006 has a number of articles about adapting cognitive and behavior therapies to clients of various ethnic groups.

It is not unreasonable to assume that of the three broad categories of interventions, culturally sensitive interventions will be utilized most often in clinical settings. This is not only because most mainstream cultural therapists have little training and experience with the other two types, but also because of the increasing professional literature on such clinically sensitive interventions, particularly adaptations of CBT for various ethnic groups and presenting problems and diagnoses.

## GUIDELINES FOR MAKING DECISIONS ABOUT CULTURALLY SENSITIVE TREATMENT

The following are guidelines for making decisions about when and if to plan and implement culturally sensitive treatments. These guidelines assume that the client's cultural identity, level of acculturation, explanatory model, and treatment expectations have been elicited and that both client and therapist are willing to discuss treatment options. It should be noted that these guidelines are tentative because they are based primarily on clinical experience rather than on quantitative research.

1. If a client identifies largely with the mainstream culture and has a high level of acculturation and there is no obvious indication of prejudice, racism, or related bias, consider conventional interventions as the primary treatment method. However, the therapist should be mindful that culturally sensitive interventions might also be indicated as the treatment process develops.
2. If a client identifies largely with the mainstream culture and has a high level of acculturation and there is an indication of prejudice, racism, or related bias, consider culturally sensitive interventions or cultural interventions for cultural concerns. In addition, it may

be useful to utilize conventional interventions for related non-cultural concerns, that is, personality dynamics.
3. If a client identifies largely with his or her ethnic background and level of acculturation is low, consider cultural interventions or culturally sensitive therapy. This may necessitate collaboration with or referral to an expert, an initial discussion of core cultural values, or both.
4. If a client's cultural identity is mainstream and acculturation level is high but that of the client's family is low, such that the presenting concern is largely a matter of cultural discrepancy, consider a cultural intervention with the client and the family. However, if there is an imminent crisis situation, consider conventional interventions to reduce the crisis. After it is reduced or eliminated, consider introducing cultural interventions or culturally sensitive therapy.

## ILLUSTRATIONS OF UTILIZATION OF CULTURALLY SENSITIVE TREATMENT

The following four cases illustrate these guidelines for making treatment decisions. The second case is inspired by Ridley and Kelly (2007), the third by Añez, Silva, Paris, and Bedregal (2008), and the fourth by Hampson and Beavers (2004).

### Case 1: Geri

This case illustrates the first guideline. We return to the now familiar case of Geri. You will recall that she is a female African American administrative assistant who experienced a 3-week onset of depressed mood and increased social isolation following word that she was to be promoted and transferred out of a relatively close-knit work team. At the start of treatment, she has only one close friend and a relative whom she can trust. She lives alone and has never been in a long-term relationship or married. She has worked at the same company since graduating from college. She is a fourth-generation African American, and she and her parents appear to be highly acculturated. Her grandparents migrated to the Midwest from Mississippi in the late 1930s. Although she attends an annual Black pride festival in the summer, she is not otherwise active in the Black community; neither are her parents. There are two other African Americans in

216

her office, but she has not become close to either of them, saying, "All they want to do is talk about men, which I'm not into." Although she was reared as a Baptist, she no longer considers herself to be religious. She identified herself as a middle-class heterosexual woman and describes herself and her parents as middle class in values and orientation, although more identified with their African American roots.

Based on the previously described cultural formulation (Chapter 10) and treatment formulation (Chapter 11), Geri's avoidant personality dynamics, rather than cultural factors, were primarily operative in her current clinical presentation. It was also forecast that no obvious cultural factors would negatively impact or interfere with therapy process or outcomes. Accordingly, conventional treatment was recommended. It would consist of combining medication and CBT with a focus on symptom reduction and returning to work.

**Case Commentary**

Although this case involves an African American female who works in a corporation that is primarily Caucasian, the question of cultural treatment is largely moot. Based on the overall case conceptualization, the recommendation was to utilize conventional interventions. The reason was that there were no obvious indications for cultural treatment be it cultural interventions, culturally sensitive therapy, or culturally sensitive interventions. However, this decision is subject to review and change if these interventions are not effective or cultural factors later become operative as the therapeutic process plays out.

## Case 2: Ana

This case illustrates the second guideline. Ana is a 25-year-old single, first-generation Mexican American female. She presented at her local community mental health center with complaints of "not feeling myself lately." Ana described her current mood as depressed and admitted that she had been isolating herself and sleeping more than usual. She had recently been diagnosed with hypothyroidism, which could account for her decreased energy and low mood. However, she thought "there was more to it than that." When asked what she meant, she said she was "not doing a good job dealing with tough issues." During the interview she presented as shy and passive while her mood was somewhat sad with constricted affect. She is the older of two siblings and reports that her father died 3 years ago

217

of cancer. She and her family migrated from Mexico to Chicago when she was in first grade, during which she took bilingual classes, which helped in adjusting and succeeding in school. Currently she lives with her mother and sister in a predominantly Hispanic community.

When her explanatory model was being elicited, Ana believed her down feeling was due to distress and disappointment about leaving medical school. She withdraw in the middle of her second year despite having a full scholarship because she felt excluded from a study group and the informal student network. She had also overheard a group of white students saying that minorities were admitted only because of affirmative action. This was hurtful to Ana because she felt she was admitted on merit, that is, high MCATs and GPA. She had always dreamed of being a physician but felt she couldn't return to school because of her fear of reexperiencing racism. She also disclosed that while in middle school, she was hit in the head with a rock during a confrontation between white and Hispanic students. Subsequently, she avoided all confrontations. It is notable that she refused to confront the medical school situation and quietly withdrew. Her expectations for treatment were for "help in being less thin-skinned and better facing tough issues." With Ana's consent, the clinician subsequently interviewed her mother and sister, who also believed that Ana's depression stemmed from her withdrawal from medical school. Ana identified herself as a "middle-class American with Mexican roots" with a high level of acculturation. It was notable that on the acculturation scale for Mexican Americans, she endorsed items such as "girls and women should defer to men and authority figures." On an assignment to log her interpersonal reactions to anyone she had contact with between the first and second sessions, she coded all of her reactions as withdrawing or submissive irrespective of whether others were males, authority figures, or other. This suggests that her avoidant and passive behavior has roots in both culture and personality.

Her situation was conceptualized as increased depressive symptoms and social isolation that were triggered and exacerbated by her experience with racism leading to her dropping out of school recently. Prominent was her avoidant behavior, which seemed to be exacerbated by both her avoidant personality as well as cultural beliefs, which appeared to be operative in her response to Caucasian medical students.

The mutually agreed-on treatment plan involved four treatment targets. The first was depressive symptoms, which would be addressed by her physician, who would continue her thyroid medication and add an antidepressant. The second target was her avoidant behavior that was culturally influenced, for which culturally sensitive interventions would be directed at dealing more effectively with "tough issues" such as prejudice and racism. The clinic's Hispanic female therapist would be involved with this treatment target as well as the third target in which she would serve as cotherapist with Ana's Caucasian therapist in group therapy. This third target involved the personality component of Ana's avoidant style for which conflict resolution and assertive communication skills training would be a central part of the group work. The fourth target involved career exploration, including the possibility of reinstatement in medical school. Her therapist would consult with and involve the school's minority affairs director, who was an African American male.

### Case Commentary

Had Ana's explanatory model of depression and avoidance and her treatment expectations been more culture based, consideration would have been given to cultural interventions. Similarly, if there had been a discrepancy on acculturation levels between Ana and her mother and younger sister, cultural interventions might have played a more prominent role in the treatment plan.

## Case 3: Francisco

This case illustrates the third guideline. Francisco is an unmarried 27-year-old first-generation Mexican American male who was court ordered for treatment at a community mental health clinic. Court-ordered psychotherapy is an option this judge has exercised with first-time offenders convicted of driving while under the influence of alcohol. Twelve sessions were stipulated, and Francisco was assigned a European American male therapist. In their first session, the therapist completed an integrative diagnostic assessment interview, with particular emphasis on the mental status exam, developmental history, and a social and cultural history. While taking the cultural history, the therapist elicited Francisco 's explanatory model and expectations for treatment.

The social history revealed that Francisco and his parents migrated from Mexico to the Chicago area when he was 10. Since graduating from high school, he has worked as a mechanic in a small body shop owned by his uncle. Francisco acknowledges that most of his friends are Hispanic, that he speaks primarily Spanish although he is bilingual, and that he is "close to the old ways." When the therapist began to elicit his explanatory model, Francisco at first denied having any problems. However, when asked why the court had ordered him to therapy, he said that his propensity to abuse alcohol "runs in my blood" and noted that his father and grandfather were alcoholics. He also believed that his drinking was due to a "hex," which, he was told by his grandmother, was placed on the men in his family by a *curandero* in their Mexican village. Francisco was insistent that this hex accounted for his craving of alcohol, particularly tequila. In terms of his expectations for therapy, Francisco believed that only a *curandero* could take away the hex on his alcohol cravings and that he hoped the clinic could arrange this.

Because this client's motivation for psychotherapy appeared to be somewhat limited, the therapist wondered what possible therapeutic leverage might be available in working with Francisco. Because of the client's low level of acculturation, the therapist considered that *confianza*, that is, the Latino value of the trust and intimacy an individual places on relationships, might be an operative cultural value for his client. Thus, with about 10 minutes remaining in the first session that therapist asked:

*Th.:*   How important is *confianza* to you when you're first getting to know somebody?

*Cl.:*   Oh, it is important to me. It's important to all my people.

*Th.:*   Exactly *how* is it important to you?

*Cl.:*   Well, you've got to know if you can trust someone with your stuff. I mean I wouldn't let somebody borrow my tools if I didn't know how he would treat them. Some people you can trust and some you can't. You just got to watch them and see what they do.

*Th.:*   I suppose that applies to me, too.

*Cl.:*   (pause) Yeah.

*Th.:*   So, on a scale from 1 to 10, where 1 is the lowest and 10 is the highest, how much *confianza* do you have in me and our relationship?

*Cl.:*   I'd say about 4.

*Th.:*   All right. So we're at a 4 right now. It makes sense that you would not have much *confianza* when you meet somebody for the first time.

*Cl.:*   Yeah.

*Th.:*   Well, why a 4 and not just a 1?

| | |
|---|---|
| *Cl.:* | (pause) Well, you're the one with the degree and the license on the wall over there (pointing). So you should know what you're doing. |
| *Th.:* | Any other reasons? |
| *Cl.:* | My friend Jaime says this clinic is good. He's doing much better now. This is a good place. You know that judge could have sent me to a worse place. (laughs) |
| *Th.:* | (laughs) So, hearing that a friend of yours had a good experience with this clinic is important to you? |
| *Cl.:* | It is very important. |
| *Th.:* | And, you trust Jaime's judgment. |
| *Cl.:* | I do. He's my best friend and he's like a brother to me. |

The therapist considered Francisco's rating of 4 meant *confianza* was average, but it also meant that the remaining distance from 4 to 10 indicated that the client was somewhat ambivalent toward therapy and the therapist. It also implied that as Francisco's rating increased, his engagement in the treatment process would increase and presumably so would his readiness and resolve to make changes in his life. To verify this conjecture, the therapist asked:

| | |
|---|---|
| *Th.:* | So, what needs to happen for the rating to go from a 4 to a 6? |
| *Cl.:* | (pause) Well, maybe you would pay more attention to me. You know, stop looking at the clock, and … |
| *Th.:* | And? |
| *Cl.:* | And, I really need your help in filling out those court papers. |
| *Th.:* | (nods head in agreement) Sure. You will have my complete attention, and I'll start filling out these court papers now and finish them after our session. I know these are important to you. |
| *Cl.:* | They really are. |
| *Th.:* | So, let's take a look at this top form. (pause) I see they want some information on you that I don't have. Can you give me it? |
| *Cl.:* | Sure, tell me what you need to know. |

Information is provided and the forms are completed. A follow-up appointment is set. As the session ends, Francisco thanks the therapist and shakes his hand. In the third session, the therapist asks Francisco to rate his *confianza* in their relationship and he says, "about a 7 or so." In their last session, the therapist summarized progress made, reflective of Francisco's increased readiness for change.

**Case Commentary**

This case illustrates the use of a cultural intervention, specifically a discussion of core cultural values to develop a positive alliance with the client. It appears that the cultural values discussion has effected some measure of clinical credibility. The therapist next discussed treatment of the alcohol craving and alcohol abuse, and his recommendation for Francisco was to become involved in a 12-step group at the clinic, consisting of other recent male immigrants from Mexico. At first Francisco resisted this plan and stated again that nothing would work until the hex was broken. The clinic had a working relationship with a *curandero* in the community whom the therapist would contact about the hex ritual. Negotiation ensued and both agreed that Francisco would become involved in the group *and* also be prayed over by the *curandero* with the expectation that the two treatments together would be more "powerful."

## Case 4: Marcos Family

This case illustrates the fourth guideline. The Marcos family were self-referred to a community mental health clinic because of a "crisis with our younger daughter." That daughter, Shelly, was 19 and a first-semester senior at a public high school. She was accompanied by her father, Fredrico, her mother, Grace, and her 23-year-old sister, Rocea. The family had emigrated from the Philippines to the southwestern United States when Rocea was 3 years old. A year later Shelly was born. Mr. Marcos holds a graduate degree and works as a research consultant for a state agency. Mrs. Marcos holds a degree in education but has not ever worked as a teacher; instead she is a full-time homemaker and mother.

The parents had been considerably troubled by Shelly's defiance and acting-out behaviors, including surreptitiously leaving home in the middle of the night, taking the car without permission, and running up her credit cards to the maximum. In defense of her behavior, Shelly complained that her parents were too strict, and she had to sneak out and defy them so that she could have a halfway "normal" life. These behaviors noticeably affected Mr. Marcos, whose hypertension worsened and migraine headaches increased in frequency. Probably because of these stressors, he was involved in three car accidents in the past 7 weeks. The parents shared the view that all of these problems were the result of Shelly becoming entirely "too American" and no longer following "the Filipino way" that was expected of her. Mrs. Marcos reported that the situation had become so serious that she feared she would lose her husband through "a stroke or car accident" and her daughter through "running away or worse."

The whole family was present at the first session and during that time the therapist observed several key interactions. The most telling of these was that Mr. Marcos controlled every exchange in the family. He directed who was to talk, he corrected "errors" of others' comments, presumably because they differed from his. Surprisingly, his wife, who said very little during this session, would occasionally redirect or contradict his comments. It is noteworthy that these exchanges were all done with little emotion, in a very mechanical tone. When Shelly disagreed or tried to defend her behavior as "normal," her father would lecture her on how she was threatening to destroy the family by not following the Filipino way. Rocea appeared to be a passive, sad, and seemingly ineffectual person who deferred to her parents. Shelly referred to her sister as "the tattler." A tone of invasiveness characterized the parents, who labeled their daughters as the "American" and their "little mama." Shelly was clearly the scapegoat in this family.

Based on these observations, the following case conceptualization of the family's dynamics was developed: A maladaptive circular interaction pattern was evident, that is, act out, ground Shelly, more acting out, and so on, in which control themes were prominent, that is, rigid control that gave way to chaos as the effectiveness of parental control was defied. Core family values were expectations for perfect behavior, condemnation for not following the "correct" culture, and dominance–submission. Compliance and impression management were evident; that is, family members needed to act "correctly" and suppress the expression of negative feelings. Shelly was the family's "black sheep," and the family was stuck and could not move forward without outside assistance. The family structure was control oriented and lacking in intimacy and spontaneity, and the family was seeking help to increase their control over their "black sheep," not to relinquish control.

Finally, while Shelly's cultural identity was that of a mainstream American and her level of acculturation was high, the rest of the family self-identified as Filipinos and had lower levels of acculturation.

The therapist concluded that any effort by the therapists to increase the control over the offender, challenge the control of the tyrant, or deal with the cultural conflict directly would result in failure. Effort to increase control would only solidify the cyclical control themes. Challenging the father's role and control would inevitably result in the controlling member pulling the family out of treatment. Dealing with the cultural dimension directly might work, but given the seriousness of the crisis on the family, especially the father's health, individual and family dynamics should be dealt with first. Instead, the only therapeutic leverage is to go below the control issues, to the underlying feelings of the family members. Presumably, because family members are upset, disappointed, and lonely, helping them address what they miss and long for can be a powerful impetus for change. The therapist expected that different factions would attempt to pull the therapist to their side of the struggle. Accordingly, the therapist was mindful of refraining from judgments and side-taking. As the therapist focused on the lost hopes and dreams of family members, it became clear that there were no specifically defined villains and victims and that they were all hurting. The therapist realized the importance of recognizing and responding to the emotional needs of Mr. Marcos, for unless he felt understood, it was quite likely that he would pull the family out of therapy.

Five therapeutic targets and goals were specified. The first was to develop a focus on the feeling level, especially with family members asking for more of what they liked, rather than rigid rule structures. The second was to emphasize individual and family dynamics rather than the cultural conflict of American versus Filipino values. Cultural dynamics were recognized but would be addressed *indirectly* because of the current crisis facing the family, that is, the seriousness of the father's health problems and his recent chain of car accidents. The third was for both parents to learn cooperation and negotiation skills and come to share parenting duties and roles. The fourth was to assist Rocea in developing some sense of autonomy in such a way that her parents would view her individuation as a sign of individual competence rather than of defiance. The fifth was that Shelly would learn that as parental control softened, she would have less need to rebel in order to meet her needs.

As the family began dealing with the first target, it became clear that each member was feeling isolated and lonely. The guilt-inducing and controlling exchanges that characterized the family began to be interspersed with questions such as "Well, what would you like to see more of?" Mr. Marcos found it much harder than others to address the feeling level. He also had more difficulty with the second target, that of personalizing rather than culturalizing the deviant behavior. However, an important breakthrough occurred when the parental dyad began to address the third target, working as a team. The more Mr. Marcos observed that his wife was reasonably competent in talking with their daughters and encouraging them to cooperate, the more he felt that he could relinquish control. Surprisingly, he "allowed" his wife and daughters to continue family therapy without him. This was a clearly major step in altering his rigid control efforts.

Once this step was reached, the three women were able to negotiate on some key matters, including a more modest social schedule for Shelly and some independence for Rocea. Rocea began taking a course at a local college and joined a few activity groups at her church, and Mrs. Marcos registered with the school system as a substitute teacher. Mrs. Marcos, Rocea, and Shelly attended a total of 15 sessions. During that last session, all reported a higher degree of satisfaction. There was less testy behavior on Shelly's part, respect for each other was higher, and negotiation and overall interactions were much smoother at home, especially since Mr. Marcos had decided that he did not need to control everyone and everything. It was also reported that Mr. Marcos was happier and significantly less stressed at home. Interestingly, throughout the course of therapy, the level of acculturation for Mrs. Marcos, Rocea, and presumably, Mr. Marcos, had increased considerably, presumably as a result of the therapeutic process.

**Case Commentary**
The decision to address cultural dynamics, that is, the clash of the "American way" versus the "Filipino way," *indirectly* rather than directly was carefully considered. Based on the therapist's negative previous experience in similar crisis situations when cultural conflicts were dealt with directly, and because of Mrs. Marcos's real concern that she might "lose" both her husband and her daughter if things didn't change quickly, the decision to focus primarily on family dynamics was made. As Mrs. Marcos and Rocea became independent and individuated, a corresponding increase in interdependence of family members was noted. Indirectly, this appeared to foster an increase in their level of acculturation. Given that family stress was significantly reduced and family harmony increased, Mr. Marcos apparently accepted this increased acculturation.

# 17

# Recognize and Resolve Treatment-Interfering Factors

*Treatment-interfering behaviors* is a term introduced by Marsha Linehan (1993) to describe behaviors that clients bring to bear within and between sessions and which impede the progress of therapy. Common treatment-interfering behaviors include failure to attend sessions consistently, failure to keep to contracted agreements, arguing with the therapist, refusal to engage in conversation, and behavior that oversteps therapist limits. While this designation gives a name to a class of behaviors that are problematic in therapy, Linehan's designation focuses entirely on the client. However, clinical observation suggests that besides clients, other factors can and do impede treatment progress. Accordingly, this book adopts a broader designation: *therapy-interfering factors,* which include client behaviors but also recognize the influences of the therapist, client–therapist relationship, and intervention factors as impediments to treatment progress.

Effective treatments require that therapists anticipate, recognize, and resolve these factors. Savvy therapists anticipate therapy-interfering factors from the first contact with the client, particularly while eliciting the developmental and social history. The potential of such therapy-interfering factors, as well as other potential treatment obstacles and challenges, should be included in the case conceptualization. Subsequently, appropriate resolution strategies can be contemplated before these factors emerge in the treatment process. This chapter provides a listing of the various interfering factors: client, therapist, client–therapist relationship, and treatment. Then it illustrates various strategies for resolving specific interfering factors.

## TYPES OF THERAPY-INTERFERING FACTORS

Four types of therapy-interfering factors are observable in clinical situations. They are client, therapist, client–therapist relationship, and treatment factors. Specific factors are listed for each category. Judith Beck (1995, 2005) and Ledley, Marx, and Heimberg (2006) provide useful descriptions and strategies for dealing with several client factors that interfere with therapy. Chapter 4 of this book addresses client resistance and ambivalence. Chapters 5 and 6 of this book provide descriptions and strategies for dealing with client–therapist relationship problems, particularly alliance ruptures and transference enactments. Table 17.1 lists some common examples.

**Table 17.1** Common Examples of Therapy-Interfering Factors

| Factor Types | Common Examples |
|---|---|
| Client | Client pathology (personality disorders) or high levels of reactance |
| | Refusal and outright resistance |
| | Ambivalence |
| | Treatment-interfering core beliefs, automatic thoughts, or other attitudes |
| | Treatment-interfering behaviors, both in session and between sessions |
| Therapist | Therapist errors, for example, inaccurate or inadequate case conceptualization |
| | Therapist inexperience, incompetence, or negligence |
| Client–therapist relationship | Alliance strains and ruptures |
| | Transference–countertransference enactments |
| Treatment and intervention factors | *Internal Factors:* |
| | Infrequency of sessions and/or scheduling problems |
| | Outside noise or distractions |
| | *External Factors:* |
| | Comorbid medical conditions |
| | Limited healthy social support system |

## PROTOCOL FOR RECOGNIZING AND RESOLVING THERAPY-INTERFERING FACTORS

Recognition is the first step in eliminating or reducing the impact of the interfering factor. The following protocol is not intended to be exhaustive in scope but rather covers the more common therapy-interfering situations.

1. Determine the most likely interfering factor or factors that are operative (e.g., shifting to another topic when distressed, avoiding self-disclosure, homework noncompliance, etc.).

   - Client
   - Therapist
   - Client–therapist relationship
   - Treatment

2. Determine the most likely explanation or cause for the interfering factor (e.g., a client factor).

   - Client-interfering belief
   - Fear of failing at change effort
   - Client's high reactance—unwillingness to relinquish any control to therapist
   - Unwillingness to deal with the consequences of change; for example, if the client's condition (e.g., anxiety) decreases, the client may have to get on with his or her career or deal with a difficult relationship
   - Transference
   - A combination of any of the above

3. Focus an intervention at that explanation or causal factor (e.g., Avoidant Personality Disorder).

   - Suspecting personality disorder dynamics are operative, identify the client's core beliefs about self and others that help identify the client's personality disorder, in this case, Avoidant Personality Disorder.
   - Recognize the typical overdeveloped and underdeveloped strategies, therapy-interfering beliefs, and therapy-interfering behaviors of the Avoidant Personality Disorder (described by Beck, 2005, pp. 55–57).

- Process a particular therapy-interfering behavior (e.g., shifting to another topic when distressed) in terms of the underlying core beliefs about self and others and the related overdeveloped strategy.
- Point out when the client shifts topics and encourage the client to recognize the distressing feeling and thought.

## ILLUSTRATION: STRATEGIES FOR RESOLVING THERAPY-INTERFERING FACTORS

This section describes three therapy-interfering factors and illustrates a strategy for dealing with each. Because client-interfering behaviors are the most common of the therapy-interfering factors, all three examples involve such client behaviors. The first and third cases are inspired by Beck (2005), and the second is inspired by Ledley et al. (2006).

### Dealing with a Client's Interfering Beliefs and Behavior

In the following example, a client's underlying core beliefs or schemas and rules are identified as the cause of the client's therapy-interfering behavior.

Jessica is a sophomore who went to the university counseling center for help because of her difficulty in choosing a major. She had completed three semesters of required core courses and was now being asked to declare a major. Her parents wanted her to get an accounting degree and do bookkeeping in the family business. She had thought about teaching art or being an anthropologist but wasn't sure that she had the "constitution" to be an elementary school teacher. An initial evaluation revealed that she was the second of four siblings and described herself as a "little runt" who was always sick. Her mother was emotionally withdrawn and demanding, and her father was physically abusive. The family owned a small printing company, which was barely successful, in a changing neighborhood. In the first session after the intake evaluation, soon after the session began, the therapist attempted to establish a treatment focus. Jessica's response was:

Cl.:     This is just useless. Nothing can help me now.
Th.:     What's useless right now?
Cl.:     I don't know.

*Th.:*     What's the main challenge you're facing right now?

*Cl.:*     I already told you: They want me to make a decision about my major.

*Th.:*     And decision making is hard for you right now, especially about your career.

*Cl.:*     (loudly) I don't want to deal with career decisions … or any decisions.

*Th.:*     Isn't the third semester the usual time for students to declare a major?

*Cl.:*     My advisor is demanding that I do something I'm not ready for. She's crazy if she thinks she can force me to be a teacher or a business major, or whatever.

Fortunately, as part of the initial evaluation, Jessica completed the *Personality Belief Questionnaire* (reprinted in Appendix B of Beck, 2005). It helped the therapist recognize Jessica's self-beliefs as being hopeless, incompetent, and vulnerable, and her beliefs about others as rejecting, demanding, hurtful, and critical. Further inquiry identified her conditional assumptions and rules: "If I avoid difficult decisions, I'll be all right," "If I blame others I'll be safe," and "I'll get hurt if I let my guard down." Related to these rules were her overdeveloped coping strategies: Avoid making major decisions, blame others, and guard against being harmed by others. This constellation is common in individuals with Borderline Personality Disorder and although the therapist decided making a definitive Axis II diagnosis now was premature, he realized that Jessica's underlying core beliefs, assumptions, and coping strategies had been activated and provided a useful explanation for Jessica's treatment-interfering behavior of resisting efforts to discuss the presenting problem.

*Th.:*     So what problem can we work on right now?

*Cl.:*     I don't know. I told you before it's useless. Nothing will make a difference. It's totally hopeless.

*Th.:*     So we can work on your feeling of being hopeless. Do you want to start off talking about school or about your parents?

*Cl.:*     I don't know. Whatever will make a difference.

*Th.:*     Would it be okay to begin with your thought: Nothing will make a difference. It's hopeless?

*Cl.:*     I suppose.

*Th.:*     Right now, how much do you believe that making a decision about your major won't make a difference?

| *Cl.:* | (pause) Pretty much. |
|---|---|
| *Th.:* | Okay, I hear that. So, Jessica, tell me, what would be the disadvantages if you did not choose a major soon? |
| *Cl.:* | Probably not being able to get into a major for another. That would mean I couldn't take any advanced courses for a while. It would delay everything. |
| *Th.:* | Any other disadvantages? |
| *Cl.:* | My parents would really be on my case. And, my dad could make good on his threat to cut off paying my tuition or board after this semester. |
| *Th.:* | So, what advantages would there be for you to choose a major? |
| *Cl.:* | Well, it would get my parents off my back. And, I guess I could keep hanging with my friends. Maybe even have a class or two with them. That would be cool. |
| *Th.:* | So, there are some clear advantages and disadvantages. Right now, which seem stronger: the advantages or disadvantages? |
| *Cl.:* | I guess the advantages have a little edge. But it's overwhelming to think about doing it. |
| *Th.:* | How overwhelming would it be? On a scale of 1 to 100, how overwhelming would it be? |
| *Cl.:* | Say about 65 or so. |
| *Th.:* | So moderately overwhelming, but it doesn't sound like it's totally hopeless. |
| *Cl.:* | Yeah. If you put it that way. |

**Case Commentary**

In the first therapy session Jessica's basic coping strategies were operative: Feel hopeless, avoid career decisions, guard against harm, and blame others. These strategies accounted for Jessica's therapy-interfering behavior of resisting efforts to discuss the presenting problem. The therapist recognized these dynamics and decided to indirectly address the underlying interfering belief of hopelessness by having her weigh advantages and disadvantages. But it would have to be done cautiously and adroitly or Jessica might be too threatened and prematurely terminate treatment. This case illustrates that therapy-interfering behaviors, reflective of the client's coping strategies, can be manifest very early in therapy, particularly when underlying core beliefs and rules are activated as the therapist endeavors to focus treatment.

## Dealing with Clients Who Use Diversionary Tactics

Seeking out treatment and being "ready" to engage in therapy do not necessarily mean the client is willing to work on the problem that brought him or her to treatment. In fact some clients engage in diversionary tactics rather than change. Diversionary tactics are client behaviors that distract, divert, delay, or deflect attention from addressing a treatment issue or engaging in a change effort. Clients may report new and overwhelming stressors in the past few days, which they want addressed now instead of proceeding with the specified treatment focus. They may say that a pressing concern that had brought them to treatment is not as important as a new concern, when in fact, it is still troublesome. Or, they may express hesitation or concern about the effectiveness or safety of a mutually agreeable treatment intervention or strategy. These are some of the many diversionary tactics that clients may display.

The following case illustrates the therapist's recognition of, and patience with, the client's uneasiness about treatment and the delaying tactic he employed.

Jack W. is a 27-year-old male attorney who presented for cognitive–behavioral therapy with an 8-month history of increasing agoraphobia. When it was first diagnosed by his primary care physician he had been tried on medication and, due to unacceptable side effects, he stopped the medication and sought therapy. He met with a psychodynamically oriented therapist for five sessions and, finding it "not useful," he dropped out. Lately, he has been becoming increasingly homebound, which was interfering with his law practice as well as with his marriage plans. When exposure treatment was introduced in the first session as the treatment of choice for his condition, he seemed reluctant and wary of an intervention in which he would expose himself to fearful situations. Nevertheless, Jack agreed to the protocol, which was to begin in the second session. As that session began he indicated that he was distraught about his law firm partner who was upset that Jack didn't show up for a deposition, and he wanted to talk about it. In the following session, he began by saying that his fiancée had just threatened to call off their engagement until he got well. Anticipating that Jack would present another crisis at the next session, the therapist suspected that diversion was operative and planned to deal with it directly. In response to Jack's mention of yet another crisis—his father had been in a car accident—in the beginning of the fourth session, the therapist asked:

*Th.:* Do you see a connection between what's been happening in your life these past few weeks and your anxiety and agoraphobia?

*Cl.:* Yeah. All this stress is making me even more fearful of being out and around.

*Th.:* That's a useful observation. What are your thoughts on how the relationship might work in the other direction? I mean, does anxiety play any role in the stressors you've been experiencing?

*Cl.:* I'm not sure what you mean.

*Th.:* Well, what about that difficult situation 3 weeks ago when Sally said that she might break off the engagement. Did anxiety have anything to do with that situation?

*Cl.:* Are you kidding? It had everything to do with it. She was just sick of it all. Just look at me; I can't do anything anymore! I can't travel, can't go to restaurants or movies, and can't even go to my health club anymore. We used to do all things together. And now with this stuff going on I can't do anything anymore.

*Th.:* What about the recent problems at your law firm?

*Cl.:* My partner has been furious with me for the last several days. We were working on two cases with tight deadlines and we're both really stressed. Then I couldn't make it to another law office for a deposition I was to do because of overwhelming fear of driving on the freeway. So at the last minute he had to drop what he was doing on his case and do the deposition. He was furious.

*Th.:* So you see a direct link between your anxiety and those stressors.

*Cl.:* Yeah, I guess I see the link.

*Th.:* And, last week your dad was in a car accident and it really affected you. So for the past 3 weeks you've come to our sessions and talked about all the stressful things that have been happening. (pause) Based on what I've just summarized, might there be another way we could address your problems?

*Cl.:* I'm not sure. All I can think about when I'm here is how bad things have gone that week.

*Th.:* Well, what if another way would be to talk about preventing such stressors from affecting you in the next week?

*Cl.:* (sarcastically) Don't I wish that could happen.

*Th.:* Well, let's look at this possibility more closely. If anxiety and agoraphobia play a direct role in these kinds of interpersonal situations, what would happen if we directly addressed the anxiety?

Cl.: Are you saying that if we had worked on my anxiety, Sally wouldn't have threatened to call off the engagement and that my partner wouldn't have become so furious with me (pause) and that my life would be great?

Th.: There's no way anyone could know the answers, and there's no way we can change what has already happened. But, maybe we could focus our work so that things would be better when a relationship problem comes up or things could be better the next time there is a deadline crunch.

Cl.: So you're saying that if my anxiety gets better, I'll have an easier time dealing with things?

Th.: Well, do you think your life would be easier?

Cl.: Huh! Right now I'm not sure Sally even wants to spend time with me much less marry me. And, I'm already dreading our next deadline. For God's sake, I can hardly leave my apartment now!

Th.: Wouldn't it be worth the effort to stay focused on your panic for the next couple of sessions and see the effect on your life outside of therapy?

Cl.: Are you talking about getting out there and practicing those exposures?

Th.: That's exactly what I mean.

Cl.: I don't really want to, but what other alternative do I have?

Th.: When we discussed other alternative treatments before, exposure came out as the most feasible to work for you. You'll recall that you couldn't continue taking those different medications because of side effects, and even though in your previous therapy you got some insight into your problems your anxiety and agoraphobia worsened. So, when we began working together a month ago, exposure seemed to be the treatment of choice.

Cl.: Yeah, I recall all that and my agreement to do the exposure. But, I'm kind of afraid that if it doesn't work, I'll be a hopeless loser, and no woman will want me and I won't be able to keep a job. It makes me panicky just to talk about this.

Th.: (empathically) I hear the distress in your voice and I can it see in your face. For many clients, the idea of taking the first step in exposure seems overwhelming. The success of taking that first step increases the client's confidence in going ahead with it. Success and confidence continue to build. (pause) As I think

235

> back, all of the clients that I have coached with this intervention have been successful. They have all greatly decreased and even eliminated their incapacitating anxiety. I have every reason to believe it will work for you, too.
>
> *Cl.:*     I remember you saying that, but I don't think I really believed you. I want to believe that it will work for me.
>
> *Th.:*     We'll start with low level exposures. As the saying goes, "Seeing is believing," and I think you'll be a believer.
>
> *Cl.:*     I want to be a believer. I want to get over this now.

**Case Commentary**

The fact that the therapist remained patient with the client and allowed him to ventilate concerns as they came up was probably necessary to solidify a therapeutic alliance. In a sense, the client "tested" the therapist sufficiently before trusting the therapist's clinical experience and judgment. Instead of confronting the matter directly, the therapist helped the client connect the proposed treatment intervention plan directly to the client's distress.

## Dealing With Client Refusal

The following case illustrates one way to deal with client refusal when the likely cause for therapy-interfering behavior is high reactance (i.e., individual reacts negatively to efforts to control him or her) rather than any specific underlying interfering core belief or rules. Two typical responses to this and other forms of resistance are to confront or coerce the individual or to withdraw and acquiesce. *The third way is the therapeutic way.* Thus, instead of confronting such resistance directly or leaving or dropping the expectation or demand, the therapist instead reflects content or feelings and rolls with the resistance (Miller & Rollnick, 2002).

Jeff is a 42-year-old chief operating officer for a software company who had been experiencing low level, chronic depression for the past 3 years. He prides himself on his independence. He has recently begun therapy at a mood disorders clinic that routinely utilizes rating scales and questionnaires. At the start of the second session (the first session involved a structured evaluation interview), the therapist began by asking:

> *Th.:*     Let's check on your depression. Have you filled out the depression rating scale?

*Cl.:*   (emphatically) No!

*Th.:*   Well, the rating scale is a good way for me to know how you've been feeling since the last time we met. Would you fill it out after our session today?

*Cl.:*   I don't really want to fill out anything. These things aren't helpful to me.

*Th.:*   Then can we come up with another way of rating your moods? Can you give me an estimate of your mood on a 1 to 10, with 10 representing the best and 1 the worst mood ever? What would be the rating this past week?

*Cl.:*   I don't know. (pause) I already said I don't like doing this. These ratings are too simplistic.

*Th.:*   Well, would you rather just say, in your own words, how you've been feeling this past week as compared to other weeks?

*Cl.:*   I just don't know. I mean I feel really rotten.

*Th.:*   I hear you. (pause) (empathically) So sorry to hear that it's been a bad week for you.

*Cl.:*   Yeah, it's been bad.

*Th.:*   When it was really bad what was going on?

*Cl.:*   The whole week was bad.

*Th.:*   Can you describe one bad time. Was it at the beginning of the week, or toward the end of the week?

*Cl.:*   Like I said before, it was all bad.

*Th.:*   Well, what about times when it wasn't so bad. For example, was there something on T.V. that you enjoyed, at least a little bit? Or, getting out, or having a pleasant conversation with somebody?

*Cl.:*   I watched the Jets game. They played the Patriots. It was a pretty good game.

*Th.:*   So, there were at least a couple brighter hours for you this week. Will you watch the Jets game next week?

*Cl.:*   Yeah. Probably. I watch most of them.

*Th.:*   Great! One reason I ask you to rate your moods is to find out what good things happened in your life. Because when we find what was good, you can then do more of it. But, if it was bad, then we can look at doing something different. (pause) So, overall, how would you say your mood was this past week compared to 2 weeks ago? Were you able to enjoy the Jets games more this past week?

*Cl.:*   (pause) I don't really think so. It wasn't much different, maybe even a little worse.

*Th.:*    Okay. We'll continue to check in on your moods at the begin-
         ning of each session, which will help me know if we're going in
         the right direction or need to change course a bit. Is that all right
         with you?

The therapist demonstrated flexibility and the willingness to compromise,
while showing respect for the client. This is shown directly when he asks
for the client's permission: "Is that all right with you?" The client's reactance is high and appears to be driving his refusal. To continue to insist
that the client fill out the clinic's rating forms could severely strain the
therapeutic alliance and so the therapist rolled with the resistance.

*Cl.:*    (with some reluctance) I suppose it'd be all right.

In the beginning of the third session, the therapist gently assesses the client's receptivity to use the rating scale.

*Th.:*    How would it be if I asked you to rate your mood this past week?
         Will it bother you?
*Cl.:*    Yeah, it will.
*Th.:*    Well, I won't ask for it then, but can you describe what it means
         to you when I ask about your mood?
*Cl.:*    It's very frustrating. It's not easy to put a number on something
         as complicated as my moods.
*Th.:*    Well, do you believe it's important for me to understand the
         level of your distress and sadness, even if it is complicated?
*Cl.:*    I guess I do, but I'd rather we'd talk about other things.
*Th.:*    I hear that. So, let's talk about something you'd rather talk about.
         What should we focus on this session?
*Cl.:*    Well, things haven't been going so well at the office. There's a big
         suit against the store and I'm having to spend twice as much time
         as what my boss originally assigned for it. I'm overwhelmed.
         And, I don't want to start screaming or get so overwhelmed
         I have to take a leave.

The therapist agreed to this focus and processed it with Jeff over the next
four sessions. By then his mood was more even keeled and he thanked the
therapist for his help. He also said he was willing to use the rating scale,
at least some of the time. The therapist's patience and flexibility had paid
off and, as a result, Jeff's reactance was less operative.

**Case Commentary**

Initially, the client's refusal is firm and emphatic. He does not want to be told what to do. Trainees love this case because they imagine that when an impasse is reached, therapy is over. They are both surprised and encouraged by the therapist's capacity to "roll with the client's resistance" and ultimately effect both a positive therapeutic alliance and treatment outcome. If trainees were not convinced that the "third way is the therapeutic way" before we discuss this case, they are solidly convinced afterward.

# 18

## *Monitor Progress and Modify Treatment Accordingly*

In this age of accountability, the expectation is that therapists will not only provide effective treatment but be able to demonstrate that the treatment is effective. This expectation has given rise to two different perspectives on how to achieve such evidence. One perspective emphasizes "evidence-based practice," which is based on the premise that specific treatment interventions must have been empirically demonstrated to be effective with specific psychological problems. The other perspective emphasizes "practice-based evidence," which is based on the premise that effectiveness is more a function of therapist–client collaboration than of specific treatment interventions. This second perspective places a premium on assessing specific treatment processes and outcomes measures, and requires therapists to monitor treatment processes and outcomes. This chapter focuses on the second perspective.

When it comes to evaluating clients' response to treatment, therapists are not particularly good at predicting the effectiveness of their client–therapist relationship or of treatment outcomes. Rather, research reveals that client ratings of the client–therapist alliance are more accurate and a better predictor of client involvement in treatment than are therapist ratings. Research also shows that a client's subjective experience of change early in the treatment process is the best predictor of treatment success compared to all other measures and predictors (Orlinsky, Rønnestad, & Willutzki, 2003). So, how can therapists know and evaluate their clients' response to treatment? The answer is simple: Monitor treatment process and outcome.

The basic premise of treatment outcome and process research is that therapists need feedback. Research rather consistently shows that when therapists receive feedback on their work with clients, their therapeutic relationships and treatment effectiveness increase significantly. One study showed that when therapists had access to outcome and thera-peutic alliance information, their clients were less likely to drop out of treatment, the client–therapist relationship was less likely to deteriorate, and clients were more likely to achieve clinically significant changes (Whipple et al., 2003). Another study evaluated client–therapist relation-ships that were at risk of a negative outcome. It found that therapists who received formal feedback were 65% more likely to achieve positive treat-ment outcomes than were therapists who did not receive such feedback (Lambert et al., 2001). A third study of more than 6,000 clients found that therapists who utilized ongoing, formal feedback measures had mark-edly higher retention rates and a doubling of overall positive effects compared to therapists without such feedback (Miller, Duncan, Brown, Sorrell, and Chalk, 2006). In short, when both therapist and client know how the client rates the therapeutic relationship and treatment outcomes, three things can be predicted: (a) An effective therapeutic relationship is more likely to be developed and maintained, (b) the client will stay in treatment, and (c) positive treatment outcomes result. Thus, ongoing monitoring of the treatment process and outcome appears to be essential to effective therapy.

This chapter identifies various ways of assessing the therapist–client relationship and monitoring treatment progress and outcomes. Both for-mal and informal methods of assessment and monitoring are described and illustrated. Emphasized in this chapter is how relationship and treat-ment factors can be modified based on this feedback.

## TREATMENT OUTCOMES AND PROCESS ASSESSMENT SCALES: COMMERCIALLY AVAILABLE

A number of commercially available outcome and process measures are available. Following is a brief description of some of the best-known and best-regarded measures.

## Polaris MH

Polaris MH is a comprehensive outcomes and diagnostic system. Like its predecessor, COMPASS-OP (Howard, Kopta, Krause, & Orlinsky, 1986; Howard et al., 1993; Sperry, Brill, Howard, and Grissom, 1996), Polaris MH is a psychometrically sophisticated, computer-based assessment system. Polaris MH provides both treatment process and outcomes feedback in addition to a number of diagnostic and critical indicators. Like other comprehensive treatment outcomes measures, Polaris MH provides the following outcomes information and indicators: suggested treatment focus, treatment progress, client satisfaction with treatment, and therapeutic alliance. Polaris MH also provides the following information and indicators: severity and nature of the patient's symptoms; the impact of the patient's problems upon his or her life functioning; the presence of comorbid conditions, such as chemical dependency, psychosis, and bipolar disorder, and the presence of critical conditions (e.g., suicidality, psychosis, violence).

The Polaris MH measures three domains: Subjective Well-Being, Symptoms, and Functional Impairment. The Symptoms scale is a composite of subscale scores: depression, anxiety, PTSD (post-traumatic stress disorder), obsessive-compulsive, somatization, panic, phobia, and an overall scale of symptomatic distress. The three subscales of Functional Impairment are personal, social, vocational, as well as a scale of overall functioning. Polaris MH also assesses for general health problems, substance abuse, psychosis, and bipolar disorder. In addition, it measures resilience, meaning, treatment motivation, satisfaction with treatment, and the therapeutic alliance or bond.

Polaris-MH consists of three measures or questionnaires. The Patient Intake form provides detailed information for treatment planning. The Patient Update form provides information concurrently with treatment about the client's condition, progress, and satisfaction with treatment. The Brief Patient Update form provides a global mental health status indicator and the severity of symptoms of depression. Polaris MH also provides reports that provide information for clinical decision support (individual patient reports) and for outcomes assessment (program-level aggregate data).

## OQ-45

The OQ-45 (Lambert et al., 2004) is probably the most commonly used commercial treatment outcomes measure today. It is a brief 45-item self-report outcome and tracking instrument that is designed for repeated measurement of client progress through the course of therapy and following termination. It measures client functioning in three domains: symptom distress, interpersonal functioning, and social role. Functional level and change over time can be assessed, which allows treatment to be modified based on changes noted. The OQ-45 also contains risk assessment items for suicide potential, substance abuse, and potential violence at work. It has been translated into more than 10 languages and is based on normative data and has adequate validity and reliability. It can be administered and scored in either electronic or paper format.

## Session Rating Scale

The Session Rating Scale (SRS; Duncan et al., 2003) is a short and easy-to-administer measure of therapeutic alliance that consists of four items. The instructions are simple and straightforward. The client is given a sheet of paper on which four horizontal lines 10 centimeters long are printed. On the first line the client rates how well understood and respected he or she felt in the just-completed therapy session. On the second line the client rates how much the client and therapist worked on what he or she wanted to talk about. On the third the client rates how good a "fit" the therapy approach was for him or her. On the fourth the client rates how satisfied he or she felt about the session. The scale is completed by the client immediately after the session has ended. Use of the SRS is free-of-charge to individual mental health practitioners by license agreement and can be found at www.talkingcure.com.

## Outcomes Rating Scale

The Outcomes Rating Scale (ORS; Miller & Duncan, 2000) is a short and easy-to-administer outcomes measure consisting of four items. The instructions are simple and straightforward. The client is given a sheet of paper on which four horizontal lines 10 centimeters long are printed. The client is asked to mark with a pen stroke, somewhere along each horizontal line, how things went in the past week. On the first line the client indicates how he or she had felt. On the second line the client rates his or her relationships. On the third the client rates his or her social and work life. On the fourth the client rates his or her well-being. The scale is typically completed by the client immediately before the session begins, although it may be administered after the first meeting. Use of the ORS is free-of-charge to individual mental health practitioners by license agreement and can be found at www.talkingcure.com.

## TREATMENT OUTCOMES AND PROCESS ASSESSMENT SCALES: CLINICIAN DEVISED

There are several ways of performing focused assessments and ongoing assessments. This section describes a set of easy-to-use self-rating measures for assessing symptoms, functional status, well-being, and therapeutic alliance, which provide an alternative to standardized and proprietary measures of treatment process and outcome.

### Self-Rating of Symptom Assessment

Symptom or symptomatic distress to a client's current level of distress attributed to fear, sadness, anger, guilt, loss, etc. Assessing and monitoring a client's subjective experience of anxiety and mood, that is, depression or mania and hypomania, are common in clinical practice. The Subjective Units of Distress Scale (SUDS) has long been employed to assist clients in rating their experience of anxiety, particularly panic and phobic anxiety. The instructions are simple: On a 1 to 100 scale where 1 represents the most calm and serenity the client imagines and 100 represents the most severe distress the client imagines, give the number that best indicates how you currently feel (or specific past situation). With a minimum amount of practice with SUDS, clients can quickly and accurately rate and communicate their distress to a therapist. The widespread use of this self-rating assessment reflects its clinical utility.

In everyday practice, therapists can assess and monitor a client's core symptom or symptoms by asking the client for their ratings. Table 18.1 provides a number of client self-rating scales, among them a 10-point Anxiety Scale and a Mood Scale. To maintain a consistent scheme for client self-rating, a 1 to 10 scale is used for the Anxiety Scale and the Mood Scale instead of the 1 to 100 scale of SUDS.

### Self-Rating of Functional Assessment

Functional status refers to a client's current or actual level of life functioning. It is assessed by client self-report or a rating scale. Presumably,

**Table 18.1**   Focused Assessment Format

**Mood Scale**

Rate your overall mood this past week on a 1 to 10 scale where 1 = the worst
  you can ever imagine feeling, where 10 = the best you can ever imagine
  feeling, and 5 = an average mood for you.

|  |  |  |  |  |  |  |  |  |  |
|---|---|---|---|---|---|---|---|---|---|
| 1 | 2 | 3 | 4 | 5 | 6 | 7 | 8 | 9 | 10 |

**Anxiety Scale**

Rate your overall feeling of nervousness and anxiousness this past week on a
  1 to 10 scale where 1 = feeling you were going to die or have a heart attack or
  go crazy, and where 10 = being perfectly calm and anxiety-free.

|  |  |  |  |  |  |  |  |  |  |
|---|---|---|---|---|---|---|---|---|---|
| 1 | 2 | 3 | 4 | 5 | 6 | 7 | 8 | 9 | 10 |

**Functional Status Scales**

Rate your level of functioning in the past week in each of the following areas on
  1 to 10 scale where 1 = lowest and 10 = highest.

| | | | | | | | | | | |
|---|---|---|---|---|---|---|---|---|---|---|
| 1. Family | 1 | 2 | 3 | 4 | 5 | 6 | 7 | 8 | 9 | 10 |
| 2. Health | 1 | 2 | 3 | 4 | 5 | 6 | 7 | 8 | 9 | 10 |
| 3. Work | 1 | 2 | 3 | 4 | 5 | 6 | 7 | 8 | 9 | 10 |
| 4. Social | 1 | 2 | 3 | 4 | 5 | 6 | 7 | 8 | 9 | 10 |
| 5. Intimacy | 1 | 2 | 3 | 4 | 5 | 6 | 7 | 8 | 9 | 10 |
| 6. Self-management | 1 | 2 | 3 | 4 | 5 | 6 | 7 | 8 | 9 | 10 |

**Well-Being Scale**

Rate your overall feeling of psychological well-being this past week on a 1 to 10
  scale where 1 = the worst it could possibly be, and 10 = the best it could be.

|  |  |  |  |  |  |  |  |  |  |
|---|---|---|---|---|---|---|---|---|---|
| 1 | 2 | 3 | 4 | 5 | 6 | 7 | 8 | 9 | 10 |

**Therapeutic Alliance Scale**

Rate your overall sense about working with your therapist, treatment focus,
  and what is being accomplished on a 1 to 10 scale where 1 = the worst it could
  possibly be, and 10 = the best it could be.

|  |  |  |  |  |  |  |  |  |  |
|---|---|---|---|---|---|---|---|---|---|
| 1 | 2 | 3 | 4 | 5 | 6 | 7 | 8 | 9 | 10 |

the Global Assessment of Functioning (GAF) scale, Axis V of DSM–IV, is a measure of functional status. In reality, it combines symptoms or symptomatic distress and functional status and thus is not a clinically useful measure of functional status. However, there are six dimensions of life functioning specified by the Social Security Administration (Sperry et al., 1996) that clinicians have found useful. They are intimacy, family, work, health, social, and self-management. A brief description of each follows:

| | |
|---|---|
| **Intimacy** | Functioning with regard to the intimate relationship with a significant other, being supportive and feeling supported by the significant other, carrying out expected responsibilities, and sexual functioning |
| **Family** | Functioning with family members, including handling of family stress and conflict, carrying out expected responsibilities, and the support of and by other family members |
| **Health** | Functioning with regard to health habits, personal hygiene and grooming, and overall sense of physical well-being |
| **Work** | Functioning at work (or school), including interactions with fellow workers and supervisors (or students and teachers), ability to complete job (school) assignments, and the like |
| **Social** | Functioning in social and community settings, including interactions with others, feeling supported by others, and carrying out expected responsibilities |
| **Self-Management** | Functioning with regard to the client's control over, conception of, and satisfaction with himself or herself |

Table 18.1 provides a set of scales for assessing levels of functioning for these six. I developed and have used these scales in my practice and supervision for several years. You are welcome to use them as well.

## Self-Rating of Well-Being

Many commercially available outcomes instruments contain a well-being scale. Well-being refers to an individual's overall feeling of psychological health, optimism, and wellness.

## Self-Rating of Therapeutic Alliance

Because of its pivotal role in treatment process and outcomes, many treatment outcome measures endeavor to assess therapeutic alliance or at least elements of it, such as therapeutic bond in the Polaris MH.

## Case 1: Geri

We return to the case report of Geri to illustrate both functional and ongoing assessment.

In terms of focused clinical assessment, Geri estimated her depressive symptoms to be 3 on the mood scale (1 = worst, 10 = best, 5 = average mood) in the past 2 weeks. This is the lowest she can recall her mood ever being. She estimates her usual mood is 6–7. Anxiety is rated as 7–8.

In terms of focused functional assessment, Geri rates herself at about 3 now, as compared to 6 prior to the job change. Her ratings on the six areas of life functioning at the present are (on a 1–10 scale where 1 = lowest and 10 = highest):

4 Self-management
2 Work
4 Family
2 Intimacy
3 Health
3 Social

Geri rates her sense of well-being at 1 out of 10. Her therapist enters these ratings in her progress note. Her notes use the O-A-P format, which stands for Observation, Assessment, and Plan.

After the second session, the therapist's progress note for Geri read:

**Observation**
It has been 2 weeks since the initial diagnostic assessment session with Geri. She did accept the referral to her family physician, L. Winslow, MD, for a medical evaluation of her depressed moods. Dr. Winslow sent a report indicating that she concurred with my diagnostic impression of major depression and prescribed Celexa 20 milligrams for 7 days and then 40 milligrams thereafter. Geri immediately began taking the medication, today being her 10th day. No side effects were reported. She reports that she has been sleeping through the night for the past 8 days and awakens

refreshed. Her energy level also has increased greatly since she has been on the medication and she has been taking daily walks. She is feeling less depressed and reports her mood to be 5 on the mood scale for the past 2 days. Her functional ratings are self-management 6; work 4; family 4; intimacy 3; health 6; and social 4. She rates her sense of well-being at 8. Discussed her job situation. She gives me written permission to talk to her supervisor and the human resources director.

**Assessment**
Some resolution of acute symptoms noted, but not much change in life functioning; reasonable response to medication and therapy.

**Plan**
Continue with medication; I will call Geri's work supervisor re: job accommodation. Scheduled appointment in 1 week.

After the third session, the therapist's progress note for Geri R. read:

**Observation**
The client reports considerable improvement since our last session, which was 1 week ago, which she attributes to medication, daily exercise, and feeling hopeful about her work situation after hearing that her job situation has been favorably resolved. She returned to work yesterday. No medication side effects were reported. Mood scale: 6/10. Functional ratings are self-management 6; work 8; family 5; intimacy 3; health 8; and social 5. She rates her sense of well-being at 8–9 out of 10. Discussed transition to psychoeducation group.

**Assessment**
Mood appears to have returned to baseline in response to medication, exercise, therapy, and job accommodation. A significant improvement in work functioning rating since the initial diagnostic assessment is noted.

**Plan**
Continue with medication and exercise. Will continue discussion of transition to group. Scheduled appointment in 1 week.

**Case Commentary**
The therapist indicates an awareness of the type and level of symptoms and functional impairment. The symptoms are of the acute type, and the

therapist is sensitive to the clinical significance of the client's rating of work functioning, as the workplace was the precipitant or trigger for Geri's presentation. Also noted is that the client is showing improvement in both symptoms and functioning over the three sessions. However, if little or no progress was noted by the third session the effective therapist would do well to reconsider the treatment formulation.

## Case 2: Cynthia

The following case illustrates the importance of utilizing treatment outcomes data to establish and maintain an appropriate treatment focus.

Cynthia G. is a 28-year-old never married Caucasian female who was referred for therapy with a history of anxiety and work issues over the past 3 months. She stated: "I've been having problems everywhere lately. My parents and I aren't getting along like we used to, my boss and I are not communicating well, and I just am experiencing a lack of satisfaction in my life. I feel tense and anxious a lot of the time but it's worse on workday mornings." As a result of the diagnostic evaluation, she was given the diagnosis of Anxiety Disorder NOS (Not Otherwise Specified). The clinic routinely collected initial and ongoing data on all clients using the Polaris MH Patient Intake (the initial assessment form) and Patient Update (the ongoing assessment of alliance and outcomes form).

Unfortunately, the therapist had been recently hired by the clinic and had no previous experience with clinical outcome measures other than the brief introduction to the clinic's treatment outcome system during his orientation. Although Cynthia had completed the Polaris MH measures, the therapist rarely, if ever, looked at the reports that appeared in Cynthia's chart.

The therapist had utilized a dynamically oriented strategy to explore the nature of the client's concerns and to uncover underlying causes. Fortunately, the clinical director routinely reviewed the "positive screens" reports on all of the clinic's clients, particularly the screens for "dangerousness to self and others" and "evidence of possible serious disturbance." After reviewing the most recent report on Cynthia, the clinic director immediately met with the therapist. The therapist was embarrassed to say that he had not noticed the positive screen regarding self-harm, nor had he reviewed any of the Polaris reports. The clinic director initialed a brief case review with the therapist on the spot. It became clear that therapy had not been addressing the main functional concern noted on all of the

Patient Update reports where the Vocational domain of functioning was in the high clinical range of 14 to 23, whereas the Personal and Social were in the nonclinical range. The therapist noted that the client had not mentioned any thoughts of self-harm and that he had focused therapy on the client's early relationship with her mother, that is, the Personal domain. The therapist agreed to contact the client immediately and evaluate possible self-harm and to refocus treatment on the Vocational domain.

In speaking with the client by phone, the therapist learned that Cynthia had in fact been feeling very hopeless in the past 2 weeks about things in general, including a concern that she might lose her job. But she denied specific intent and plan, stating that suicide was forbidden in her church and that she was a practicing Christian. In subsequent sessions, the focus of treatment shifted to job and career issues. It was not surprising that the client's subsequent Patient Update reports reflected a shift of the Vocational domain of functioning closer to the nonclinical range.

### Case Commentary

Here the therapist had not monitored outcomes information and could have been found negligent if the client had engaged in self-harmful behavior. Fortunately, the clinical director was monitoring this indicator. Of particular note is that once the therapist used the Polaris feedback and shifted the focus on treatment to job and career issues, the client's functioning improved. In short, feedback played a significant role in the client's life and at the same time convinced the therapist of the clinical value and utility of monitoring outcome measures.

## Case 3: Rosa

Rosa is a 42-year-old recently separated Hispanic female who presented for therapy because of uncertainty regarding getting back together with her estranged husband of 18 years. During the initial evaluation it was noted that Rosa had no children by choice, was highly acculturated, had worked as a nurse practitioner for 14 years at a local hospital, and had separated from her husband after she learned that he had had an affair with one of her friends.

As she was to leave their first session, her African American female therapist, Jerina, asked her to complete the ORS and the SRS. Rosa was asked to be as honest and forthright as she could so that Jerina could better focus her approach in working with Rosa. Rosa was then told that they would talk about the results at the beginning of their next session. Immediately after the scales were completed, Jerina reviewed the results.

On the ORS Rosa had scored herself at about 2 on the Interpersonal scale and about 4 on the other scales. It appeared that her conflicted relationship with her husband was affecting her satisfaction with other areas of her life. While the relationship rating was quite consistent with Rosa's stated reason for therapy, Rosa had not communicated how much the rest of her life was being affected by relational distress. Accordingly, Jerina made a chart note to focus on this during their next session. On the SRS, a measure of therapeutic alliance, Rosa had rated each scale at about a 9. Jerina felt confident that their work together was heading in the right direction. By soliciting feedback from her client at the beginning of therapy, Jerina was conveying her intent to enter into a partnership with her client and give Rosa the unequivocal message that her opinions and ideas about change were important information to Jerina.

Based on her previous experience, Jerina was convinced that the earlier any problems or challenges in the therapeutic alliance were revealed, the greater the likelihood was of the client's continuation and collaboration with the treatment process. Similarly, Jerina was also convinced that client feedback on outcomes rating was essential to effectively collaborating and focusing treatment to ensure that mutually established treatment goals were most likely to be achieved. In short, Jerina was convinced of the value of monitoring treatment process and outcomes and incorporated these measures into everyday practice.

### Case Commentary
This case points out that useful client data can be quickly assessed, reviewed, and monitored. For clients who are willing to spend a minute or so providing feedback in the form of a brief rating scale after each session, the ORS and SRS are a welcome addition to clinical practice.

# 19

# *Evaluate Progress and Prepare Client for Termination*

Eventually the treatment process ends. Termination is an event that may or may not have been planned, and the process of treatment may or may not have been successful. But termination is much more than an event; it is also a process. It is a process of ending a relationship focused on support and change, and this process can be a source of significant healing and growth for many clients. Facilitating this process and making it a positive experience is the therapist's primary role in the last phase of treatment. The basic task of this phase is to provide clients the opportunity to express their thoughts and feelings about what therapy and the therapist have meant to them. Preparing for termination is a time to review the client's progress in achieving treatment goals. It is also a time to plan for maintaining treatment gains and for the inevitable lapses that may ensue. Finally, preparing for termination is a time to reflect about what remaining therapeutic tasks the client might work on in the future and what additional therapeutic contact with you or other therapies might be indicated.

Like some other clinical competencies addressed in this book, this clinical competence has captured relatively little time and attention in the curricula of many training programs and is not even addressed in some textbooks. For this reason, some practical considerations in preparing for termination are addressed in this chapter. The chapter begins with a brief discussion of the relationship of the case conceptualization and termination and then briefly addresses the process of relapse prevention planning. Next it discusses some guidelines for preparing for termination. Finally,

HIGHLY EFFECTIVE THERAPY

it illustrates the process of preparing for termination and developing a relapse prevention plan.

## CASE CONCEPTUALIZATION AND TERMINATION

As noted in Chapter 9, the case conceptualization is more than a plan that guides treatment decisions. The case conceptualization also functions as a guide for therapists in recognizing when the most important therapy goals and treatment targets have been addressed and for identifying when and how to prepare for termination. Because the case conceptualization anticipates the roadblocks and challenges therapists are likely to face in the various phases of treatment, the case conceptualization helps the therapist anticipate the particular difficulties clients may experience with termination. Clients who commonly have difficulty with termination have a history of losses or a pattern of clinging to, or dependency on, others (Cucciare & O'Donohue, 2008).

## RELAPSE PREVENTION PLAN

Relapse prevention is a procedure for anticipating and reducing the likelihood of relapse or recurrence of symptoms or maladaptive behavior. Relapse prevention planning (Marlatt & Gordon, 1985) begins with the assessment of a client's likely interpersonal, intrapersonal, environmental, and physiological risks for relapse and specific stressors and situations that may precipitate it. Once these potential triggers and high-risk situations are identified, cognitive and behavioral techniques are implemented that incorporate specific interventions to prevent or manage them if they do occur. It also involves a discussion of more global strategies to address lifestyle balance, craving, and cognitive distortions that could expose the client to high-risk situations where relapse is most likely. Such a relapse plan is likely to increase the client's sense of self-efficacy and effectiveness in maintaining treatment gains (Carroll, 1996).

## GUIDELINES FOR PREPARING FOR TERMINATION

Following are some guidelines that can facilitate the process of preparing for termination such that it is a positive and growth-producing process.

254

For many clients, three or more sessions may be sufficient for this process in briefer therapies (i.e., 25 or fewer sessions), whereas four or more sessions may be needed for longer term therapies.

## 1. Discuss the Prospect of
## Termination and the Client's Reactions

Begin by providing a framework and time for clients to talk about their feelings about termination as well as about personal feelings they might have about their therapist. Clients are then asked to speculate about how their experience in ending therapy is related to other endings in their lives. They may feel a sense of accomplishment, a sense of anger, or a sense of sadness at the prospect of ending contact with the therapist. They may be apprehensive about maintaining their gains or feel relieved of the commitment of time and money that treatment involves. When there are mixed reactions, the therapist's role is to normalize them. Most clients are receptive to sharing positive and negative thoughts and feelings about treatment and termination but may be somewhat reluctant to share feelings about therapists.

## 2. Discuss Progress Toward Treatment Goals

Make a list of what the client reports as his or her treatment gains. Then the therapist adds other gains that have been noted by the client. Next, this list is compared to the stated treatment goals. Even if these goals have only partially been achieved, they are noted and framed in a positive manner, for example, through pointing out that therapy is an ongoing process. Giving this list to clients can be quite meaningful. Clients can be encouraged to view this list in the future, particularly when things seem less than optimal, because even a cursory review of the list can remind them of all their gains as well as their strengths.

## 3. Discuss How Gains Can Be
## Maintained and Relapse Prevented

Discussing how to maintain and consolidate hard-won gains is a part of ending treatment for most therapeutic approaches. A formal discussion and plan for preventing relapse is more likely to be a part of behavioral and cognitive–behavioral therapies, although effective therapists of all orientations seem to engage in this process albeit more informally. In any event, these discussions can be of inestimable value to clients.

## 4. Discuss Continued Personal Growth

One indicator that the treatment process is ready to end is that clients become more able to rely on themselves and their own internal resources to neutralize negative thoughts and feelings and to solve problems without the constant oversight of the therapist. Some clients find this easier than others. Nevertheless, it is useful to discuss how clients can continue to build on their newly developed capacities and confidence to accomplish new goals or to continue to work on those not fully realized during treatment. If indicated, the therapist engenders a discussion of additional therapy-related work, such as a support or self-help group, referral to a specialty therapist, or other follow-up activities.

## 5. Discuss Remaining Sessions and Future Contacts

Discussion and negotiation of additional contact with the client as therapy winds down and ends are essential. It is not unusual for some therapists to schedule the remaining few sessions on a biweekly rather than weekly basis. For some clients scheduled follow-up or booster sessions (Beck, 1995) at 3 and 6 months after treatment ends can serve as a lifeline to those clients who have become quite dependent on their therapist. If there is some future likelihood that the therapist might have contact with the client in a social context, it is useful for both to discuss how such contact can be best handled such that the former client's privacy is protected.

## ILLUSTRATIONS OF THE PROCESS OF PREPARING FOR TERMINATION

The following two cases illustrate many of the points made in this chapter. The first case emphasizes the process of preparing for termination, whereas the second emphasizes relapse prevention. The first case is inspired by Seligman (2005) and the second by Beck (1995).

## Case 1: Geri

We return a final time to the case of Geri. As you recall she is an African American female who was referred by the human resources director of her company for depression and increased social isolation. She collaborated in a combined treatment involving medication, individual therapy, and group psychoeducation. Her primary care physician monitored her medications. The plan was for sixteen individual cognitive–behavioral therapy sessions and six group sessions. Given her shy and avoidant style, she participated in four individual sessions which prepared her for transition into the psychoeducation group. She continued in individual sessions while also participating in six group sessions, after which she was to continue in six additional individual sessions. The individual sessions focused on symptom reduction, cognitive restructuring of maladaptive schemas, and returning to work, while group sessions focused on increasing social relatedness and friendship skills training.

Because the therapy was cognitive–behaviorally oriented, a brief discussion and preparation for termination began in the first therapy session. The case conceptualization anticipated that Geri would likely have difficulty with termination given her limited social network and tendency to be overly reliant on the few individuals whom she could trust, of which the therapist would be one. To reduce the likelihood of difficulty with termination, treatment very early focused on increasing her social network and friendship skills. In their 13th individual session the discussion focused on planning for termination given that only four sessions remained. The therapist began the session saying:

Th.:     So as we talked briefly last session, counting today we have four sessions remaining of our contracted sixteen individual sessions. Today, we were going to talk about treatment progress and your reactions to what we have done together.

Cl.:     Sure, let's do it. I'm a bit nervous about it (pause), but I'm also quite pleased, too.

Th.:     How about listing some of the accomplishments you've made over the course of our individual and those group sessions.

Cl.:     I guess the main ones I see is that I'm back at work, which is really important to me. It was really good that I was able to stay in the same unit with my same boss and my close friend. I never thought it would work out this way. But the HR [human resources] director, bless her heart, figured a way to send my boss's administrative assistant to the new location and I then would take over her responsibilities. My boss is really pretty good. He's very understanding of my shyness and he's been pretty good about the way he gives me feedback on my work. So that's the main thing. Another thing is that I have another friend, Jannella. As I think I told you before, I met her in the psychoeducation group and we are a lot alike so we can be comfortable with each other. I've also been in more touch with my auntie in Macon. I call her every week. That's good because she's getting pretty old. (pause) I guess that's the progress I've made.

Th.: That's great and I can see you are proud of what you have accomplished. There are also a couple of other achievements that I have observed. Do you want to hear them? (Yes.) Well, I'll mention them and maybe we can add them to the list. I'll begin with your moods. They seem so much better. You look brighter and happier and you haven't mentioned depression in a long time. You report that you are sleeping better, and you're more hopeful about things. That's quite a difference compared to how you were when we first got together. Next, you have developed some important skills in relating to others. Because of those social relationship and friendship skills, you've been able to feel more comfortable around others. As a result, you've made a new friend, Jannella. I'll bet that's just the beginning. Another achievement is that you seemed to be a little less worried about other people criticizing and making fun of you.

Cl.: Well, you did mention some extra things that I didn't. They are changes. So, go ahead and add them to our list.

Th.: Okay. Now can you compare this list to the list of goals we came up with when we began our work together. (hand list to client) Here is the list. [The treatment goal and target list reads: 1. reduce depressive symptom; 2. return to work; 3. extend social network at work; 4. establish a supportive social network off the job, including relatives and people in neighborhood; 5. increase interpersonal skills, assertive communication, trust, and friendship skills.]

Cl.: Interesting. It looks like I met number 1 and number 2. And, maybe a little bit of number 3. I wouldn't say my boss is a friend, but I think I can trust him more than most people. Maybe number 4 also. I do have more contact with my auntie. I'm not sure how to measure those skills in number 5, but I probably am a little better. Wow. That's not bad.

Th.: You are really proud of yourself and all that you have achieved.

Cl.: Yes, I am. In a way, I am a different person.

Th.: A person who is so much more confident and able to do things that 6 months ago she couldn't do.

Cl.: Probably things I couldn't even imagine myself doing 6 months ago. (pause) But it has taken a lot of raw effort on my part. And a lot of support and hard work on your part. (pause) And …

Th.: And?

Cl.: And, I'm not sure what it will be like when I'm not seeing you anymore. (pause) That's what worries me. That's what I meant when I said when we started talking today that I was nervous.

Th.: You have made so much progress, and you're afraid that you might lose it. That you won't have me to support and encourage you anymore. And, that thought makes you frightened and sad.

Cl.: It does. I don't want to regress back to the way I was before. A basket case who wasn't sure she even wanted to live anymore.

Th.: You don't want to regress back to the way you were. We've already started a relapse prevention plan and we'll do some more work on it. (pause) You've come such a long way.

Cl.: I really appreciate your confidence in me. It really boosts me up. I think I can keep growing. It really helps to be able to call Jannella. She just listens when I tell her about things that worry me.

Th.: It's so good for you to have someone you trust, someone who will listen and will support you. (Yes.) You can rely on people like her. And, you can even support yourself. You can tell yourself that things may be hard at times, but that you can conquer them, that you can conquer those worries. You have done it already, and you can continue to do it.

Cl.: I have to keep telling myself that and believing it. (pause) You're right, I have done it and I can keep doing it. (pause) That probably is a new goal for me, to keep my thoughts positive. More positive about people, especially the ones I trust. And more positive about myself. You know when you asked me to write out those positive self-talk statements a while back, I did them and they seemed to help. I can do them again.

*Th.:* Sounds like that strategy worked and that you can continue to use it to achieve that new goal. It can really help you continue growing without therapy. It is really a form of self-therapy.

*Cl.:* Yes, it can work. But, if I really get off track in the future would I be able to I come back and meet with you again?

*Th.:* Certainly. Just call me for an appointment. But, I'd ask you to first remember and think about what you have accomplished. Look at this list of the gains you have made in therapy and the new skills you have learned and have put into practice.

*Cl.:* Yes, I can do that. And, I appreciate that I can call you if things really get tough.

*Th.:* You can. Before we stop our session today, I'd like us to talk about the therapy process and our work together. It would be very useful for me if you can say what was particularly useful to you and what would have made our work together even better.

*Cl.:* Well, the main thing is you never criticized me. You were very patient with me.

*Th.:* Patient?

*Cl.:* You know when I kept calling in the beginning to change appointments and stuff. You didn't hassle me about it or get flustered or anything. You weren't like other people.

*Th.:* I remember. I know you needed time to get comfortable with me and see if I was someone whom you could trust. Someone that wouldn't get upset with you or criticize you.

*Cl.:* I did and I do appreciate it. Thanks.

*Th.:* So, next week we will continue to review and wind down. You said earlier you don't want to regress back to the way it was, so let's do some more work on maintaining your gains and on your relapse prevention plan. (Okay.) Before we meet next week, can you see yourself making a list of the thoughts, feelings, and situations that are likely to trigger your worries and fears about people hurting you, and thoughts, feelings, and situations that make you want to get away from others and just be by yourself?

*Cl.:* Yes, I'll do it. It should help.

The session winds down and an appointment time for the next session is finalized.

**Case Commentary**
Because Geri's shy and avoidant style predisposes her to the likelihood of experiencing difficulties with termination, the therapist planned pro-actively to reduce this likelihood. Early work in both individual and group sessions emphasized increasing her social network, becoming more asser-tive, and making friends. The fruits of these labors are evident in this session. For instance, Geri is able to share that she is proud of her achieve-ments, particularly making a new friend, Jannella, in whom she trusts and can confide.

## Case 2: Jeffries

The following case illustrates a discussion of lapses or setbacks and the development of a relapse prevention plan. Jeffries is a 57-year-old married Caucasian male who sought therapy for help with depression following the loss of his wife in a car accident. He had made good progress in the first 17 of the 20 sessions his HMO (health maintenance organization) had authorized. In the 18th session Jeffries and his Caucasian male therapist began talking of termination, and in the beginning of 19th session he and his therapist discussed relapse and a prevention plan.

*Th.:* You sure have been making wonderful progress. You should be very proud of your progress. I certainly am. Your anxiety and depressive symptoms are pretty much gone, and you've been able to move forward with your life.

*Cl.:* Yes, I am feeling and doing much better. And, I am proud of what we've accomplished together.

*Th.:* We discussed setbacks in our very first session. Do you remember?

*Cl.:* Vaguely.

*Th.:* Well, because it is possible to have a relapse or setback during and after therapy is over, it can be helpful for you to know in advance how you can handle a setback.

*Cl.:* That sounds reasonable.

*Th.:* Please imagine, if you will, that you have had a really bad couple of days. I mean, almost nothing seems to be going well. Things start looking hopeless, and you get down on yourself. Can you imagine this scenario?

*Cl.:*    I sure can. I had many days like this before starting therapy.

*Th.:*    Okay. Can you tell me what thoughts you are having right now?

*Cl.:*    I'm thinking it isn't fair. I've been doing so well, and now look what happens. Things are caving in all around me.

*Th.:*    All right. Now, how will you respond to these thoughts?

*Cl.:*    (pause) I'm not sure.

*Th.:*    It's a choice. You can either continuing thinking these frightening and depressing thoughts, or you can do something about them.

*Cl.:*    You're right, it is a choice. But, it doesn't mean it's easy.

*Th.:*    That's right. It isn't easy, but it is probably a lot easier now than it was before.

*Cl.:*    I'd agree with that.

*Th.:*    Okay. So what do you suppose will happen to your mood if you continue to have those kind of thoughts?

*Cl.:*    It'll get worse.

*Th.:*    Yes, if you let those thoughts take over, your mood will get worse. But, you can choose to recall that this is only a setback. That it is to be expected, that it is normal, and most importantly; that it is temporary. (pause) If you do that, how do you imagine you'll feel?

*Cl.:*    Better. I imagine that my mood will be better rather than worse.

*Th.:*    Now, lapses can also occur when you put yourself in high-risk situations. We talked before about how your feelings can be affected by being around certain individuals or certain situations. For example, being around negative individuals could trigger negative thoughts that lead to feeling anxious or depressed.

*Cl.:*    Yeah. That's true. There are some individuals that sure seem to be toxic for me.

*Th.:*    There is another factor we need to discuss. That is, putting yourself or deciding to stay in certain situations can also affect how you feel. For instance, I recall your mentioning how being in your apartment alone on a Saturday afternoon with no plans for the evening had set you in a downward spiral.

*Cl.:*    It sure did. In that situation I started to think that nobody cares about me and that life is hopeless and that it's unfair that I'm not married anymore or have a caring partner. Then I really started to feel depressed.

Th.: So, it's critically important that you can remind yourself that setbacks do occur, that those negative thoughts and feelings can come back, that they can be expected, and most importantly, that they can be neutralized or reversed.

Cl.: Yeah. I see that.

Th.: Now, what specifically could you do to short circuit those thoughts and feelings when you find yourself in the situation of being alone with no plans for Saturday?

Cl.: Well, I could call some friends and get something set up with them to go out or do something.

Th.: Good. That's a great short-term plan. What about a longer term plan?

Cl.: You mean like not wait until I'm all alone on Saturday and starting to feel sorry for myself?

Th.: Precisely.

Cl.: Well, sure, I could make plans earlier in the week to do things on the weekend with people. Maybe even plan for some friends to come to my place for poker. I really like doing things like that.

Th.: That's a very good plan. Proactive behaviors like planning ahead can greatly reduce the likelihood of relapses.

Cl.: Yeah. That makes sense.

Th.: So, it comes down to making decisions and doing things that result in more positive feelings and actions, or making decisions and doing things that result in more negative feelings and actions.

Cl.: I see what you're saying. I've got to have a plan in place for when setbacks come up.

Th.: Definitely. And, in our next couple of sessions we can make a list of potential setback situations and develop a setback prevention plan for dealing with each.

The session winds down and the next appointment is made.

## Case Commentary

The therapist has engaged Jeffries in an action-oriented discussion of relapses and how they can be dealt with directly and, as importantly, how they can be anticipated and prevented with proactive planning.

# 20

# *Utilize Supervision Effectively to Develop and Evaluate Competencies*

At first glance, this competency may seem somewhat tangential to the overall topic of essential competencies. It might seem that this competency would be better included in a book or training manual on supervisory competencies. Actually, because supervision is a primary means of developing and evaluating psychotherapy competencies, many consider the effective use of supervision by trainees to be an essential intervention competency (Haynes, Corey, & Moulton, 2003). For this reason, this competency is addressed in this book.

Using supervision effectively begins with preparation for supervisory meetings. The first segment of this chapter briefly describes and illustrates this competency. Because client engagement in the treatment process is critical to positive clinical outcomes and because client-therapist relationship issues can significantly influence client engagement and clinical outcomes, the second segment focuses on utilizing supervision to deal with therapeutic relationship issues. The final segment addresses the importance of reflection in developing and evaluating competencies, particularly in the context of self-supervision.

## BEING PREPARED TO USE SUPERVISION EFFECTIVELY

There are at least two ways to use clinical supervision. One way is for supervisees to show up for supervision meetings and expect that somehow their time will be well spent and that they will learn something. The other way is for supervisees to come well prepared for supervision meetings. Specifically, this means having a prioritized agenda for that session, as well as the expectation they will further develop the learning outcomes, that is, specific knowledge, skills, and professional attitudes, that they recognize as essential for this training experience. Typically, they have already articulated—maybe even in a written plan—and discussed these learning outcomes with their supervisor. Trainees who are evaluated as having achieved minimal competence in utilizing supervision in their internship or practicum experience will manifest this level of preparation.

## USING SUPERVISION TO DEAL WITH CLIENT RELATIONSHIP CONCERNS

Earlier it was noted that fostering the client's engagement in the therapy process is critical to positive clinical outcomes. Earlier chapters—chapters 2 to 6—described and illustrated various types of client–therapist relationship issues that can significantly influence client engagement and clinical outcomes. Recognizing and resolving resistance, ambivalence, alliance ruptures, and transference–countertransference enactments are key competencies that therapists must master on the journey to becoming highly effective therapists. Not surprisingly, client–therapist relationship issues are a common consideration in clinical supervision. This assumes that the trainee or therapist recognizes the issue and is not embarrassed to bring it to supervision.

Clearly, trainees who downplay such client relationship concerns are not utilizing clinical supervision effectively.

## SELF-SUPERVISION

A critical function of clinical supervision is to assist supervisees in developing the capacity and competency for self-supervision. Self-supervision is the active, ongoing conversations that therapists have with themselves about their clients. Unlike the reflection and direction provided by a clinical supervisor, self-supervision involves therapists' own reflection about their clients, their case conceptualizations, their interventions, and treatment outcomes. It also includes the therapists' assessment of their own professional effectiveness and their attention to the political and ethical effects of their clinical work with their clients (Sperry, 2007). Reflective practice is clearly the central dimension of self-supervision, and it involves reflecting on all aspects of clinical experience. Such practice is essential in the day-to-day development of therapists (Bennett-Levy & Thwaites, 2006). Why is self-supervision so important? Because it is through self-supervision that therapists learn to trust their intuitions and clinical judgment, both of which are important in developing expertise and becoming effective therapists (Haynes et al., 2003).

## ILLUSTRATIONS OF UTILIZING SUPERVISION TO ENHANCE AND EVALUATE COMPETENCIES

### Case 1: Being Prepared to Effectively Use Supervision

In the following case, Phyllis is an intern this semester in the counseling center at a local university. This is her third week at the counseling center and she is eager to learn from her clients and from Dr. Benton, the associate director of the center. She feels fortunate that she was assigned to be supervised by him. He has an enviable reputation as a supervisor and she knows from their first meeting that he expects her to be well prepared to make the most of their supervisory time. So she goes into her second supervisory meeting with an agenda, a videotape, and case folder of her five clients.

*Spe:*  I've really been looking forward to our meeting today. I've got a couple of things I'd really like your input on.

*Spr:*  I'm also looking forward to working with you today. So what's on your agenda?

*Spe:*  First, I guess, is a technical concern. It's about note-taking during sessions. They told us in our graduate program that note-taking is a distraction and can interfere with the therapeutic alliance. Anyway, I'd like to talk about that.

*Spr:*  Good. That's one agenda. Are there others?

*Spe:*  Yes, Andrea, the client I started with last week is conflicted about whether to abort or not. This raises some concerns and questions for me, and I'm not sure that I should remain her therapist.

*Spr:*      Sounds like that's a pressing concern to discuss. Any others?

*Spr:*      Finally, there was an unexpected transference enactment in my session with one of my male clients, and I wanted to review the video of that with you. Thanks to the protocol you shared with all of us interns in last week's group supervisory meeting, I tried it with Jackson Tyre. It was only the second time I saw him and I haven't staffed him with you yet, so I brought his file. (pause) Anyway, I think my intervention went pretty well, and I would like to go over that segment of the tape with you.

*Spr:*      Fine. So, where do you want to start?

*Spe:*      Well, the abortion issue is time sensitive for Andrea and a source of some distress for me, so maybe that would be the first to discuss. And, I definitely want to get your feedback on the video, so I want to make sure there is time for that.

*Spr:*      All right, so let's begin with Andrea. Let's organize our time so that we can spend sufficient time reviewing the video segment on you dealing with transference enactment, say, at least 20 minutes. If we need more time we can pick it up next time you and I meet. Then, if time permits we can turn to the matter of note-taking. If we don't have time for the last topic, what do you think of bringing it to group supervision later this week? It might be a concern for other interns as well.

*Spe:*      I think that the note-taking issue is of concern to other interns as well. Sure, I'd be willing to bring it up in group supervision.

*Spr:*      Okay, so tell me about Andrea.

The session continues with Phyllis's concerns, both personal and professional, about Andrea's situation. After that, the videotape of Phyllis's effort to deal with the transference enactment was reviewed and discussed. She was quite pleased with Dr. Benton's feedback on how she had successfully dealt with transference.

**Case Commentary**

This session transcription illustrates the beginning of a typical supervisory session and particularly illustrates how a trainee effectively utilizes supervision. Phyllis was not only prepared for the meeting with an agenda, a videotape, and case folders, she had spent time reflecting about what she needed to learn and how to best utilize her time with Dr. Benton.

## Case 2: Using Supervision in Client Relationship Concerns

In the following case, the supervisee, Alexis, is an intern who has been at a mental health clinic for the past 2 months. Alexis shows up for the fifth supervisory meeting with a client relationship concern. She has had four previous sessions with Nancy Jeffers, a 42-year-old new car salesperson, who came for counseling because of difficulty adjusting to the breakup with her lesbian partner. Alexis wants to use supervision to resolve this matter. Subsequently she brings it to her next supervisory session. She begins by saying:

*Spe:*     I'm really struggling with my therapeutic relationship with Nancy. It almost seems like she doesn't want to be in therapy any more. Maybe she wishes that someone else was treating her. She just seems to talk incessantly as if I'm not there. (pause) I don't know how to deal with this situation.

*Spr:*     Say some more about your relationship with her. What's it like for you?

*Spe:*     Well, it's kind of emotionally impoverished.

*Spr:*     Emotionally impoverished?

*Spe:*     It's like there's no chemistry between us. It's as if I'm at a firing range just observing her shooting away with her words like a rapid fire automatic weapon with no feeling. And, she doesn't act as if I'm even there.

*Spr:*     Uhm-hmm. It is troubling to you that she doesn't seem to acknowledge you and what you to have to offer. (pause) What would you like that therapeutic relationship to be like?

*Spe:*     Well, first I'd like there to be an emotional connection. You know, be closer and warmer emotionally. And, I'd like the relationship to be more mutual, more collaborative.

*Spr:*     Can you think of some things you could do to foster the relationship being closer and more collaborative?

*Spe:*     Well, I'd like to feel an emotional connection. (pause) Could it be that she speaks in such a rapid fire way because she's anxious lately, or because it's her basic pattern of relating? (pause) Maybe I'm intimidated by her.

*Spr:*     You feel intimidated by her?

*Spe:*     I think so. I didn't realize before now that I was internalizing that feeling. (pause) Maybe I was really acting like a small kid in

269

the sessions, and I was bringing about this distant relationship. It wasn't her, it was me.

*Spr:* So what does that mean for your next session with your client?

*Spe:* It will be different. I'll go in there and relate to her as an adult, as a therapist who can establish a bond of trust and caring.

*Spr:* You sound hopeful that things can be different.

*Spe:* Yeah! In the past I almost dreaded sessions with her, but now I'm really look forward to our next appointment.

## Case 3: Self-Supervision

The following case illustrates the process of self-supervision by means of reflective practice. There are several methods of reflective practice, including reflective writing, self-evaluation of audiotapes and videotapes, and actively seeking and using client feedback (Bennett-Levy & Thwaites, 2006). The case that follows illustrates the use of reflective writing in reviewing, analyzing, and planning subsequent therapeutic action.

Patricia has been a staff therapist in a large private psychiatric clinic for 2 years. She keeps a journal in which she engages in reflective writing about notable experiences with clients she has worked with that day. After her last client today she made the following entry in her journal:

> I know I messed up my session with Andrea today. It was a really stupid error. The session shifted from being collaborative to non-collaborative. I think I took her to a place that she said rather clearly that she didn't want to go [discussing her breakup with Vince]. I clearly did not respect her request. I guess this may have strained our therapeutic alliance. Why did I do such a thing? It was most likely because I felt that at some level her relationship with Vince was absolutely absurd. Why would she cling to and idolize a womanizer like him? Could this be something like my relationship with Jack? Sure he's not a womanizer but … [reflects on similarities between her own experience with her former lover and comes to the conclusion that her own issues—and subsequent counter-transference—were activated by Andrea's material]. … There's no doubt that my response was not therapeutic. It seems I need to begin our next session with an apology. For now I need to process her issues more gently. After all she's avoided facing and expressing emotions for years now, so I can't expect her to change overnight. So I'll go slow for now. I also need to check with her to see how this session affected her, and I may need to apologize.

As the next session began, Patricia asked Andrea how the last session had been for her. Andrea said that she had had a sleepless night after the session and wondered if it was worth continuing in therapy because it seemed so painful. Patricia apologized and said that it was ill-advised to bring up the matter of Andrea's relationship with Vince. She also indicated that she wouldn't bring up that relationship until Andrea agreed to talk about it. Andrea sighed with relief and accepted the apology. Her involvement and responsiveness in the next few sessions suggested that the strained alliance had been repaired.

# REFERENCES

Ackerman, S., & Hillensroth, M. (2003). A review of therapist characteristics and techniques positively impacting the therapeutic alliance. *Clinical Psychology Review, 23*, 1–33.

Adler, A. (1963). *The practice and theory of individual psychology.* Patterson, NJ: Littlefield, Adams.

American Psychiatric Association. (2000). *Diagnostic and statistical manual of mental disorders* (4th ed., Text rev.). Washington, DC: Author.

Añez, L., Silva, M., Paris, M., & Bedregal, L. (2008). Engaging Latinos through the integration of cultural values and motivational interviewing principles. *Professional Psychology: Research and Practice, 39*, 153–159.

Arkowitz, H., Westra, H., Miller, W., & Rollnick, S. (Eds.). (2007). *Motivational interviewing in the treatment of psychological problems.* New York: Guilford Press.

Arnkoff, D. (2000). Two examples of strains in the therapeutic alliance in an integrative cognitive therapy. *Journal of Clinical Psychology, 56*, 187–200.

Beck, J. (1995). *Cognitive therapy: Basics and beyond.* New York: Guilford Press.

Beck, J. (2005). *Cognitive therapy for challenging problems: What to do when basics don't work.* New York: Guilford Press.

Beitman, B. (1999). Sex, love and psychotherapy. In B. Beitman & D. Yue (Eds.), *Learning psychotherapy: A time-efficient, research-based, and outcome-measured psychotherapy training program* (pp. 265–279). New York: Norton.

Beitman, B., & Yue, D. (1999). *Learning psychotherapy: A time-efficient, research-based, and outcome-measured psychotherapy training program.* New York: Norton.

Bender, D. (2005). The therapeutic alliance in the treatment of personality disorders. *Journal of Psychiatric Practice, 11*, 73–87.

Bennett-Levy, J. (2006). Therapist skills: A cognitive model of their acquisition and refinement. *Behavioural and Cognitive Psychotherapy, 34*, 57–78.

Bennett-Levy, J., & Thwaites, R. (2006). Self and self-reflection in the therapeutic relationship. In P. Gilbert & R. Leahy (Eds.). *The therapeutic relationship in the cognitive behavioral psychotherapies* (pp. 255–282). London: Taylor & Francis.

Bhui, K., & Bhugra, D. (2004). Communication with patients from other cultures: The place of explanatory models. *Advances in Psychiatric Treatment, 10*, 474–478.

Binder, J. (1993). Is it time to improve psychotherapy training? *Clinical Psychology Review, 13*, 301–318.

Binder, J. (2004). *Key competencies in brief dynamic psychotherapy: Clinical practice beyond the manual.* New York: Guilford Press.

Blatt, S., Sanislow, C., Zuroff, D., & Pilkonis, P. (1996). Characteristics of effective therapists: Further analysis of data from the National Institute of Mental Health Treatment of Depression Collaborative Research Program. *Journal of Consulting and Clinical Psychology, 64*, 1276–1284.

Bordin, E. (1979). The generalizability of the psychoanalytic concept of the working alliance. *Psychotherapy: Theory, Research and Practice, 16*, 252–260.

Cardemil, E. (2008). Commentary: Culturally sensitive treatments: Need for an organizing framework. *Culture Psychology, 14,* 357–367.

Carlson, J. (2006). *Psychotherapy over time.* Washington, DC: American Psychological Association.

Carlson, J., Sperry, L., & Lewis, J. (2005). *Family therapy techniques. Integrating and tailoring treatment.* New York: Routledge.

Carroll, K. M. (1996). Relapse prevention as a psychosocial treatment: A review of controlled clinical trials. *Experimental and Clinical Psychopharmacology, 4,* 46–54.

Committee on Cultural Psychiatry of the Group for the Advancement of Psychiatry. (2002).*Cultural assessment in clinical psychiatry.* Washington, DC: American Psychiatric Press.

Constantine, M., & Ladany, N. (2000). Self-report multicultural counseling competence scales: Their relation to social desirability attitudes and multicultural case conceptualization ability. *Journal of Counseling Psychology, 47,* 155–164.

Cucciare, M., & O'Donohue, W. (2008). Clinical case conceptualization and termination of psychotherapy. In M. O'Donohue & W. Cucciare (Eds.), *Terminating psychotherapy: A clinician's guide* (pp. 121–146). New York: Routledge.

de Shazer, S. (1985). *Keys to solutions in brief therapy.* New York: W. W. Norton.

Dreyfus, H., & Dreyfus, S. (1986). *Mind over machine.* New York: Free Press.

Driscoll, K., Cukrowicz, K., Reardon, M., & Joiner, T. (2004). *Simple treatments for complex problems: A flexible cognitive behavior analysis system approach to psychotherapy.* Mahwah, NJ: Lawrence Erlbaum Associates.

Duncan, B., Miller, S., Sparks, J., Claud, D., Reynolds, L. R., Brown, J., & Johnson, L. (2003). The Session Rating Scale: Preliminary properties of a "working" alliance measure. *Journal of Brief Therapy, 3*(1), 3–12.

Eells, T., Lombart, K., Kendjelic, E., Turner, L., & Lucas, C. (2005). The quality of psychotherapy case formulations: A comparison of expert, experienced, and novice cognitive-behavioral and psychodynamic therapists. *Journal of Consulting and Clinical Psychology, 73,* 579–589.

Engle, D., & Arkowitz, H. (2006). *Ambivalence in psychotherapy: Facilitating readiness to change.* New York: Guilford Press.

Erickson, K. (Ed.). (1996). *The road to excellence: The acquisition of expert performance in the arts and sciences, sports and games.* Mahwah, NJ: Lawrence Erlbaum Associates.

Fiedler, F. (1950). Comparisons of therapeutic relationships in psychoanalytic, nondirective, and Adlerian therapy. *Journal of Consulting Psychology, 14,* 436–445.

Gabbard, G. (1999). An overview of countertransference: Theory and technique. In G. Gabbard (Ed.), *Countertransference issues in psychiatric treatment* (pp. 1–25). Washington, DC: American Psychiatric Press.

Gelso, C., & Hayes, J. (2007). *Countertransference and the therapist's inner experience: Perils and possibilities.* Mahwah, NJ: Lawrence Erlbaum Associates.

Gelso, C., Hill, C., Mohr, J., Rochlen, A., & Zack, J. (1999). Describing the face of transference: Psychodynamic therapists' recollections about transference in cases of successful long-term therapy. *Journal of Counseling Psychology, 46,* 257–267.

Gendlin, E. (1996). *Focusing-oriented psychotherapy.* New York: Guilford Press.

Goldfried, M., & Davison, G. (1976). Clinical behavior therapy. New York: Holt, Rinehart & Winston.

Goldfried, M. R., Raue, P. J., & Castonguay, L. G. (1998). The therapeutic focus in significant sessions of master therapists: A comparison of cognitive-behavioral and psychodynamic-interpersonal interventions. *Journal of Consulting and Clinical Psychology, 66,* 803–810.

Good, G., & Beitman, B. (2006). *Counseling and psychotherapy essentials: Integrating theories, skills, and practices.* New York: Norton.

Greenberg, L. (2002). *Emotion-focused therapy: Coaching clients to work through their feelings.* Washington, DC: American Psychological Association.

Greenberg, L., & Watson, J. (2006). *Emotion-focused therapy for depression.* Washington, DC: American Psychological Association Press.

Hampson, R., & Beavers, R. (2004). Observational assessment of couples and families. In L. Sperry (Ed.), *Assessment of couples and families: Contemporary and cutting edge strategies* (pp. 91–116). New York: Routledge.

Hansen, N., Randazzo, K., Schwartz, A., Marshall, M., Kalis, D., Fraziers, R., et al. (2006). Do we practice what we preach? An exploratory survey of multicultural psychotherapy competencies. *Professional Psychology: Research and Practice, 337,* 66–74.

Haynes, R., Corey, G., & Moulton, P. (2003). *Clinical supervision in the helping professions: A practical guide.* Pacific Grove, CA: Thomson–Brooks/Cole.

Hays, P., & Iwamasa, G. (Eds.) (2006). *Culturally-responsive cognitive-behavioral therapy: Assessment, practice and supervision.* Washington, DC: American Psychological Association.

Hays, P. (2006). Introduction: Developing culturally responsive cognitive-behavioral therapies. In P. Hays and G. Iwamasa (Eds.). *Culturally-responsive cognitive-behavioral therapies.* (pp. 3–20). Washington, DC: American Psychological Association.

Hill, C. (2004). *Helping skills: Facilitating exploration, insight, and action* (2nd ed.). Washington, DC: American Psychological Association.

Hill, C. (2005). Therapist techniques, client involvement, and the therapeutic relationship: Inextricably intertwined in the therapy process. *Psychotherapy: Theory, Research, Practice, Training, 42,* 431–442.

Horvath, A., & Symonds, B. (1991). Relationship between working alliance and outcome in psychotherapy: A meta-analysis. *Journal of Counseling Psychology, 38,* 139–149.

Howard, K., Kopta, S., Krause, M., & Orlinsky, D. (1986). The dose-effect relationship in psychotherapy. *American Psychologist, 41,* 159–164.

Howard, K., Lueger, R., Maling, M., & Martinovich, Z. (1993). A phase model of psychotherapy: Causal mediation of outcome. *Journal of Consulting and Clinical Psychology, 61,* 678–685.

Jennings, L., & Skovholt, T. (1999). The cognitive, emotional and relational characteristics of master therapists. *Journal of Counseling Psychology, 46,* 3–11.

Johnson, S. (2004). *The practice of emotionally focused couple therapy* (2nd ed.). New York: Brunner-Routledge.

Jongsma, A. (2006). *The complete adult psychotherapy treatment planner* (4th ed.). New York: Wiley.

Kabat-Zinn, J. (1990). *Full catastrophe living.* New York: Delta.

Kaslow, N. (2004). Competencies in professional psychology. *American Psychologist, 59,* 774–781.

Kaslow, N., Borden, K., Collins, F., Forrest, L., Illfelder-Kaye, J., Nelson, P., et al. (2004). Competencies conference: Future directions in education and credentialing in professional psychology. *Journal of Clinical Psychology, 80,* 699–712.

Kendjelic, E., & Eells, T. (2007). Generic psychotherapy case formulation training improves formulation quality. *Psychotherapy: Theory, Research, Practice, Training, 44,* 66–77.

Lambert, M. (1992). Psychotherapy outcome research: Implications for integrative and eclectic therapists. In J. Norcross & M. Goldfried (Eds.), *Handbook of psychotherapy* (pp. 94–129). New York: Basic Books.

Lambert, M., Morton, J., Hatfield, D., Harmon, C., Hamilton, S., & Reid, R. (2004). *Administration and scoring manual for the Outcome Questionnaire-45.* Orem, UT: American Professional Credentialing Services.

Lambert, M., & Okishi, B. (1997). The efficacy and effectiveness of psychotherapy supervision. In C. Watkins (Ed.), *Bergin and Garfield's handbook of psychotherapy and behavior change* (5th ed., pp. 139–193). New York: Wiley.

Lambert, M., Whipple, J., Smart, D., Vermeersch, D., Nielsen, S., & Hawkins, E. (2001). The effects of providing therapists with feedback on patient progress during psychotherapy: Are outcomes enhanced? *Psychotherapy Research, 11*(1), 49–68.

Lambie, G. (2004). Motivational enhancement therapy. *Professional School Counseling, 8,* 268–276.

La Roche, M., & Christopher, M. (2008). Culture and empirically supported treatments: On the road to a collision? *Culture and Psychology, 14,* 333–356.

Lazarus, A. (1966). Behavioral rehearsal vs. non-directive therapy vs. advice in effective behavioral change. *Behavior Research and Therapy, 4,* 209–212.

Leahy, R. (2002). A model of emotional schemas. *Cognitive and Behavioral Practice, 9*(2), 177–191.

Leahy, R. (2003). *Cognitive therapy techniques: A practitioner's guide.* New York: Guilford Press.

Ledley, D., Marx, B., & Heimberg, R. (2006). *Making cognitive-behavioral therapy work: Clinical process for new practitioners.* New York: Guilford Press.

Levenson, H. (1995). *Time-limited dynamic psychotherapy.* New York: Basic Books.

Li, C., & He, Y. (2008). Morita therapy for schizophrenia. *Schizophrenia Bulletin, 34,* 1021–1023.

Linehan, M. (1993). *Cognitive-behavioral treatment of borderline personality disorders.* New York: Guilford Press.

Marlatt, G. A., & Gordon, J. R. (1985). *Relapse prevention: Maintenance strategies in the treatment of addictive behaviors.* New York: Guilford Press.

Martinez-Taboas, A. (2005). The plural world of culturally sensitive psychotherapy: A response to Castro-Blanco's. *Psychotherapy: Theory, Research, Practice, Training, 42* (1), 17–19.

Martinez-Taboas, A. (2005). Psychogenic seizures in an *espiritismo* context: The role of culturally sensitive psychotherapy. *Psychotherapy: Theory, Research, Practice, Training, 42* (1), 6–13.

McCullough, J. (2000). *Treatment for chronic depression: Cognitive behavioral analysis system of psychotherapy.* New York: Guilford Press.

McCullough, J. (2005). *Treating chronic depression with disciplined personal involvement.* New York: Springer.

Miller, S., & Duncan, B. (2000). *The outcome rating scale.* Chicago: author.

Miller, S., Duncan, B., Brown, J., Sorrell, R., & Chalk, M. (2006). Using outcome to inform and improve treatment outcomes: Making ongoing, real-time assessment feasible. *Journal of Brief Therapy, 5,* 5–23.

Miller, S., Duncan, B., & Hubble, M. (1997). *Escape from Babel: Toward a unifying language for psychotherapy practice.* New York: Norton.

Miller, W., & Rollnick, S. (2002). *Motivational interviewing: Preparing people for change* (2nd ed.). New York: Guilford Press.

Neufield, S., Pinterits, E., Moleiro, C., Lee, T., Yang, P., & Brodie, R. (2006). How do graduate student therapists incorporate diversity factors in case conceptualizations? *Psychotherapy: Theory, Research, Practice, Training, 43,* 464–479.

Ochoa, E., & Muran, J. (2008). A relational take on termination in cognitive-behavioral therapy. In W. O'Donohue & M. Cucciare (Eds.), *Terminating psychotherapy: A clinician's guide* (pp. 183–204). New York: Routledge.

Orlinsky D., Grawe, K., & Parks, B. (1994). Process and outcome in psychotherapy. In A. Bergin & S. Garfield (Eds.), *Handbook of psychotherapy and behavior change* (4th ed., pp. 270–376). New York: Wiley.

Orlinsky, D., Ronnestad, M., & Willutzi, U. (2003). Fifty years of psychotherapy process-outcome research: Continuity and change. In M. Lambert (Ed.), *Bergin and Garfield's handbook of psychotherapy and behavior change* (5th ed., pp. 307–389). New York: Wiley.

Ornstein, E., & Ganzer, C. (2005). Relational social work: A model for the future. *Families in Society, 86,* 565–572.

Paniagua, F. (2005). *Assessing and treating culturally diverse clients: A practical guide* (3rd ed.). Thousand Oaks, CA: Sage.

Perry, S., Cooper, A., & Michels, R. (1987). The psychodynamic formulation: Its purpose, structure, and clinical application. *American Journal of Psychiatry, 144,* 543–551.

Pos, A., & Greenberg, I. (2008). Emotion focused therapy. In K. Jordan (Ed.), *The quick reference guide: A resource for expert and novice mental health professionals* (pp. 285–298). New York: Nova Scientific Publishers.

Prochaska, J., DiClementi, C., & Norcross, J. (1992). In search of how people change. *American Psychologist, 47,* 1102–1114.

Ridley, C., & Kelly, S. (2007). Multicultural considerations in case formation. In T. Eells, (Ed.), *Handbook of psychotherapy case formulation* (2nd ed., pp. 33–64). New York: Guilford Press.

Rogers, C. (1961). *On becoming a person.* Boston: Houghton Mifflin.

Safran, J., & Muran, J. (2000). *Negotiating the therapeutic alliance: A relational treatment guide.* New York: Guilford Press.

Safran, J., Muran, J., Samstag, C., & Stevens, C. (2002). Repairing alliance ruptures. In J. Norcross (Ed.), *Psychotherapy relationships that work: Therapist contributions and responsiveness to patients* (pp. 235–254). New York: Oxford University Press.

Samstag, C., Moran, J., & Safran, J. (2003). Defining and identifying alliance ruptures. In D. Chairman (Ed.), *Core processes in brief dynamic psychotherapy: Advancing effective practice* (pp. 182–214). Mahwah, NJ: Erlbaum.

Schön, D. (1983). *The reflective practitioner.* New York: Basic Books.

Seligman, L. (2005). *Conceptual skills for mental health professionals.* Columbus, OH: Merrill.

Skovholt, T., & Jennings, L. (2004). *Master therapists: Exploring expertise in therapy and counseling.* Boston: Allyn & Bacon.

Smith, K., & Greenberg, L. (2007). Internal multiplicity in emotion-focused psychotherapy. *Journal of Clinical Psychology, 63,* 175–186.

Sperry, L. (2005a). Case conceptualization: A strategy for incorporating individual, couple, and family dynamics in the treatment process. *American Journal of Family Therapy, 33,* 353–364.

Sperry, L. (2005b). Case conceptualizations: The missing link between theory and practice. *The Family Journal: Counseling and Therapy for Couples and Families, 13,* 71–76.

Sperry, L., Blackwell, B., Gudeman, J., & Faulkner, L. (1992). *Psychiatric case formulations.* Washington, DC: American Psychiatric Press.

Sperry, L., Brill, P., Howard, K., & Grissom, G. (1996). *Treatment outcomes in psychotherapy and psychiatric interventions.* New York: Brunner/Mazel.

Sperry, L., Carlson, J., & Kjos, D. (2003). *Becoming an effective therapist.* Boston: Allyn & Bacon.

Spruill, J., Rozensky, R., Stigall, T., Vasquez, M., Bingham, R., & Olvey, B. (2004). Becoming a competent clinician: Basic competencies in intervention. *Journal of Clinical Psychology, 60,* 741–754.

Sue, D., & Zane, N. (1987). The role of culture and cultural technique in psychotherapy: A critique and reformulation. *American Psychologist, 59*(4), 533–540.

Sue, S., & Zane, N. (1987). The role of culture and cultural techniques in psychotherapy. A critique and reformulation. *American Psychologist, 42*(1), 37–45.

**278**

Thwaites, R., & Bennett-Levy, J. (2007). Conceptualizing empathy in cognitive behaviour therapy: Making the implicit explicit. *Behavioral and Cognitive Psychotherapy, 35,* 591–612.

Watson, J., & Greenberg, L. (2000). Alliance ruptures and repairs in experiential therapy. *Journal of Clinical Psychology, 56*(2), 175–186.

Westra, H. (2004). Managing resistance in cognitive behavioural therapy: The application of motivational interviewing in mixed anxiety and depression. *Cognitive Behaviour Therapy, 33,* 161–175.

Whipple, J., Lambert, M., Vermeersch, D., Smart, D., Nielsen, S., & Hawkins, E. (2003). Improving the effects of psychotherapy: The use of early identification of treatment and problem-solving strategies in routine practice. *Journal of Counseling Psychology, 50,* 59–68.

Wright, J., Basco, M., & Thase, M. (2006). *Learning cognitive-behavioral therapy: An illustrated guide.* Washington, DC: American Psychiatric Press.

**279**

# INDEX

CBASP, *see* Cognitive-behavioral
  analysis system of
  psychotherapy
CBT, *see* Cognitive-behavioral therapy
Change, *see* Readiness for change;
  Strategies to promote change
Change talk
  cases, 41, 42, 44
  types of, 50
Childhood and Adolescence Disorders,
  101
Chronic fatigue, 204–211
Clients
  case conceptualization by, 113–114
  expectations of (*see* Expectations
    of clients)
  explanatory models of (*see*
    Explanatory models of clients)
  frustration of, 75
  hope of, 38
  impasses and, 47
  progress monitoring by, 241–242
  resistance and ambivalence of (*see*
    Resistance and ambivalence)
  resources of, 89, 155, 159
  tasks of, 25–26, 32, 73–74
  termination difficulties of, 254,
    257–261
  transference and, 61
  treatment-interfering factors of, 227,
    228, 229, 230–239
Clinical case reports, *see* Integrative
  clinical case reports
Clinical formulation
  case conceptualization and, 116,
    118–120, 123–124, 127, 141–142
  in clinical case report, 155, 160–161
  overview of, 112, 113
Clinical formulation statement, 116,
  118–120, 123–124, 127, 141–142
Clinicians, *see* Therapists
Cognitive-behavioral analysis system
  of psychotherapy (CBASP),
  166, 167–168, 185–194

Cognitive-behavioral therapy (CBT)
  cases, 51–55, 185–194, 204–211,
    233–236 (*see also* Geri R.)
  culturally sensitive, 215
  overview of, 10–13
  relapse prevention in, 255–256
  strategies in, 11, 12–13, 184–194,
    204–211
  treatment focus in
    conceptual maps and, 11, 12–13
    master therapists and, 172–173
    specifying, 166, 167–170
    treatment formulation and,
      142–143, 145
Cognitive Disorders, 100
Cognitive map, 20
Cognitive restructuring strategy,
  189–194
Commercial process assessment
  scales, 242–245
Common factors approach, 24
Competencies; *see also specific core and
  essential competencies*
  developmental stages and, 3–4
  learning and, 5–8
  overview of, 1–2, 5, 7, 8
  psychotherapy practice and, 4–5
  skills versus, 2–3, 6
Competency-based training, 1
Competent stage of development, 3–4
Conceptual maps
  cognitive-behavioral, 10–13
  dynamic, 11, 13–15
  experiential, 11, 16–18
  integrative, 11, 20–22
  overview of, 9–11
  relational-systemic, 11, 18–20
  treatment focus and, 166
  treatment formulation and, 145
*Confianza*, 220–222
Conflict split, 49–50
Confrontation rupture, 75
Contemplation stage of change, 36, 37,
  40–43

**T**

Tailoring treatments, 145
Tasks of clients, 25–26, 32, 73–74
Termination
    case conceptualization and, 111, 254
    cases, 256–263
    guidelines for, 254–256
    overview of, 253–254
    relapse prevention plan for, 254,
        255–256
    theoretical approaches to, 13, 15, 18,
        20, 22
Theoretical frameworks, *see*
        Conceptual maps
Therapeutic alliance; *see also*
        Relationship building and
        maintenance
    assessment of, 243, 244, 246, 248
    cases, 27–34, 75–81, 267, 270–271
    cultural formulation and, 25
    integrative view of, 24–26
    overview of, 23–24
    as process, 24
    ruptures in (*see* Therapeutic
        alliance ruptures)
    therapists and, 26–27
    transference and (*see* Transference
        and countertransference)
    treatment-interfering factors and,
        236, 239
Therapeutic alliance ruptures; *see also*
        Relationship building and
        maintenance
    cases, 75–81
    definition of, 73–74
    resistance compared to, 74–75
    strategies for, 75
    transference-countertransference in,
        74
Therapeutic empathy, 2–3, 52–54
Therapists
    assessment scales devised by,
        245–248

case conceptualization by, 113–114
credibility of, 38, 110, 222
feedback needed by, 242, 250–251,
    252
impasses and, 47
as master therapists, 172–173
orientation of (*see* Conceptual maps)
reasoning of, 113
reflective writing by, 79–81, 270–271
self-integration of, 63
therapeutic alliance and, 26–27
training of, 1, 5–6 (*see also*
    Supervision)
transference-countertransference
    and, 61, 63–64, 268, 270–271
treatment-interfering factors of, 228
Therapy, *see* Psychotherapy; *topics
    beginning with intervention or
    treatment*
Thoughts in transference-
        countertransference, 62
Time-limited dynamic therapy
    cases, 166–168
    overview of, 11, 13–15
    treatment focus in, 166–168, 172–173
Training psychotherapists, 1, 5–6;
        *see also* Supervision
Transference and countertransference;
        *see also* Relationship building
        and maintenance
    cases, 64–72, 79–81, 148, 163
    overview of, 59–61
    recognizing, 61–62
    strategies for, 63–64
    supervision and, 268, 270–271
    in therapeutic alliance ruptures, 74
    treatment formulation and, 146, 163
Treatment, *see* Psychotherapy; *topics
        beginning with intervention
        or treatment*
Treatment focus
    approaches to (*see* Treatment focus
        approaches)